Representational Mind

A Study of Kant's Theory of Knowledge

Studies in Phenomenology and Existential Philosophy

Representational Mind

A Study of Kant's Theory
of Knowledge

Richard E. Aquila

Indiana University Press · Bloomington

This book was brought to publication with the assistance of a grant
from the Andrew W. Mellon Foundation.

Manufactured in the United States of America

Library of Congress Cataloging in Publication Data

Aquila, Richard E., 1944–
    Representational mind.

    (Studies in phenomenology and existential philosophy)
    Includes bibliographical references and index.
    1. Kant, Immanuel, 1724–1804—Knowledge, Theory of.
2. Knowledge, Theory of—History—18th century.
I. Title. II. Series.
B2799.K7A63   1983   121'.092'4   83-47918
ISBN 0-253-35005-0
1 2 3 4 5 87 86 85 84 83

For my family and friends

CONTENTS

Preface

Most recent analyses of Kant's theory of knowledge as presented in the *Critique of Pure Reason* proceed rather quickly to an assessment of his reasoning in the Transcendental Deduction, the second edition Refutation of Idealism, and the Analogies of Experience. At least this has tended to be so among Anglo-American philosophers, for whom Kant's claims about sensation, intuition, and the "forms" of intuition in the Transcendental Aesthetic are too often regarded as representative either of a provisional stance requiring drastic revision in the light of the Transcendental Analytic or else of a precritical position best left behind. In contrast to this attitude, I have found it fruitful to see in the Aesthetic the development of a theory of "mental representation" (*Vorstellung*) that is historically significant in its own right and that requires carrying over into the Analytic the recognition of a fundamental power of the mind that is not explicable in the terms of the later analyses. No doubt a number of different approaches to the Analytic are compatible with this recognition, especially in the formulation of the arguments of the above-mentioned sections. Though I do not offer more than generalities in this regard, I try to shed some light on certain fundamental notions that, first introduced in the Aesthetic, are then carried into those arguments: that of a concept and those of the distinctions between things in themselves and appearances and between inner and outer sense.

Much of the recent Kant interpretation on the Anglo-American side has been in terms of issues and distinctions of undeniable importance to Kant but since his day more adequately formulated by philosophers more directly concerned with problems of meaning and reference in semantics. Such approaches, though valuable in various ways, are one-sided and anachronistic unless enriched by means of ideas that are more phenomenologically oriented. The Kantian notion of an irreducible form of intuition, I argue, embodies the recognition of a basic intentional or object-directed capacity of the mind that is inexplicable by appeal to the sorts of conceptual and judgmental abilities treated in the Transcendental Analytic. The notion of a sensible appearance, in turn, is to be understood in terms of that of an intentional object of sensory awareness, with corresponding implications for the Kantian theory of space and time. The key idea in the latter case is that the regions of space and stretches of time occupied by sensible appearances are also intentional objects in their own right.

Within the community of Anglo-American philosophers, it has been Wilfrid Sellars who has accorded the greatest attention to the notion of intentionality in the interpretation of Kant's philosophy, and my own ideas have developed in part under the influence of his writings. Throughout this work, at appropriate points in the notes, more specific reference will be made to these writings. The same will be the case with respect to the writings of Gerold Prauss, which, despite a difference in terminology, defend a position similar to that of Sellars. In both cases we find an interpretation that avoids ascribing to Kant certain unsophisticated conceptions of sensation as the immediate object of sensory awareness. In both cases, indeed, sensations (in the sense in which they are the basic "material" of perceptual awareness) are not themselves objects of awareness at all, but something much more like theoretical entities or postulates of a transcendental theory of consciousness. Failure to grasp this point has inevitably led to failure to comprehend Kant's theory of mental representation, which rests precisely on an analysis of the cognitive features required for the constitution of an intentional reference to objects of awareness *through* possible sensations.

In placing the problem of "representation" at the center of my concern with Kant's theory of knowledge, many readers will know that my terminological choice is not in all respects the most desirable as an equivalent for Kant's *Vorstellung*. But it has come to be standard in English translations. Furthermore, despite the presence of undesirable connotations, it expresses an important part of what Kant was after. This is the notion that we, as cognitively active beings, represent the world to ourselves as being of a certain sort (whether or not in every case it really is of that sort). The undesirable connotations involve the suggestion that representations are peculiarly mental objects. But that supposition is by no means implied in the notion that we are capable of representing the world as being of such-and-such a sort. One might represent certain facts as obtaining without producing some *object* that represents those facts.

To some philosophers, the cognitive means by which we represent reality to ourselves must be defined in terms of peculiarly mental objects. These, for example, would be the "ideas" of Berkeley and Hume, and at least to some extent also those of Descartes and Locke. To thinkers of this stripe, cognitive dealings with reality are effected via cognitive involvement with a reality (ideas) internal to the process of cognition itself. To others the possibility of cognitive contact with extra-mental reality is not something calling for explanation at all, and it stands in no need of mediation by means of something more primordial. In either case Kant's predecessors tended to take one thing as basic: the occurrence of cognitive relationships, the presentation of "objects" to the faculty by which they are then to be cognized.

The Kantian insight is that cognitive relations must in every case rest upon the foundation of cognitive *states*. They must rest, that is, upon states of the knower whose internal constitution is such that it is in the first place *possible* for those states to present it with objects of possible cognition. Even those pre-Kantian sceptics or "idealists" who questioned the possibility of cognitive relations in regard to extra-mental reality failed to see this point. They limited cognitive relations to those objects that are internal to the process of cognition itself. What they continued to take for granted was the possibility of cognitive contact as such, the possibility of cognitive contact with *any* sort of object.

Kant discovered (or perhaps he invented) the notion of a cognitive state. What might be called "cognitive states" among Kant's predecessors were really nothing more than would-be mental, or cognitive, *relations* of various sorts. Cognitive states, in the sense that was new with Kant, are not cognitive relations with objects, nor are they themselves peculiar objects supposed to mediate the occurrence of cognitive relations. They are simply the perceiver's awareness of possible objects. They are, as one might thus put it, *possible* cognitions. The distinction may appear trivial at first, but the difference is vast. On the one side we have cognitive relations; on the other we have states that stand (though in some cases they also might fail to stand) *in* cognitive relations. The latter view, unlike the former, allows for something important. It allows for the possibility of one and the same cognitive state involving more than one kind of cognitive relation; the alternative view at most allows for one and the same *knower* standing in more than one kind of cognitive relation with reality. More specifically, the new epistemology brought with it a dramatic new possibility for Kant: the possibility of uniting, in a single cognitive state, the cognitive quality peculiar both to fully perceptual content (empirical "intuitions") and to the content of intellection and judgment proper.

It is with respect to the problem of the relation between intuitional and conceptual factors that I have been unable to follow the approaches of Sellars and Prauss. While both regard sensation as merely part of the transcendental material through which the mind's intentional activities are directable—part of the material to be animated (to use Husserl's term) by those activities—both suppose that the business of such animation is fundamentally a conceptual one. For Sellars, the intuitions that animate sensation are "minimal conceptual episodes"; for Prauss, sensations (which he tends to equate with empirical intuitions) function solely in virtue of their "interpretation" (*Deutung*) by means of concepts. In neither case is a fundamental intentional component to be found in the faculty of intuition as such. The only factors at work in an empirical intuition are sensations and the conceptual episodes constituting intentional reference through them. By contrast, it seems to me that Kant's distinction between forms of intuition and forms of understanding, and hence of the Aesthetic from the Analytic, was aimed precisely at the recognition of a factor neglected by any such interpretations. The sensory side of human cognition does more than contribute an element making intentional reference *sensory* on occasion. Far from our referential power being fundamentally a conceptual one, its direction upon human sensibility is rather to be regarded as an enrichment or determination of a basic power already at hand.

The conceptualization of intuition involves a kind of potentiation of a characteristic already to be found in the latter. Adopting this point of view, I think, allows for a more satisfying theory of the relation between judgment and percept than is possible on Sellars's or on Prauss's account. For in the latter cases we are at most dealing with a relation between two distinct components; one is responsible for sensory content, the other for intentional reference. The alternative also allows for a more adequate point of view with respect to the *object* of perceptual reference. It allows, namely, for a more adequate recognition of the fact that the immediate objects of perceptual awareness, and of imagination, are not merely objects of *thoughts*, appropriately connected to sensory or imaginative content, but quite properly and immediately objects of a *sensibility* to which thoughts have been directed. This point should not be obscured even by the concession, should some (such as Kant himself at times) require it, that apart from conceptual determination no fully *conscious* intention could be operative. In the face of such a concession, the fact would still remain that conceptualization of an intentional object involves a kind of *reference* to an object that is constituted neither by concepts that enter into it, nor by the sensations in virtue of which it is "sensory," nor by a combination of the two. What more it involves will of course be indefinable. But Kant at least attempts to shed some light on it, and to confirm its presence, with his theory of space and time (or of regions thereof) as individuals which, though in a sense mere intentional objects, are irreducible to the conceptual descriptions predicable of them.

It should be evident to what extent I interpret Kant in Husserlian terms in this work. My emphasis on the unity of conceptual and intuitive factors, reflected especially in the treatment of imagination and schematism, also seems to me to capture at least part of what Heidegger saw in Kant, though the difference in ontological perspective should be particularly evident from Chapter Four. However, I do not make an effort in this work to pursue the details of Kant's relation to Husserl and Heidegger. This is no doubt at least partly due to the fact that, in my own mind and in the course of my studies, I have only gradually moved from an occupation with more "analytical" perspectives to an eventual appreciation of the phenomenological dimensions in Kant. In any case, I hope to have contributed to the current tendency toward "dialogue" between the two approaches.

Some of the material in this book has been presented, or is an improvement on material that has been presented, in previous publications. These are "Categories, Schematism and Forms of Judgment," *Ratio*, XVIII (1976); *Intentionality: A Study of Mental Acts* (University Park: Pennsylvania State University Press, 1977); "Two Lines of Argument in Kant's Transcendental Aesthetic," *International Studies in Philosophy*, X (1978); "Things in Themselves and Appearances: Intentionality and Reality in Kant," *Archiv für Geschichte der Philosophie*, 61 (1979); *Akten des 5. Internationalen Kant-Kongresses*, ed. Gerhard Funke, et al. (Bonn: Bouvier Verlag Herbert Grundmann, 1981); "Intentional Objects and Kantian Appearances," *Philosophical Topics*, 12/2 (1981). Appreciation is extended to the editors in each case.

I am also indebted to my colleagues in the Philosophy Department of the University of Tennessee for the creation, over the years, of an extremely congenial working environment. In this regard special thanks are owed to John Davis, our Department Head; to Dolores Scates; and to Barbara Moser, whose expertise and patience in typing the manuscript have belied the many ways in which these labors are insufficiently rewarded by academic institutions.

Representational Mind

A Study of Kant's Theory of Knowledge

Chapter 1

The Background of
Kant's Representationalism

I. Introduction

A REVOLUTION in Western philosophy was instigated by concepts commonly supposed to be the invention of Descartes. These concern the human capacity for having and forming "ideas." The point of comparison with Kant concerns the Kantian notion of *Vorstellung*. The latter is perhaps most naturally equated with "presentation," as when we speak of our mental faculties as "presenting" various objects or matters, or at least permitting their presentation, to the mind for possible perusal. However, 'idea' is also a common translation. Kant himself equates it with the Latin *repraesentatio* (A320/B376).[1] Cognitive faculties are regarded, then, as the means by which the mind "represents" various objects to itself or, at the very least, has something represented to (or "in") it. This may suggest that (re)presentations are peculiar mental entities of some sort. However, the term need not be used to indicate the apprehension of one entity that represents, or is supposed to represent, another one. It might simply indicate an instance of a certain sort of (cognitively relevant) occurrence. To be sure, such occurrences may be an object of our concern. As Kant says, "all representations have, as representations, their object, and can themselves in turn become objects of other representations" (A108); "Everything, every representation even, in so far as we are conscious of it, may be entitled object" (A189/B234). But these statements do not show that representations are peculiar entities that one's representational faculty has constructed or produced, or that in some other way have been presented to that faculty for its utilization.

In the Cartesian tradition a human mind is some sort of (nonphysical) locus, internal to a person, for a system of representations (or misrepresentations) of reality. The mind, that is, is where our ideas are. Kant doesn't talk about the "mind" (*Gemüt*) very much, but most often of our knowledge, or our faculty of knowledge (*Erkenntnisvermögen*). This,

though, is largely a terminological point. The operative assumption remains that of an internal system of representations of reality. Given this
assumption, of course, the philosophical challenge seems clear: to investi-
gate the *nature* of our representative faculty; to analyze the *possibility* of an
(internal) power for the representation of (external) reality:

> There can be no doubt that all our knowledge begins with experience. For
> how should our faculty of knowledge be awakened into action did not
> objects affecting our sense partly of themselves produce representations,
> partly arouse the activity of our understanding to compare these repre-
> sentations, and, by combining or separating them, work up the raw mate-
> rial of the sensible impressions into that knowledge of objects which is
> entitled experience? . . . But though all our knowledge begins with experi-
> ence, it does not follow that it all arises out of experience. For it may well be
> that even our empirical knowledge is made up of what we receive through
> impressions and of what our own faculty of knowledge (sensible impressions
> serving merely as the occasion) supplies from itself. If our faculty of knowl-
> edge makes any such addition, it may be that we are not in a position to
> distinguish it from the raw material, until with long practice of attention we
> have become skilled in separating it. (B1–2)

Kant is often supposed to have held that the immediate objects of sense
perception are peculiarly mental entities ("sensations") that the mind
somehow organizes and structures under the guidance of its own internal
principles. This much is typically seen as stemming from a Cartesian
heritage. Descartes, one may be told, made the error of regarding the
distinction between immediately sensory and properly conceptual representations as a distinction between two *sorts* of mental entities. "Sensations" or "sense impressions" are the immediate objects of sense perception. Corresponding to these are the immediate objects of truly conceptual
ideas. The triumph of Kant, one may then be told, lies in his discovery that
acts of the intellect do not at all involve a peculiar species of mental entity.
For Kant, there are no peculiarly intelligible *objects*; only more or less
intelligent activities.

This reading supposes that Kant adopts two quite different approaches to
mental representation. With respect to the representations involved in a
properly intellectual context (that is, wherever a judgment or a concept is
in question), the mind's representations are the various ways in which we
represent the world to ourselves, the various ways that we think about it.
But something quite different may be suggested when Kant distinguishes
the "intuitions" of sense perception from judgments of the intellect. In the
latter case we may only be dealing with an instance of judgment or
conception. In the former case we are dealing with an instance of something actually presented as an object of perception, something that Kant

also refers to as a species of representation. These, it seems, are nothing other than our own sensations. This reading of Kant, as I shall be arguing, is a quite definitely mistaken one. It fails to perceive the extent to which Kant's theory of mental representation breaks not only from its antecedents in the seventeenth and eighteenth centuries, but also from a pattern of thinking extending for centuries earlier.

So far we have distinguished two notions of mental representation. One of these is an entirely ordinary one that involves no element of philosophical speculation or analysis. It is simply that we represent the world to ourselves as being of such and such a sort, that we *take* it to be of that sort, or that it *appears* to be of that sort. The second notion stems to a large extent from Descartes. This is the notion of some peculiarly mental entity whose presence in consciousness is what makes it *possible* for us to represent the world as being of some particular sort, or what serves to explain the fact that it appears to be of that sort. We now need to make a further distinction.

Prior to Kant there were two patterns for understanding the mind's ability to represent a world to itself. On one, the primary "element" of human knowledge is an unexplained ability of the knower to enter into cognitive relations with reality as it is in itself. The most elaborately thought out form of this pattern uses a metaphor to make the point. It speaks of the knower's ability to "receive" the actual "forms" of things into its cognitive apparatus. This is the Scholastic theory to which I turn in the next section. We shall see that Kant, like Descartes, formulated the basic principles of his own theory of knowledge at least partly, and very self-consciously, in opposition to this way of thinking. A second approach takes as its primary element the ability of the knower to enter into cognitive relations, not with reality as it is in itself, but rather with peculiarly mental representations of reality. As I have suggested, Kant offers an alternative to both approaches.

What is important is that both approaches regard mental representation as fundamentally a kind of mental *relation*. Where they differ is with respect to the terms of the relation. One of the terms is of course the human knower. The other is then supposed to be either the various aspects of reality in itself or else the various mental entities that serve as our representations *of* reality. On either of these approaches mental "states" are mental relations; they are the relations in which the knower stands either to reality in itself or else to those peculiar entities constituting its representations of reality.

Let us suppose, in contrast to the relational approach, that a state of awareness or conception is not as such some special sort of relation with any object. Rather, it is a state of the knower that may or may not *involve* that knower in some cognitive relation with an object. We must suppose, in other words, that human knowers are able to stand in cognitive relations because they are able to experience internal states that *allow* them to stand in such relations. This will then yield a further notion of mental representation. In this sense, mental representation comprises whatever internal states of a knower place (or fail to place)[2] that knower in genuine cognitive contact with some object. So mental representations are not peculiarly mental objects, nor are they, as such, peculiarly mental relations with objects. At best they are (part of) what makes such relations possible.

On this suggestion, one should note, but not on the relational approach, a single cognitive state might exhibit more than one kind of cognitive relation. A single representation, for example, might be characterized both by the kind of relation typical of sense perception and by the kind typical of intellection. According to some philosophers (Plato, for example) the object of the former kind of "idea" is particulars; the object of the latter is the universal conceptions, or the intellectual "essences," or the "natures" or defining "forms" *of* (possible) particulars. Other philosophers draw the distinction differently. For Kant, as we shall see, the object of sense perception (which he also calls "sensible intuition") is particulars; and so is the object of conception or understanding. But the former involves an "immediate" sort of reference to particulars, while the latter involves a different kind of reference to them. It refers to them not qua actual particulars, but only qua possible instances of certain *kinds* of particulars.

It has been difficult, as the examples in this chapter will show, for philosophers to see how precisely the same cognitive state might possess both a sensory and an intellectual content. For the sensory and intellectual seem to involve two different ways of representing reality. Thus a state that combines both sorts of cognitive relation would seem at best a conjunction of distinct states. But this supposition stems, as Kant saw, from failure to see an alternative to the relational approach. On that approach a cognitive state just *is* a kind of cognitive relation. So it is difficult to see, on that approach, how the same state might be characterized by two distinct kinds of cognitive relation, or how it might involve two distinct ways of representing reality.

II. The Scholastic Approach

What characterizes the Scholastic account is the notion of some kind of "identity" uniting the knower and what it knows. This is elaborated in terms of a distinction between "matter" and "form" with respect to things known. The form of a thing is the characteristic "what" of it. It is that in virtue of which it can be said to be a thing of the sort that it is. The distinction of matter from form, correspondingly, is what we require in order to speak of *a* particular thing of the sort. Matter is what permits distinguishing several different things of some sort. These things are then formally but not materially identical. But there is a sense, on the Scholastic account, in which the knower, via its cognitive faculties, may also be said to be formally "identical" with the objects known *through* those faculties. Not of course that the form that defines a certain species of object is in the knower in the same way in which it is in the members of that species. But it is nevertheless by means of a special sort of presence in our cognitive faculties that species, and hence their members, come to be known by us.

This account was offered by Aristotle, and later by St. Thomas Aquinas. It was offered with respect both to the "sensible" and to the "intelligible" forms of things. The sensible form of a thing is that in virtue of which the thing is describable in terms of immediately perceptible features, e.g., color and shape.[3] Intelligible form is what is involved in asking what sort of thing *has* the sensible features in question. Is it, for example, a statue or a woman? Thus the form of the thing perceived is "in the intellect" in an even more abstract and immaterial way than when forms are merely in our sense organs:

> Now by matter the form of a thing is determined to some one thing. Therefore it is clear that knowledge is in inverse ratio to materiality. Consequently, things that are not receptive of forms, save materially, have no power of knowledge whatever—such as plants, as the Philosopher says. But the more immaterially a being receives the form of the thing known, the more perfect is its knowledge. Therefore the intellect, which abstracts the species not only from matter, but also from the individuating conditions of matter, knows more perfectly than the senses, which receive the form of the thing known, without matter indeed, but subject to material conditions.[4]

The "what" of a thing, as apprehended through the senses, is embedded in a context of details that are irrelevant to its being just the sort of thing it is known to be (though not of course to its being this particular example of that sort). So while sensible form is present immaterially in the organ of sense (or, through what Aquinas calls a "phantasm," within imagination or memory), it still contains "material conditions" from which the intellect must make further abstraction. The upshot is the reception of the intelligible form into the intellect.[5]

St. Thomas also describes the reception of forms as the reception of a similitude or likeness of the object.[6] Perhaps Descartes took this too literally, when he objected to the Scholastic approach. In any case the mind is a purely spiritual, nonspatial, "unextended subject" for Descartes, hence cannot receive into itself the resemblances of corporeal things:

> Here you ask, how I think that I, an unextended subject, can receive into
> myself the resemblance or idea of a thing which is extended. I reply that no
> corporeal resemblance can be received in the mind, but that what occurs
> there is the pure thinking of a thing, whether it be corporeal or equally
> whether it be one that is incorporeal and lacking any corporeal semblance.[7]

With respect, to be sure, to imagination (and, it seems, the original
perceptions from which the images therein functioning derive), some sort
of image or resemblance of the external object plays a role. But Descartes
excludes the possibility of describing this role in terms of a reception of the
image in question into the mind itself (as opposed to the brain):

> But as to imagination, which can only be exercised in reference to corporeal
> things, my opinion is that it requires the presence of a semblance which is
> truly corporeal, and to which the mind applies itself, without, however, its
> being received in the mind.[8]

In addition, the respects in which an image is required are fewer than is
commonly supposed: "It is sufficient that images resemble their objects in
some few respects."[9] (These, it turns out, exclude anything not formulat-
able as geometrical relationships.) Finally, images are not in any case
received into the mind from something outside the mind in which they are
also present:

> We must be careful not to suppose that in order to sense, the mind has to
> contemplate images which are [emitted by objects and] despatched by
> them to the brain, as our philosophers commonly assert. . . . When I see a
> staff, it is not to be thought that [minute images flying through the air
> commonly called] *intentional species* fly off from it and reach the eye, but
> merely that rays of light reflected from the staff excite certain motions in the
> optic nerve and, by its mediation, in the brain as well. . . . [10]

    Descartes formulated his epistemological doctrines in opposition to the
Scholastic approach. What is less well known is that Kant does the same.
Now Kant's view concerning the distinction between sensory and intellectual cognition underwent considerable change during the course of his
development. In the dissertation "On the Form and Principles of the
Sensible and Intelligible World" (the so-called *Inaugural Dissertation*) he
held that understanding or intellect has a twofold use. In its purely "logical" use, intellect merely systematizes a variety of possible items of cognition. It functions, that is, by formulating concepts useful for the classifica-
tion, according to common marks (*notis communibus*), of otherwise
apparently diverse matters; and also by the pursuit of logical reasoning
concerning such matters. But where the matters involve "sensitive cogni-

tion," derived from perception by the senses, the corresponding knowledge is limited to claims about the way the world appears to us, not about how it really is. However, our understanding also has a "real" use, for Kant, where its activities are not restricted to generalizations and inferences concerning such matters. Here it deals with matters that are proper to itself, and not derived from some other source. It deals, that is, with "intellectual things strictly as such." And when it does, according to Kant, it finally deals with things as they really are, and not just as they appear to be.[11]

Kant argues, then, that the application of intellect to sense yields no knowledge about the way things really are. What is noteworthy, though, is that Kant infers that this is so on the ground that, contrary to the Scholastic account, the forms of things, existing in themselves, cannot enter or be received into our senses:

> *Sensuality* is the *receptivity* of a subject by which it is possible for the subject's own representative state to be affected in a definite way by the presence of some object. *Intelligence* (rationality) is the *faculty* of a subject by which it has the power to represent things *which cannot by their own quality enter into the senses* [emphasis added] of that subject [*quae in sensus ipsius per qualitatem suam incurrere non possunt*]. The object of sensuality is the sensible; that which contains nothing but what is to be cognized through the intelligence is intelligible. . . . [12] In this way whatever in cognition is sensitive is dependent upon the special character of the subject to the extent that the subject is capable of this or that modification by the presence of objects. . . . Consequently it is clear that things which are thought sensitively are representations of things *as they appear*, but things which are intellectual are representations of things *as they are*.[13]

What the perceiver "receives" in perception is not some feature or form that is taken from an object. What is received is merely some internal *effect* upon the perceiver, or a modification of the perceiver's internal state. Hence knowledge gotten by applying the intellect to what is received is not of the forms or species of things as they really are, but only as they are represented by the forms of our own faculties:

> In a representation of sense there is first of all something which you might call the *matter*, namely the *sensation*, and there is also something which can be called the *form*, namely the *species* of the sensibles which arises according as the various things which affect the senses are coordinated by a certain natural law of the mind. . . . For objects do not strike the senses in virtue of their form or *species*. So, for the various things in an object which affect the sense to coalesce into some representational whole there is needed an internal principle in the mind by which those various things may be clothed with a certain *species* in accordance with stable and innate laws.[14]

Kant later abandoned the view that intellect has a "real use" distinct from the possibilities of its application to sense. (He also concluded that a purely "logical" use, as originally described, was not the only alternative to that real use.) But Kant did not change his view that such application fails to yield knowledge of things in themselves, nor that it follows from the untenability of the Scholastic account that this is so:

> I can only know what is contained in the object in itself if it is present and given to me. It is even then incomprehensible how the intuition of a present thing should make me know this thing as it is in itself, as its properties cannot migrate into my faculty of representation [da ihre Eigenschaften nicht in meine Vorstellungskraft hinüberwandern können]. . . . [15]

It is difficult to know how seriously to take the Scholastics' talk about the immaterial cognitive existence of the forms or "species" of knowable and perceivable things. Perhaps both Descartes and Kant took that account too literally. Perhaps, one might even object, only too literal a reading supports the supposition that the view is an instance of the relational approach to cognition. St. Thomas says that knowledge is via states that contain the natures of objects, but not as those natures are present in the objects themselves. He also maintains that this involves a "likeness" or "similitude" of the object in the knower. Perhaps, though, this is just a metaphorical way of saying that cognitive relations with objects require that one's internal state be suited, according to its nature, to directing the knower precisely to such objects. The "identity" between forms or species in the knower and the thing known, and their "resemblance," is a metaphorical identity and resemblance. The point is simply this. Sensing would not be sensing *of* this or that particular thing unless it had some nature of its own, in virtue of which it "points at" (constitutes an "intention" of) precisely that thing. And similarly for acts of the intellect. After all, "The likeness between two things may be considered in two ways. First inasmuch as they agree in a common nature. . . . Second, from the point of view of representation; and such a likeness of the knower to the object known is necessary."[16] Thus cognitive states contain a "resemblance" of some object known, or its form, only in that they contain a feature in virtue of which they constitute a way that such objects may be *represented*.

If this is St. Thomas's meaning, then it would be wrong to interpret his account as an instance of the relational approach. For on the present suggestion, a cognitive relation is possible only in virtue of the presence in the knower of a cognitive state with a nature of its own (a nature that is suited precisely for the making *possible* of just such a relation). So a cognitive state is not merely a unique sort of relation with objects, but it is a state one of whose *properties* is that it stands in a special relation (or that it brings the knower to stand in a special relation) with objects. And this will only be one of the properties of that state. For another, namely, will involve some facts about the intrinsic nature of the state, in virtue of which it is *able* to stand in that sort of relation (or to bring the knower to do so). One might simply choose to describe this nature in terms of a metaphorical "resemblance" borne by the states in question. In this case, however, it will always be possible for those states to occur in the absence of genuine cognitive relations with objects. This will always be possible precisely because each such state has an intrinsic nature; it is a state of a particular sort. When a state of that sort occurs, then the knower is in the sort of state that might at least constitute the apprehension of some object; but then again it also might not. Suppose, on the other hand, that the presence of a cognitive form or species in the knower is ipso facto a cognitive relation with the very form or species of some possible object. Perhaps it is not a genuine cognitive relation with any *particular* object. However, suppose that it is at least a cognitive relation with the form or the species of some possible object. Then in that case there will be no such thing as a cognitive state's "intrinsic nature." There will be no such thing as a state of a sort whose occurrence might or might not constitute a form of awareness or knowledge of some reality, or some aspect of reality. For the form or species thereby apprehended will in each instance itself be an appre-hended reality. However, except when performing some internal reflec-tion, the "species" by which one knows an object is not itself the object of cognition, but merely (part of) the means by which an object is cognized:

> Some have asserted that our intellectual powers know only the impressions made on them; as, for example, that sense is cognizant only of the impres-sion made on its own organ. According to this theory, the intellect under-stands only its own impressions, namely, the intelligible species which it has received. This is, however, manifestly false. . . . First, because the things we understand are also the objects of science. Therefore, if what we understand is merely the intelligible species in the soul, it would follow that every science would be concerned, not with things outside the soul, but only with the intelligible species within the soul. . . . Therefore it must be said that the intelligible species is related to the intellect as that *by which* [emphasis added] it understands. . . . But since the intellect reflects upon itself, by such reflection it understands both its own act of understanding, and the species by which it understands. Thus the intelligible species is secondarily that which is understood; but that which is primarily under-stood is the thing, of which the species is the likeness.[17]

A certain ambiguity attaches to the notion of an "object of knowledge." On the one hand the proper object of knowledge is precisely the defining form, nature, essence, or species of some thing or class of things: " . . . the essence of a thing is the proper object of the intellect. . . . [18] On the other hand, our concern to know the essences of things is precisely to know something about the things of which they are the essences. In this sense, it is the things themselves that are the "proper object" of cognition, and the forms and species which we abstract from them are merely part of the means by which we know them:

> The human intellect holds a middle place; for it is not the act of an organ, and yet it is a power of the soul, which is the form of the body. . . . And therefore it is proper to it to know a form existing individually in corporeal matter, but not as existing in this individual matter. But to know what is in individual matter, yet not as existing in such matter, is to abstract the form from individual matter which is represented by the phantasms. Therefore we must needs say that our intellect understands material things by abstracting from phantasms. . . . [19]

So it is no objection to a relational reading that the forms or species by which things are known are not themselves an object known (except "reflectively") but merely the means by which an object is known. For if the forms are the very forms of the things to be known, then in knowing an object the form itself perforce also is known. What complicates the issue is that while forms in the intellect are the same forms as are present in the things to be known, they are present in a different way in the intellect. Hence while their presence in the intellect is their being known, it is only through internal reflection that they are known precisely *as* they are in the intellect. In the nonreflective case, the forms of course function as the means by which some object is known. Hence while they are themselves ipso facto known, they are thereby known only "in the object, not as they are in the intellect."[20]

Consider another complication. On the relational approach the cognitive presence of the forms or species of things is not so much an internal *state* as it is a cognitive *relation* of some sort. However, consider now our cognitive relations precisely with those things of which these are forms or species. According to St. Thomas, these relations are mediated by the sensible forms received from objects, or by the "phantasms" remaining in imagination and memory from the original reception of sensible form. Thus I know some particular thing when my intellect "turns to" the phantasms in question, abstracting the intelligible form from them and receiving it into the intellect. The cognitive relation to the particular, then, does indeed involve some internal state with the property of representing an object:

> Now what is abstracted from individual matter is universal. Hence our intellect knows directly only universals. But indirectly, however, and as it were by a kind of reflexion, it can know the singular, because, as we have

said above, even after abstracting the intelligible species, the intellect, in order to understand actually, needs to turn to the phantasms in which it understands the species, as is said in *De Anima* iii. Therefore it understands the universal directly through the intelligible species, and indirectly the singular *represented by the phantasm* [emphasis added]. And thus it forms the proposition, *Socrates is a man.*[21]

As we shall see more clearly later, the phantasm plays a role in Aquinas analogous to that of Kantian intuitions. It is that element in our "faculty of representation" which represents the particular to be conceptualized by the intellect. But two points should be noted. First, though singular reference is mediated by the phantasm, hence by something that is an internal state and not a mere relation, nevertheless that state is not itself the state by which the object is known. The latter simply turns out to be a more complex relation, namely between (a) knower, (b) form abstracted from the phantasm, (c) phantasm (in its organ), (d) particular represented by the phantasm. No one of these is the cognitive state by which the knower is directed to the object. Furthermore, consider the sense in which the phantasm itself is a cognitive "state" that represents some object to us. That, apparently, would be nothing but the fact that the phantasm is the "immaterial" presence, within the organ for memory and imagination, of a certain form received originally from sense (or imaginatively "composed" from forms thus received).[22] Thus the internal state that represents the particular to be known turns out to be itself a complex relation. It is a relation between (a) knower (or a certain organ of the knower), (b) object from which certain sensible forms are received, (c) the forms in question. Thus all cognitive "states," it seems, are really certain sorts of relational *states of affairs*, and the object of a cognitive state is contained within it in the sense in which any entity is contained in the states of affairs involving it.

III. Descartes

The view most commonly attributed to Descartes involves, as suggested earlier, a special notion of mental representation and a corresponding new use for the term 'idea'.[23] Ideas, on this view, are entities of a distinctively "mental" sort. These, furthermore, are the immediate objects of cognition, or what one "directly perceives" (in a broad sense of the term). However, insofar as ideas are adequate representations of reality, we might also regard them not as immediate objects of knowledge, but merely as the means by which we attain to knowledge of the reality in question.

As some commentators have recently argued, there is question as to the extent to which Descartes departed from the Scholastic theory. With respect, at least, to the theory of sensation, the departure is clear. It is most dramatically clear with respect to his view about colors. For the colors, on

Descartes's account, that we are conscious of "in our senses" are in no sense identical with some feature of the objects that, by affecting our senses, cause them to be "received." Perceived colors, in this respect, are like pains. There is no more reason to suppose that they are in objects than there is to suppose that pain is in the knife that cuts me: "I found . . . that colours, odours, savours, and the rest of such things, were merely sensations existing in my thought, and differing no less from bodies than pain differs from the shape and motion of the instrument which inflicts it.[24]

Descartes takes "the term idea to stand for whatever the mind directly perceives."[25] In this sense, then, colors, odors, savors, etc., are ideas. (In fact, though, Descartes does not appear particularly comfortable calling sensations *ideas*, preferring to speak rather of our ideas *of* sensations.[26] This no doubt reflects his own uneasy recognition of the vast difference that his own view acknowledges between sensations and other sorts of ideas.) But these particular sorts of ideas are especially inadequate from the representational point of view. In this respect, they are unlike certain other ideas:

> Size in the body which is seen, or figure or movement . . . or situation, or duration, or number, and the like, which we clearly perceive in all bodies, as has been already described, are known by us in a quite different way from that in which colour is known in the same body, or pain, odour, taste, or any of the properties which, as hitherto mentioned, should be attributed to the senses.[27]

I shall call the more inadequate of these two types of ideas *sensations*. Descartes himself does so, though there is something misleading in this. It blurs a distinction between sensation as certain sorts of immediately perceived qualities (e.g., colors) and sensation as the state of apprehending those qualities. It also implies that there are no sensations of shape. The issues connected with both of these points will occupy our attention when we turn more explicitly to Kant.

Except for one respect, sensations typify the approach to ideas that is commonly thought to be Descartes's. They are mental entities; they are immediate objects of awareness; and they represent, albeit inadequately, aspects of the "external world." Most importantly, they represent aspects of that world without, as the Scholastics held, being *identical* with those aspects. But sensations, of course, are not present when we're merely thinking about the world, or dealing with it in purely intellectual terms. So there must be some other ideas that are not sensory but intellectual. Nevertheless, these must share all of the other features of sensations (except of course for the inadequacy of their representation). Thus the idea before my mind when I merely contemplate something is also something mental (hence "immaterial") that more or less adequately represents the thing that I am contemplating.[28]

Though the Cartesian account of sensation constitutes a radical departure from the Scholastic theory, it is important not to assume that Descartes thereby formulated a nonrelational account of sensation. The account is anti-Scholastic, inasmuch as the sensations we perceive are in no way identical with the objects that they represent to us. Nevertheless, so long as the perceiving of them (e.g., seeing a color) is some sort of unique relation between the mind and the sensation in question, then the account remains a relational one. Colors are objects of perception, but the question hinges precisely on the account of that perception. Is seeing a color simply a kind of relation with that color? Or is it rather an internal state with the (possibly relational) property of being (a seeing) *of* that color? The relational approach regards an instance of seeing as a relation between a perceiver (for Descartes, a "mind") and an object seen. The seeing is that relation. A nonrelational approach would regard an instance of seeing as some sort of internal state or event that at most has the *property* of relating the perceiver to some object (and which in other cases may in fact only seem so to relate the perceiver).

An alternative to the relational approach requires abandoning the standard interpretation of Descartes. What we might suggest is this. Strictly speaking, there are no such things as the colors that we see. There is of course such a thing as the seeing *of* all those colors. But none of those colors is something that really exists; they are all a kind of fiction generated by the mechanisms of sense perception. It is important to be clear how this differs from the standard interpretation. On that approach, all the colors that we see really do exist. But they exist in a special mental realm; they exist in the mind of the perceiver. Thus there are two things that we might mean by supposing that colors are only mental or that they exist only "in the mind." Taken one way, what we mean is that they do not really exist at all, but only the seeing of them exists. Taken another way, what we mean is that they really do exist, in just as real a fashion as the seeing of them does, but they do not exist in the material world.

There is some sense in which Descartes, no doubt unconsciously, took a step in the direction of the new approach. For precisely because Descartes, unlike the Scholastics, tended to confuse the color seen with the state of seeing the color, he opened the door to the notion that the mind has its own internal contents quite *apart* from its cognitive relations to the objects which it knows. (And he thereby opened the door to the notion that it is only on the basis of such internal content that cognitive relations are possible in the first place.) But Descartes himself, it seems, regarded colors as mental entities whose presence in the mind constitutes perception of those entities. For Descartes, that is, the "state" of seeing the entities in question just *is* the relation which those entities bear to the mind (their "presence in" it); it is not a state with some internal content of its own. On the other hand, it is hard to square the standard view with the rest of

Descartes's theory. If color is a mental entity, for example, then in Descartes's view it cannot be something that is really spread out in some spatial form. For the mind is something unextended. Nonetheless, the colors we see do seem to be extended in spatial forms. And at one point Descartes himself refers to the extension of the colors that we see.[29] (According to the Scholastic account, of course, this is no problem. The colors that we see are indeed spread out on the surfaces of objects.) Strictly speaking, this does not constitute a contradiction on Descartes's part. Descartes could always maintain that the colors we see are not really spread out to fill spatial forms; they merely seem to be. Now certainly if the shapes that we see are themselves the surfaces of objects (hence certain "modes of extension"), this is just what Descartes would be expected to say: the colors that we see are not really on the surfaces of those objects; all that is located there are the various shapes and motions responsible for the reflection of light (itself constituted, for Descartes, by other motions) to the organs of sense. But on the standard approach to Descartes the shapes *that we see* ought themselves to be certain ideas in our mind, ideas that at best *represent* (in a much better way than the colors do) the shape of the object in question. On the alternative approach, of course, one might simply concede that what we see is a colored shape, but no such shape exists; only the seeing of it does.

There is a strong tendency in Descartes's thinking to associate our cognitive relations with the spatial aspects of reality exclusively with our intellect rather than the senses. Thus there is a tendency to suppose that even in sense perception the awareness of spatial form involves an element of intellection that is not involved in the awareness of the colors that seem to fill that form.[30] As a number of commentators have recently argued, however, Descartes's view of *intellectual* activity is in fact hardly distinguishable from the Scholastic account.

Sometimes when Descartes thinks of "ideas" he is thinking about a certain sort of (mental) object. This at least is so, though not without some confusion, in the case of sensations. But other times he seems to have something different in mind:

> *Idea* is a word by which I understand the form of any thought, that form by the immediate awareness of which I am conscious of that said thought. . . .[31] For, since ideas themselves are forms, and are never composed of any matter, when we take them as representing something, we regard them not *in a material guise* but *formally*; but if we were to consider them not in so far as they represent this or that other thing, but in the respect in which they are *operations of the intellect* [emphasis added], it might be said that they were taken materially, but then they would have no reference to the truth or falsity of objects.[32]

In these passages Descartes seems to use the term 'idea' in two ways. In one way the term signifies the occurrence of a mental act, not an object of some sort. In a second sense the term signifies the "form" of a mental act. And in regard to the latter, Descartes seems to say two things. First, it is that aspect of an act in virtue of our awareness of which we are *conscious* of it. Second, it is that aspect of an act that has to do with the specific representational quality of the act, i.e., with the specification of what it is (an act of thinking) *about*. As one might expect, these points are connected: awareness of mental activity is of course awareness precisely of what one is thinking about. Thus the "form" in question is that by which I am conscious of the thought *"in such a way that,* when understanding what I say, I can express nothing in words, without that very fact making it certain that I possess the idea of that which these words signify" [emphasis added].[33]

What this suggests, one might argue, is precisely that Descartes has departed from the relational theory. A mental act ("operation of the intellect") is some sort of internal state, occurrence, or episode that constitutes a thought about something in virtue of some particular quality or feature of itself. Only in virtue of possession of that quality or feature is the episode a representational one, hence only that possession allows it to place the knower in a specific cognitive relation with some object. A mental act, in other words, is not itself a cognitive relation, but an occurrence which, through its internal "form," makes such relations possible.

But in another passage Descartes takes pains to distinguish ideas considered "materially" (as operations of the intellect) from ideas considered with respect to what determines their specific content:

> In this term *idea* there is here something equivocal, for it may either be taken materially, as an act of my understanding, and in this sense it cannot be said that it is more perfect than I; or it may be taken objectively, as *the thing which is represented by this act,* which, although we do not suppose it to exist outside of my understanding, may, none the less, be more perfect than I, because of its essence [emphasis added].[34]

One might of course suggest that there are *three* uses of the term for Descartes. Ideas are either acts, the "forms" of acts, or the (mentally "inexisting") *objects* of acts. But if ideas taken objectively are merely mentally inexisting objects, then it is at least difficult to interpret this claim according to the standard representational approach. On that approach an idea (qua mental object) is a mental entity that represents (what we take to be) the actual external object that we are thinking about. It is in no sense identical with that object. But in that case it is difficult to see why an idea taken objectively is any more likely to be something "more perfect than I" than an idea considered as an operation of the intellect. Clearly Descartes is saying that if the object about which I am thinking is, in virtue of its nature or essence, something more perfect than I, then the idea by which I *represent* that object is something more perfect than I. Descartes's (Third *Meditation*) argument for the existence of God, as a being whose nature or essence is infinite perfection, rests precisely on this assumption. The passage we are now discussing is part of his reply to an objection to that argument. But this assumption is illegitimate unless an idea taken objectively *is* identical with the object in question, at least with respect to its essence.

Furthermore, Descartes himself seems to grant that the representational quality of an act simply *is* the fact that the act's object is "objectively present" in the mind:

> If the question be, what the idea of the sun is, and the reply is given, that it is the object thought of in so far as that exists objectively in the understanding, he will not understand that it is the sun itself, in so far as that extrinsic attribute is in it . . . but that it is in the mind in the way in which objects are wont to exist there. Hence the idea of the sun will be the sun itself existing in the mind, not indeed formally, as it exists in the sky, but objectively, i.e. in the way in which objects are wont to exist in the mind. . . . [35]

Descartes of course wants to insist that the sun is not in the mind in the way that it is in the sky. It is in the mind, presumably, via its nature or essence (at least as we understand that nature or essence). Thus Descartes makes it clear elsewhere that what is in the understanding, by way of our ideas, is not "substances" but the "attributes" of substances. The attributes in question, when really characterizing some substance, are said to be "formally" in it; they are only in our thought "objectively" (or as Descartes sometimes seems to prefer, the thing itself is thereby in our thought):

> Neither do we have any other idea of substance itself, precisely taken, than that it is a thing in which this something that we perceive or which is present objectively in some of our ideas, exists formally or eminently. For by means of our natural light we know that a real attribute cannot be an attribute of nothing.[36]

Thus while the attributes are not in our understanding formally, but only objectively, it is nonetheless the presence of those attributes that constitutes the "form of the thought" in question. So an idea considered materially (an operation of the intellect) simply *is* the "objective presence" of the object of the idea. It is nothing but the relation of objective presence, not an episode which, in virtue of its internal quality, makes such relations possible. In this sense, an idea is a mere "form."

Thus Descartes's own account of ideas (other than sensations)[37] seems indistinguishable from the Scholastic approach. And so would be his account of the singular reference of ideas to particular things. Corresponding to the role of sensible forms and phantasms, and their causal relations with the particular things in question, Descartes would presumably appeal to the causal factors involved in the production of sensations and the corresponding images in the brain. The latter, though, unlike the Scholastics, he viewed as wholly material.[38]

To sum up, finally, and to anticipate. Kant is often supposed to have held that the immediate objects of sense perception are just our own sensations, or at least our own sensations structured into objects of "intuition" in accordance with certain of our own innate tendencies. A Cartesian basis for this sort of view is also supposed, and Descartes in fact often does espouse such a doctrine. But there is reason to believe that Descartes himself wavered between two points of view. On one of these sensation involves some kind of relation of the perceiving mind to immediately perceived qualities. As on the Scholastic account, too, the relation in question is regarded as a kind of presence of those qualities within the cognitive faculties of the perceiver; specifically within the mind itself. By contrast with the Scholastics, though, these qualities are not taken to be in any way identical with the forms or qualities of external objects. At most they "correspond" to such forms. However, Descartes also seems to lean toward a different conception. On this conception mere sensation does not as such involve the apprehension of perceptible objects or qualities, but is merely an essential ingredient *within* the apprehension of perceptible objects or qualities. This is Kant's view too.

To the extent that Descartes does lean toward the second of these points of view, he also leans toward a second doctrine that is definitely not Kantian. For he then inclines toward the view that every bit of object-directedness on the part of one's cognitive faculties is totally a function of the *intellectual* ideas that are attached to, or associated with, mere sensations. However, the whole point of Kant's distinction between forms of intuition and forms of the understanding is that the direction of our cognitive faculties to objects of apprehension involves an element that is *not* wholly a function of the understanding or of purely intellectual ideas. Many people are inclined to think that this signifies regression to the supposition that the immediate objects of sense perception are our own sensations, or at least include them as aspects in some way. However, Kant's attempt to attribute some primitive sort of object-directedness to mere intuition, as opposed to genuine conception and understanding, signifies neither return to the Scholastic conception of sensation as immediate cognitive contact with reality "in itself" nor return to a Cartesian conception of the immediate objects of sense perception as sensations themselves. In any case, finally, we have seen that Descartes himself adheres to a basically Scholastic conception of intellect. Conceptual "forms" for Descartes are just instances of the mind's reception of the intelligible forms or aspects of external reality. For Kant, by contrast, conceptual forms are at most aspects of cognitive states themselves.[39]

IV. Leibniz

The notion of representation is central to Leibniz's philosophy. Leibniz also uses the term 'expression' to signify it. The latter term may seem especially adapted to certain theological and ontological issues in Leibniz, rather than epistemological ones:

> Every individual substance expresses the entire universe in its own way and in a certain relationship, or from that point of view, so to speak, from which it regards it. It follows also that its subsequent state is the result, though free or contingent, of its preceding state, as if there were only God and itself in the world. . . . Yet this independence does not prevent the intercourse of substances with each other, for since all created substances are a continual production of the same sovereign being, by the same designs, and expressing the same universe or the same phenomena, they correspond exactly with each other.[40]

In fact, though, the notion of representation/expression extends, for Leibniz, beyond both ontological and epistemological contexts. Thus in a purely logical or mathematical context, the projection of a solid figure onto a plane may be said to represent or express that solid figure, or the model of a machine to represent or express the machine.[41] Still, there is a single genus according to Leibniz under which these as well as the other species of representation fall:

> One thing expresses another, in my usage, when there is a constant and regular relation between what can be said about the one and about the other. It is in this way that a projection in perspective expresses a geometric figure. Expression is common to all the forms and is a genus of which natural perception, animal feeling, and intellectual knowledge are species. In natural perception and feeling it suffices that what is divisible and material and is found dispersed among several beings should be expressed or represented in a single indivisible being or in a substance which is endowed with a true unity. The possibility of such a representation of several things in one cannot be doubted, since our soul provides us with an example of it. . . . Now this expression takes place everywhere, because every substance sympathizes with all the others and receives a proportional change corresponding to the slightest change which occurs in the whole world. . . . [42]

The primacy of epistemological representation is guaranteed, however, by a rather peculiar doctrine to which Leibniz adheres. This is that, first of all, reality is comprised of nothing but "single indivisible" beings or "true unities"; anything else is nothing but aggregations of such beings. Second, the only internal characteristic of such beings is their perceptions (in a suitably broad sense of the term, including both sensory and intellectual "perception"): "this is the only thing—namely, perceptions and their changes—that can be found in simple substance."[43] Our knowledge of the world of bodies extended in space, then, merely reflects the various perceptions that are possible from the positions which single substances "occupy." These are linked to one another solely in virtue of divinely established "constant and regular" correspondences relating what is perceived from one with what is perceived from another position. Thus corresponding to a position in my visual field (say some position that I locate on the wall across the room) will be a set of perceptions different from but related to what I perceive from here. (That is just what that spot's being there rather than here means to me.) Knowledge of the principles of visual perspective, of course, permits *inferences* from what I perceive to what is perceived from there. The reality of the world of extended bodies, then, is just the reality of the set of perceptual points of view related by such principles. Their constant and regular operation assures that all the substances "occupying" those points "express" or "represent" all the others in their perceptions:

> Now this mutual connection or accommodation of all created things to each other and of each to all the rest causes each simple substance to have relations which express all the others and consequently to be a perpetual living mirror of the universe. . . . Just as the same city viewed from different sides appears to be different and to be, as it were, multiplied in perspectives, so the infinite multitude of simple substances, which seem to be so many different universes, are nevertheless only the perspectives of a single universe according to the different points of view of each monad.[44] God could give to each substance its own phenomena independent of those of others, but in this way he would have made as many worlds without connection, so to speak, as there are substances, almost as we say that when we dream, we are in a world apart and that we enter into the common world when we wake up. Not that dreams do not also correspond with the organs and the rest of the body, but in a less distinct way.[45]

And in virtue, of course, of the constant and regular divine activity involved, each thing will also express God in its perceptions.

Now it is clear from the start that on Leibniz's view perceptual representation cannot be explained in terms of a Scholastic model of reception within the subject of forms or natures really existing outside of itself. To be sure, Leibniz does not reject the notion that in some sense perceptions involve reception from God. But even here reception is reduced to a purely *causal* notion. (So it is in Kant's case as well.) We receive our experiences and thoughts from God in the sense that God is the ultimate explanation of our ability to have them. Beyond this, there is no notion that *what* we experience, or *what* we perceive or think is in some way identical with some nature or form received from things outside of us. At best, Leibniz seems to hold, our perceptions "represent" what is real apart from ourselves:

> Being constrained, then, to admit that it is impossible for the soul or any other true substance to receive something from without, except by the divine omnipotence, I was led [to the view that] . . . God has originally created the soul, and every other real unity, in such a way that everything in it must arise from its own nature by a perfect *spontaneity* with regard to itself, yet by a perfect *conformity* to things without . . . these perceptions internal to the soul itself come to it through its own original constitution, that is to say, through its representative nature. . . . [46]

The Scholastic account, as noted, need not be taken as literally entailing the reception and subsequent containment of objects within the knower. Nonetheless, objects are at least always contained within the mental acts of the knower. This, as we saw, makes representation a basically relational matter. Now Leibniz does not deny the possibility of representational "relations." But apart from the common relation in which everything stands to divine agency, relations involving substances, on his view, are simply coordinated conjunctions of *internal states* of substances. Thus, considering the status of "chains" of monads, each linked by some sort of relation to the others, Leibniz says:

> Since no modification can subsist by itself but essentially entails a substantial subject, these chains will have what reality they possess in the modification of each monad and in the harmony or agreement of the monads with each other. I do not believe that you will admit an accident that is in two subjects at the same time. My judgment about relations is that paternity in David is one thing, sonship in Solomon another, but that the relation common to both is a merely mental thing whose basis is the modifications of the individuals. . . . [47]

That a monad represents, through its cognitive states, precisely what it represents involves nothing more than a conjunction of facts about its own internal "state" or "modification," together with the corresponding facts about the internal states of everything else.

It has been argued that Leibniz did not really regard relations as totally reducible to conjunctions of internal states of substances.[48] Certainly he often makes only a weaker claim, but even this claim supports the conclusion of the preceding paragraph. For even if relations are not wholly reducible to conjunctions of facts about the internal states of substances, nonetheless, Leibniz insists, they are made *possible* only in virtue of such facts:

> It follows further that *there are no purely extrinsic denominations* which have no basis at all in the denominated thing itself. . . . Likewise, whenever the denomination of a thing is changed, some variation has to occur *in the thing itself* [emphasis added].[49]

Thus "there must be something in me *which not merely leads me to the thing [expressed] but also expresses it.*"[50] That is, one might so interpret, cognitive relations with something represented are themselves made possible only in virtue of internal features of the representation itself. And so Leibniz continues: "That is said to express a thing in which there are relations [*habitudines*] which correspond to the relations of the thing expressed . . . [such that] we can pass from a consideration of the relations *in the expression* to a knowledge of the corresponding properties of the thing expressed" [emphasis added]. It is this feature of Leibniz's view that leads one writer to observe: "Introducing the concept of "expressive content" of ideas signifies clear refutation of the naive Cartesian tendency to identify the idea itself with its mere representative content."[51]

There are, however, two ways to understand Leibniz's talk about relations "in the expression." I shall try to explicate the first of these with the help of some ideas derived from the philosophy of Franz Brentano. Brentano puts to his own use the notion of "intentional inexistence," which he derives from his understanding of Scholastic philosophy:

> Every mental phenomenon is characterized by what the scholastics of the Middle Ages called the intentional (and also mental) inexistence of an object, and what we could call, although in not entirely unambiguous terms, the reference to a content, a direction upon an object (by which we are not to understand a reality in this case), or an immanent objectivity.[52]

What Brentano has in mind is the phenomenon of mental "directedness" to an object, but he wants to emphasize the possibility of the occurrence of that phenomenon in the absence of the object's real *existence*. The Scholastics, of course, had their own view about such possibilities. For them, it was also perfectly possible to "intend" nonexistent objects. But this was only so because one's intention includes some form or nature which, by the very fact that it "inexists" in the knower, is not something completely nonexistent. Brentano, however, does not accept any ontological account of intentionality.[53] He uses the term 'intentional inexistence' to signify the

fact that some psychological state has an object, while remaining completely neutral with regard to questions concerning the object's ontological
status. Brentano of course does not deny that many psychological states are
directed toward real objects. His only point is that a necessary condition for
that being the case is that the state also possess a feature in virtue of which
it would still have been describable as object-directed, even were the
object in question to have failed to be real. Brentano uses the term
'intentionality' to stand for this feature. The feature is not a genuine
relation, since the object need not exist, but it is, according to Brentano,
something like a relation.[54] Furthermore, the presence of this feature is a
necessary condition for the obtaining of genuine cognitive relations with
objects.

Now the notion that I want to introduce involves the "intentional object"
of a cognitive state. The description of a state's intentional object, I shall
say, is whatever description of its object is licensed by the mere occurrence
of the state itself, without regard to extrinsic questions concerning the
ontological status of its object, or concerning that object's own nature
(should it differ from our representation of it). It is clear that for Leibniz any
representative state should necessarily be describable with respect to an
intentional object. For it is part of the *intrinsic nature* of a monad that it
represent the world as it does. Hence that world should be in principle
describable merely as the correlate of the representation of it, without any
further question as to the true nature or ontological status of what might in
fact correspond to or agree with that representation. But we do need to
make one qualification here, with respect to the notion of intentionality as
we have taken it from Brentano. For Leibniz, namely, but not for Brentano, states may be representative states, and hence involve the perception
of objects, without involving any *consciousness* of those objects.[55] What
Leibniz seems to have in mind is the possibility of perceiving something
without perceiving *that* one is perceiving it. Leibniz reserves the term
'apperception' for this additional feature. Such unconscious perceptions,
according to Leibniz, are also part of most ordinary perceptions, as when,
for example, one perceives the roar of a multitude without distinctly
perceiving each of the component sounds that go to make it up. In that case
one simply fails to perceive distinctions within the total auditory intentional object. One fails to perceive distinctions that would correspond to
those present in at least some of the intentional objects defined by the
infinitely many other points of view that there are.[56]

In a certain way, one might attempt to broaden the notion of an intentional object beyond what is useful in an interpretation of Kant. Suppose I
happen to be thinking that there is a certain sort of object in my vicinity.
Then someone might contend that an object of that sort is, or is part of, the

"intentional object" of my thought on that occasion. This, however, would blur an important distinction. It would blur the distinction between my merely thinking *that there is* an object of that sort and my actually *imagining* such an object (forming, one might say, an "image" of it). I shall have a good deal more to say about this distinction in later chapters, as well as concerning the relation between the intentionality of imagination and that of sense perception. We might simply register here that the notion of an intentional object, insofar as it is useful for elucidation of such Kantian notions as those of "appearance" and of "forms of intuition," must be understood in a way that relates it to our capacity for actually imagining an object of some sort, and not merely to our capacity for thinking (or indeed imagining) *that there are* objects of that sort (or that some otherwise identifiable objects might *be* of that sort).

The term '*Vorstellung*' most naturally suggests, in ordinary usage, the case of imagination. Kant, like many philosophers, extends it beyond this realm. He extends it, as suggested, to the case of sense perception, and he also extends it to include concepts and judgments. The first two cases, as we shall see, play a very special role. These involve what Kant calls "intuition" (*Anschauung*). Any given intuition might be conceptualized in various ways; it might, as I put it later, be "informed" by any number of different concepts. The concepts determine how one is *thinking* about (or "of") the object in question. The "form of intuition," on the other hand, determines that, in any such instance, one is not merely thinking (even hypothetically) *that* something is the case, but rather thinking *about* some (perhaps merely imaginary) object presented in imagination or through sensation. It is in this latter regard that the notion of an "intentional object" is useful in an interpretation of Kant.[57]

Kant himself was ambivalent with respect to the possibility of unconscious intuitions. This, as we shall see in Chapter Five, is connected with Kant's concern with the possibility of unconceptualized intuitions. Certainly it seems to be his view that, in some important sense, unconceptualized intuitions would have to be unconscious ones. (Like Leibniz, in addition, Kant connects the notion of unconscious representations with that of representations that are not also the object of some kind of *self-consciousness*.) To the extent to which Kant is prepared to tolerate a notion of unconscious intuition, he of course appears to tolerate an idea foreign to Brentano, namely of an "intentionality" and of "intentional objects" associated with the occurrence of unconscious "mental" activity. However, one might, by a kind of stipulation, remove the apparent difference at this point. As we shall see later, all that Kant's arguments require is the admission that within any *conscious* instance of imagination or of sense perception, an intentionality is operative that is not itself determined by whatever conceptual factors might be involved and which guarantees that any such factors are serving precisely to conceptualize some properly intentional *object* of consciousness.

To return to Leibniz, in any case, we now have one sense in which a monad might be said to "contain" relations corresponding to the reality which it expresses: it contains them in that its intentional *object* contains those relations. Correspondence between expression and what is expressed, or between representation and represented, is simply correspondence between the intentional object comprising the world of any monad, and the elements that it contains, and those comprising the worlds of all the others.

Viewed in this way, Leibniz's conception appears to involve a departure from any form of the relational account. On this conception, the primary ingredient in the subject's ability to represent "external" reality is not some primitive relation in which it stands to reality's knowable aspects. Rather, it is the subject's coming to be in states that make such relations possible. In other words, the primary ground for cognitive relations among monads is the primitive fact of each monad apprehending a *possible* reality. That reality also is an actual reality for Leibniz. But so far as the immediate internal state of any monad is concerned, it might not have been. What is represented by a monad is a represented reality only because God has created other monads with corresponding representations. Consider, for example, the tree that one perceives across the quad. This perceived tree also is a real one. But it is a real one only because God has created infinitely many other perceivers (monads), defining infinitely many other "points of view" on that tree. Each point of view, as an intrinsic state of the monad, is defined, on this interpretation, by a distinct intentional object.

If we do interpret Leibniz along these lines, we can then regard Kant's innovations as developing Leibnizian insights. For the central notion in Kant's conception of representation rests precisely on that of an intentional object. But Leibniz's representations would still not be "inner states" in the Kantian sense. Representational states will be inner for Leibniz simply in the sense that they are intrinsic properties of a perceiver; not as such relations, they are only the foundation for relations. But the very fact that representational states are properties of the perceiver is what makes them unsuitable as Kantian representations. The point relates to one upon which Brentano was later to insist. It would be wrong, according to Brentano, to suppose that any particular psychological state is nothing other than the *property*, exemplified by some perceiver, of apprehending an ("intentional") object of a certain description.[58] The reason for this, on Brentano's view, is that the very same psychological state that intends a given intentional object will also have the property of intending itself. Were a psychological state *itself* the property of intending an object, then we never could say that the same state both intended that object and also intended itself. The most we could say is that any state intending an object is necessarily connected with a state intending the original one. This for Brentano was quite impossible, since it leads to an infinite regress. The only way to avoid the regress is to suppose, not that the self-consciousness connected with any given psychological state involves a distinct psychological state, but simply that any psychological state exemplifies two distinct intentional, or representational, properties. It exemplifies the property of intending its (primary) object, and it exemplifies the property of intending itself. So a psychological state cannot be identified with intentional or representational properties. Rather, a psychological state itself *exemplifies* representational properties.[59]

Kant's view of self-awareness is, despite some similarities, importantly different from Brentano's. Nevertheless the general consideration applies in Kant's case as well, insofar as only such a notion of representation as Brentano's approach involves (whatever the account of *self*-representation) will permit one and the same psychological state to exemplify both the cognitive quality of sense perception and also that of intellection. Kant's conception of representations, not as Scholastic forms received within the perceiver, but as internal states that nonetheless *have* their own "forms," does in fact offer such an account. Leibniz's conception fails to do so. Leibniz does grant the possibility of *concepts* or *thoughts* that are both sensory and intellectual.[60] But that is simply the possibility of thoughts that combine a reference to the way in which things appear to the senses with a reference involving an intelligible content of a different sort. What Leibniz does not allow is the possibility of a sensory state, as opposed to a thought, that also has intellectual content (and is not merely connected to a distinct state that does). This is impossible, as we shall see shortly, precisely in virtue of Leibniz's view that sensation is inherently "confused." Leibniz also drew the distinction in terms of action and passion:

> The created being is said to *act* outwardly insofar as it has perfection and to *suffer* from another insofar as it is imperfect. Thus *action* is attributed to a monad insofar as it has distinct perceptions, and *passion* insofar as it has confused ones.[61]

Unlike the other way of drawing the distinction, Kant agrees with this association of sensation with passivity and intellection with activity. But what Leibniz failed to account for was precisely the interrelationship between these factors in experience.

Now we have been taking as our point of departure Leibniz's suggestion that representation rests upon a correspondence among the representational states of various perceivers. What Leibniz says is that there must be a

set of relations within any representational (or "expressive") state that
corresponds to relations in what that state represents (or "expresses"). This
doctrine, as we have seen, leads Leibniz to the conclusion that there must
be intrinsic differences within any given perceiver corresponding to all the
distinctions within the reality perceived by it. So far we have not tried to
take that notion very literally. We have not supposed that Leibniz really
means that within the internal state of a perceiver there must be distinctions and relations corresponding to all those within a perceived reality.
We have rather taken him to mean only that it must be possible (at least for
a divine intellect) to draw such distinctions, and to establish such correspondences, within and among the (intentional) *objects* apprehended by
perceivers. Kant, as we shall see, took Leibniz more closely at his word.

It is not easy to tell from Leibniz's express words just how literally he
supposed that any ordinary perceptual state must be a complex system of
representational states. He does say that the sense in which a perception
must "enfold a multitude" in the unity of a single state requires a multitude
of "affections and of relations in the simple substance, even though it has
no parts."[62] That the monad has no parts might at once suggest that any
multiplicity within its representational state could be nothing other than
multiplicity within its intentional object. As we have already seen, however, a multiplicity of representational states would in any case amount
only to a multiplicity of *properties* exemplified by a perceiver for Leibniz,
not of literal parts of that perceiver. Thus an ordinary perceptual state
might be regarded as a complex property of a perceiver, without prejudi-
cing the perceiver's ontological simplicity.

It is possible that Leibniz inclined toward two contrary conceptions.
There is reason to suppose, in any case, that he did in fact incline toward
the second of the two views that I have distinguished. This is reflected in
Leibniz's acceptance of a doctrine for which Kant in fact criticizes him. The
point emerges just as soon as we ask what could be the objects of those basic
perceptions of which all ordinary perceptions would be composed, on the
second of the views that I have suggested. What could be the objects of the
infinitely many subrepresentations that go to make up a total representation of some particular spatial expanse? On Leibniz's view, "corresponding" to the infinite divisibility of a perceived spatial expanse, as an
intentional object, is some particular set of infinitely many indivisible
monads.[63] Obviously, then, if a total representation of such an expanse is
itself composed of infinitely many subsidiary representations, the objects
of these representations could only be precisely those monads. So somehow the members of a set of perceptions would have to be so interrelated
within a single perceptual state that the object of the state as a whole
becomes a spatial expanse, even though the objects of its component parts
are not spatial. This leads immediately to a doctrine that Leibniz in fact

accepts, and for which he is criticized by Kant. It leads to the view that the difference between properly intellectual and merely sensory representations of reality is that the latter presents the objects of the former to our mind in what is merely a "confused" manner.

Leibniz's view seems to be just what Kant thought it was, when Kant supposed that for Leibniz both sense perception and a truly intellectual grasp of reality are directed to the same "objects." They are directed to what Kant called things "in themselves." The difference is that intellection represents those objects (by thinking about them) in ways corresponding to their actual nature. Sense perception represents them merely as they appear to us. It represents them, that is, as they are "expressed" in our ordinary sense perceptions. And this difference, Leibniz holds, corresponds to a distinction between representations that are "distinct" and those that involve "confusion": "Therefore whatever follows from the laws of body must necessarily be represented in order by the soul to itself, some of it distinctly but some confusedly. . . . In the former case, the soul understands; in the latter, it senses."[64]

Kant objected most strenuously to what he took to be the point of this distinction:

> The concept of sensibility and of appearance would be falsified, and our whole teaching in regard to them would be rendered empty and useless, if we were to accept the view that our entire sensibility is nothing but a confused representation of things, containing only what belongs to them in themselves, but doing so under an aggregation of characters and partial representations that we do not consciously distinguish. . . . The representation of a body in intuition . . . contains nothing that can belong to an object in itself, but merely the appearance of something. . . . The philosophy of Leibniz and Wolff, in thus treating the difference between the sensible and the intelligible as merely logical, has given a completely wrong direction to all investigations into the nature and origin of our knowledge. (A43–44/B60–61)

On Kant's own view, as I would suggest, the immediate object of sense perception is an intentional object. At one time, as we saw, Kant agreed with Leibniz that the object of intellect (at least in its "real" use) was "things in themselves" (though even then he rejected the view that this was also the object of sense perception). But in the *Critique of Pure Reason* he held that the proper function of intellect is merely the representation of relations *among* (the intentional objects of) sense perceptions. It is not a difference between more or less adequate ways in which things in themselves are represented, not simply because the distinction is not one of degree, but because *neither* faculty involves the representation of "things in themselves."

On the other hand, Kant's own view is influenced by the view he ascribes to Leibniz. Recall the passage that I quoted earlier, from the *Inaugural Dissertation* (II, 4), concerning representations of sense:

> In a representation of sense there is first of all something which you might call the *matter*, namely the *sensation*, and there is also something which can be called the *form*, namely the *species* of the sensibles which arises according as the various things which affect the senses are coordinated by a certain natural law of the mind. . . . For objects do not strike the senses in virtue of their form or *species*. So, for the various things in an object which affect the sense *to coalesce into some representational whole* [emphasis added] there is needed an internal principle in the mind by which those various things may be clothed with a certain *species* in accordance with stable and innate laws.

The "species" of perceptual objects are not for Kant received into the faculties of the perceiver. All that is received there is a manifold of internal *effects* on that faculty. The set of these affection relations corresponds to the manifold of basic representations in a Leibnizian "representational whole." The latter, as Kant interpreted Leibniz, is comprised of a multitude of more basic representations of external reality. On Kant's view this is not so. The components in question at best represent effects within the *subject*: "A perception which relates solely to the subject as the modification of its state is *sensation*" (A320/B376). As on Leibniz's view, then, a perception always involves a structured whole (a whole possessing the right kind of "form") comprised of more basic elements. Like Leibniz, too, Kant was inclined to regard these more basic elements in terms of some relation between the percipient and "things in themselves." But for Kant this relation was at most a causal relation, not a relation of representation. The latter arises only through the representational whole itself. So the (intentional) object of the latter is not whatever things in themselves might in fact be in question. Kant calls this object "appearance." For Leibniz, of course, there are no relations of "affection" between monads; only God can affect a monad's internal state. So Leibniz, it seems, has no choice but to regard the relations constituting the manifold of "matter" for some representational whole as (in some now inexplicable sense) relations of *representation* of some reality outside the perceiver.

What seems to be the case, then, is that there is something of a contradiction in Leibniz's thinking about mental representations. On the one hand is the desire to hold that genuine cognitive relations presuppose a basis in internal states that are not themselves relational at all. This leads to a conception which is very much Kantian. It leads to a notion of perception as the apprehension of intentional objects; as the perception of objects that, in any particular case, might or might not correspond to any external reality. On the other hand, Leibniz's supposition that every perceptual state must "enfold" an infinitely complex multiplicity within itself seems to lead most naturally to a quite contrary conclusion. It leads to the view that every ordinary perception is a complex whose basic elements are unanalyzable (and quite unconscious) perceptions of things in themselves.

V. Berkeley and Hume

Kant was at least as concerned to clarify his relationship to the empiricists, especially Berkeley and Hume, as he was with regard to rationalistic thinkers like Descartes and Leibniz. It was Hume who interrupted Kant's "dogmatic slumber" by causing him to reflect more deeply on the possibility of "knowledge a priori."[65] That notion will occupy us in subsequent chapters. With regard to Berkeley, Kant's aim was to distinguish his own view of knowable reality as mere appearance from Berkeley's view that material objects are merely "collections of ideas."

Though Kant may not fully have understood Berkeley, he seems in the main to have adopted a fairly standard interpretation. On this interpretation, Berkeley accepted the view that the immediate objects of sensation are mental entities, which he called "ideas." These are all the "sensible qualities" that we are capable of perceiving. This view has also been attributed to Locke. Now both Locke and Berkeley agreed that sensuously perceived ideas do not, as such, exist apart from actually being perceived. But for Locke, it seems, they represent other entitities that do, namely physical objects (and qualities). Berkeley argued, on the other hand, that it makes no sense to suppose that such a "representational" relation obtains. So if physical objects are anything at all, they are themselves nothing other than ideas that are perceived.

We have seen that, despite a standard interpretation, Descartes's representationalism is more Scholastic than at first may strike us. It has been argued that the same goes for Locke.[66] I won't pursue the point here. There has also been considerable debate concerning the interpretation of Berkeley's view. Most of the debate concerns the meaning of Berkeley's claim that perceived ideas exist only "in the mind" of the perceiver of them. A number of things might be meant by this. First, ideas, we might suppose, are sensible qualities that inhere in the mind in the way that many philosophers regard qualities as inhering in substances.[67] The problem with this is that philosophers who talk about the "inherence" of qualities in substance usually have in mind the *qualification* of some substance. But Berkeley is clear that the presence of, for example, extension and figure in the mind does not make the mind in any way extended or shaped. Rather, "Those qualities are in the mind only as they are *perceived by it* [emphasis added]—that is, not by way of *mode* or *attribute*, but only by way of *idea. . . .* "[68] Of course, defenders of the "inherence account" could hold that the sort of inherence in question is simply not of a "qualifying" sort. But then it remains unclear what inherence is supposed to amount to. Furthermore, other passages seem to make it clear that ideas are in the mind only in the sense that they are *perceived* (or conceived) by the mind: "My meaning is only that the mind comprehends or perceives them".[69] "I know what I mean when I affirm that there is a spiritual substance or support of ideas, that is, that a spirit knows and perceives ideas."[70]

This suggests that we might adopt an intentional object approach.[71] When I earlier introduced the notion of an "intentional object," I did not suppose that the intentional object of a representation might not also be regarded as real apart from that representation. The point was simply to remain neutral with regard to the question. On this approach to Berkeley, though, ideas would be intentional objects that do *not* have any reality apart from the perception of them. This interpretation conforms to Berkeley's suggestion that ideas do not "exist" in the same sense that other things do: "*Spirits* and *ideas* are things so wholly different that when we say 'they exist,' 'they are known,' or the like, these words must not be thought to signify anything common to both natures. There is nothing alike or common in them . . . ."[72] But sometimes people speak of two radically different kinds of existence, or ways of existing, when all that they really mean is that the things in question are two radically different sorts of *things*.

A third interpretation makes pretty much the same point as this one. But it does less justice to Berkeley's terminology. On this approach, what Berkeley means by an "idea" is a *sensory state*, e.g., an instance of seeing a certain color, and Berkeley's point is simply that to say that some color exists is just to say that such a state exists.[73] On this view, however, ideas are not objects of sensation, nor are they identifiable with "sensible qualities" such as perceived colors, though Berkeley certainly speaks as if they are. To be sure, Berkeley does say there is no distinction between a sensory quality and the sensation of it.[74] But that claim can of course be given an interpretation on the intentional object approach as well. (That in fact is what I suggest Kant has in mind in claiming that "appearances" are not distinct from our representations of them. For Kant, though, the objects are not as for Berkeley sensible qualities, but particulars that we represent as *having* such qualities.)

I would suggest a fourth interpretation: Ideas for Berkeley are entities that exist in the mind in the sense that they exist only as constituents of the very *state* of perceiving them. A perceptual state, on this reading, is only a certain kind of relation. It is a relation between some mind and an idea that it perceives. The latter thus comprises the object *of* that state. So ideas are not in the mind in the way that qualities of a thing might be in it. To this extent critics of the inherence account are right. Rather, ideas are in the mind only in the way that perceived *objects* are. At the same time, however, ideas are also in the mind in an ontological sense. For they are entities contained as actual constituents within perceptual states (which latter, of course, are themselves at least "qualities" of some mind). And what of Berkeley's suggestion that there is no distinction between a perceptual state and its object? Obviously, that is a claim that itself calls for interpretation. On the present reading, it simply amounts to the assertion that ideas don't exist apart from their containment in perception. (And conception: Berkeley, like Leibniz and others, uses the term 'perception' very broadly.)[75]

In any case, there seem to be no such things in Berkeley as perceptual "states" in the Kantian sense. Even if ideas are construed as the intentional objects of perception, for example, there is no supposition that perceptions themselves are in that case anything other than cognitive qualities of the perceiving mind. But then it is still quite impossible (as on the other interpretations) to regard perceptions as states that might themselves *possess* (more than a single) representational ("ideational") quality. It is impossible to suppose that a single perception, for example, might possess both sensory and conceptual content. This will be so, of course, simply because perceptions don't possess representational characteristics in the first place. Rather, they simply *are* the perceiver's representational characteristics. Thus conceptualization of a given sensory idea can involve nothing other for Berkeley than the occurrence of some additional ideas. These are like sensory ideas, but they are weaker in some way. The only difference, for example, between an idea of fire when I think about it, and one when I sense it, is that the latter can burn me.[76] This is Hume's view as well.[77] For Berkeley and Hume, then, conceptualization of a sensory idea amounts to nothing other than association of it with distinct but related ideas.[78]

Were sensory representations states that themselves *possess* representational characters, then we could make sense, in a way that Berkeley and Hume could not, of the possibility of a single perception that both presents a sensory object and also conceptualizes it in some way. This, as Kant recognized, requires distinguishing between the object immediately presented in any representation and the "act" or the "state" of conceptualizing that object. Even when the object is regarded as an intentional object, this is a distinction that Kant allows us to draw. He does so, as we shall see, by distinguishing within any given perception the representational form in virtue of which it is a sensory presentation, and a distinct form in virtue of which it is a specific sort of conceptualizing act. Kant calls the former element the form of "intuition." The latter involves "concepts." (Thus on Kant's view concepts are not peculiarly mental objects. Rather, they are part of the "form" of our representations *of* objects.) Berkeley, as one might expect, rejects the distinction between an act and an object of perception. This is not because he denies an active mind altogether, as something over and above the perceptions that are in it. He rejects the distinction because, even if we can distinguish between mental activity and the sensible qualities that we find in sensory (or imaginative) presentations, we can't find that distinction *within* any instance of such presentation.[79] This in turn, we may surmise, is simply because the Berkeleian "presentation" of sensible qualities is nothing but the *presence* of those qualities in one's mind, i.e., in mental "states." So over and above the relation of "presence-in" itself, there is no room in such states for additional mental content. The only possible variation in representational content has to be provided by the objects comprising it; there is no distinction between presented objects and the specific content of our presentations *of* those objects.

As we shall see, Kant's own view is not free from an important ambiguity regarding the notion of a mental act. We need to draw an act/object distinction (even if in certain cases the object should prove to be, though "intended," nonexistent) in order to highlight the cognitive state, which is possessed of internal representational quality independently of any real relations with reality outside of itself. And this representational quality will involve both the sensible forms of intuition and the conceptual forms of understanding. As we shall see, however, the introduction of the latter into a representational state introduces an element of *spontaneity*, and hence of "activity," that would not otherwise be present. In this sense, forms of intuition do not contribute anything to mental "acts" after all.

Chapter 2

Concepts and Intuitions

I. Five Kinds of Representation

THERE ARE, as we have discovered, several things that might be meant by a subject's "representations" of reality (or of a would-be reality). One of these involves the notion of a cognitive relation in which a subject might stand to something, insofar as it is true of that thing that the subject is perceiving it or thinking of it or in some way aware of it; or at least insofar as it enters directly *into* whatever the subject is perceiving or thinking or otherwise aware of. Such relational states of affairs might legitimately be considered representational, since they are different ways in which the subject represents the world to itself as being of a certain sort. Or, if one prefers, they are ways in which the world represents itself to the subject.

We need to distinguish a faculty of representation in this first sense from one that might rather be defined by reference to those quasi relations that Brentano meant to indicate with his notion of intentionality. The latter is, in itself, at most a capacity for (quasi)relations with *possible* realities, with objects that reality *might* be represented as containing. Some will maintain that, while such a capacity exists, the quasi relations that it involves are ultimately explicable in terms of the genuine relations in which a person might stand to actual realities and the actual world. Brentano did not think so, nor, I believe, did Kant.

The supposition that the representation of possible realities is more basic than that of actual ones may appear to contradict one of the most central Kantian doctrines. The doctrine emerges from the combination of arguments presented in the Transcendental Deduction and in the Refutation of Idealism that Kant added in the second edition of the *Critique of Pure Reason* (B274ff.). In the former of these places Kant considers the general conditions involved in the occurrence of any conceptualized representation. This, as we shall see later, involves the consciousness of some kind of rule-governed element with respect to such a representation and its relation to other possible ones that the subject might have or have had instead.

It follows that a necessary condition for the occurrence of a conceptualized representation is that the subject be self-conscious in a certain way. As already suggested, Kant also holds that in some important sense only conceptualized representations are fully conscious in the first place. So on Kant's view all fully conscious representations presuppose a capacity for self-consciousness on the part of the subject in question. Now in the Refutation of Idealism Kant argues that a necessary condition of self-consciousness is a consciousness of oneself as perceptually related, in a direct manner, to actual bodies in space. As he puts it there, "outer sense" is a necessary condition of "inner sense." He also makes it clear, to be sure, that this is compatible with any *given* representation proving to be purely imaginary or hallucinated (B278). Nevertheless, Kant seems to insist, the very capacity for self-consciousness presupposes that in *general* one is capable of obtaining direct perceptions of bodies in space. Or at the very least the capacity for self-consciousness presupposes that one *conceive* of oneself as thus relatable to bodies in space. It follows that a presupposition of the subject's ability to experience *any* representations, with any real degree of consciousness, is that the subject conceive of itself by means of the concept of a genuine cognitive relatedness to bodies in space. In this sense, one might say, the concept of representation in general (at least insofar as it is conscious) presupposes the concept of such relatedness. This may appear to contradict the view I have suggested is Kant's.

The two doctrines are not, I think, incompatible. The Brentanian aspect of Kant's view lies, as I suggested earlier, in Kant's acknowledgment of an irreducible "form of intuition" that accounts for the distinction between merely thinking or supposing *that* something is or might be the case and thinking or supposing something *about* a (possibly merely imaginary) object. The claim that the form in question is irreducible implies that it cannot be explicated in terms of possible cognitive relations with actual objects. Now the point of the doctrines sketched above is that the aspect of any representational state in virtue of which it is conscious in the fullest sense relates to the subject's ability to conceive of itself precisely in the latter terms. This, it seems to me, is perfectly compatible with holding that the *other* aspect of a representational state, in virtue of which whatever concepts it involves are being applied to a (possibly imaginary) *object* presented in it, is an irreducible feature of such a state.

Now I have distinguished so far two notions of representation, one according to which representations are a kind of relation and another according to which they cannot strictly be so regarded. As suggested in the preceding chapter, this second notion allows of two alternatives. On one, which appears to be Leibniz's, the representational "states" of a subject are simply various sorts of (quasi-relational) *properties* that the subject exemplifies, different ways in which the subject *is* at any moment, representationally. This, as we have seen, makes it impossible to ascribe two different sorts of representational properties to one and the same representational state, even though we might of course ascribe them both to the same subject. Brentano's *Vorstellungen* and that particular species that Kant calls intuition (*Anschauung*) are representational "states," I have suggested, in a sense that allows the possibility in question. It is sometimes thought, however, that they are representations in what must yet be acknowledged as a fourth sense, namely that they are peculiar mental *objects* supposed to perform, in virtue of their presence to (or in) the mind, the function of "representing" reality *to* that mind.[1]

Kant sometimes speaks of *Anschauungen* and *Vorstellungen* as if they were objects of ordinary awareness. He also says that the latter are something that, strictly speaking, exist only "within us." These sorts of statements have suggested that for Kant the objects of human knowledge are aspects of our own mental condition. As we shall see, however, the sense in which the objects of knowledge are mere representations, and exist only within us, is not at all the same as the sense in which our own mental states, or literal "contents of the mind," exist only within us. Again, Kant speaks of intuitions, or at least those which he calls "empirical" intuitions, as involving sensation (*Empfindung*) as their "material," together with something that he calls the "form" of intuition, and he also uses 'form of intuition' to refer to the spatial form exhibited by objects of perception. Sensations furthermore are internal states of the perceiver in Kant's view, or at least aspects of such states. Many readers conclude, then, that in Kant's view the objects of immediate perception are internal states somehow spatially organized and projected into a space (only) apparently outside of us. In fact, though, there are *two* notions of "form of intuition" in Kant, one referring to an aspect of our (intuitively) representational states and the other to the form of what is perceived *through* those states. Our sensations are the material aspect of the former, but not of the latter.

The status of sensation may require a notion of representation additional to the four we have already recognized. Though Kant regards sensation as a kind of representation, it is not clear that we ought to regard it as in itself possessed of cognitive quality.[2] It would seem more accurate to regard it as a (potential) ingredient in, or aspect of, an internal state possessed of such quality. So we would have to introduce, for Kant, an additional notion of representation, namely of an aspect or ingredient that *contributes* to the cognitive quality of an internal state. A similar point will have to be made with respect to the kind of representation that Kant calls a "concept" (*Begriff*). This too, in its primary sense, can only be regarded as a representation in a "contributory" sense, although it cannot be regarded, as perhaps sensation can be, as some kind of internal state in its own right.

II. Intuition as Singular Reference:
A Semantical Approach

The notion of intuition is, as I have already noted, an ambiguous one in Kant. Sometimes, certainly, Kant uses it to stand for objects of human cognition. Thus he uses the term to refer to "appearances" (*Erscheinungen*) on occasion, though he had originally introduced the latter term to signify what are properly the objects *of* intuition (A20/B34). This he does, for example, at A168/B204 and in *Prolegomena*, §13. He also speaks of intuition as an ingredient in, or an aspect of, appearances, namely their spatial and temporal form (B202, A163/B203–204). And space and time themselves, he says, are "pure" or purely "formal" intuitions (B147, B207). However, with respect to the primary use of the term, Kant makes three claims about intuitions. (1) They are means by which cognition is in "immediate" relation to objects; (2) they are means by which objects are "given" to consciousness; (3) they are "singular representations" (A19/B33, A320/B376–377). In all three respects, intuitions are distinguished from concepts.[3]

Unlike intuitions, concepts lack immediacy according to Kant because they refer to objects only by way of certain characteristics or features (*Merkmale*) that objects might possess. This of course might lead us to suppose that while concepts do not relate immediately to, or immediately represent, objects, they do nonetheless relate immediately to the *features* of possible objects.[4] But Kant says that concepts relate immediately only to other concepts, or else to intuitions themselves (A19/B33, A68/B93). This suggests that Kant is not prepared to distinguish concepts from intuitions on the ground that these are representations of two distinct sorts of things, objects and features of objects. Rather to refer to objects "by way of certain features" of them would seem to involve a special sort of representation of (possible) objects themselves.

Thus it would not be accurate to say, for Kant, that while an intuition might represent, or refer to, particular trees in some immediate way, the concept *tree* immediately represents the feature *treehood*. Rather the concept also represents trees, but not any particular tree or trees. Now does this imply that Kant is committed to the supposition that, in addition to whatever particular trees might be represented in intuition, there is also an infinitude of merely possible trees which the concept *tree* represents? There is no need to suppose this. Rather, we might suppose, the concept *tree* represents trees, without representing any particular ones, simply in the sense that, unless precisely that concept were present in some actual intuition, then even if the intuition were the intuitive representation of a tree, it would nonetheless not amount to the representation of it precisely *as* a tree:

> In every cognition we must distinguish the *matter*, i.e., the object, and the *form*, i.e., the *way in which* we cognize the object. Suppose, for example, a primitive person sees a house in the distance, whose use he has no knowledge of. Then he indeed has before him, in his representation, the very same object as another person who definitely recognizes it as a dwelling constructed for human beings. But with respect to its form, this cognition of one and the same object is different in the two cases. In the one case it is *mere intuition*, in the other *intuition* and *concept* together.[5]

(As I mentioned earlier, Kant also distinguishes between the matter and the form of an *intuition*. In that case, as we shall see later, the form in question appears to be something preconceptual.)

The role of concepts as "forms" is apparently what allows Kant to hold that concepts are themselves *Merkmale* and not just representations *of Merkmale* (or representations of objects in virtue of being representations of *Merkmale*):

> All our concepts are therefore *Merkmale*, and all *thinking* is nothing other than a representing by means of *Merkmale*. Every *Merkmal* may be considered from two sides: First, as a representation in itself; second, as belonging as a partial concept (*Teilbegriff*) to the complete representation of a thing, and thereby as a ground of knowledge of this thing itself.[6]

And again: "*Merkmal* is a partial representation (*theilvorstellung*). . . . It is either intuitive . . . : a part of intuition, or discursive: a part of the concept."[7] The concept *tree* might of course be part of the more complex concept *blooming tree*, but "all thought must, directly or indirectly, by way of certain *Merkmale*, relate ultimately to intuitions" (A19/B33). Thus the status, ultimately, of the concept *tree* as a representation potentially included in other concepts is secondary to its status as an element in virtue of which intuitions might be intuitions not simply of things that are trees but of such things as recognized in intuition precisely *as* trees.

This way of distinguishing between the immediacy of intuitions and the mediacy of concepts might also appear adequate for explaining Kant's claim that intuitions are the means by which objects are "given" to us and concepts the means by which objects are "thought" (A19/B33). Thus when I merely think, in a general way, that some tree (or trees) or other must be in bloom, no intuitions are involved, because no particular "given" tree is in question. But when I think, of some particular tree, that it must be in bloom, then the concept *tree* as well as the concept *blooming* are combined with some particular intuition. Intuitions, then, seem to function by constituting the actual reference to, and not just a general thought about, the things about which we are able to entertain thoughts. And in this sense, we might suggest, intuitions are the means, or at least part of the means, by which such things are "given" to us to think about.

At least sometimes, Kant appears to have something else in mind, when he claims that intuitions are the means by which objects are given to us as possible objects of thought. For Kant often distinguishes between intuition and understanding (the faculty of conceptualization) on the basis of a distinction between passive and active, or between "receptive" and "spontaneous," faculties of the mind:

> Intuition takes place only in so far as the object is given to us. This again is only possible, to human beings at least, in so far as it affects the mind in a certain way. (A19/B33) Our knowledge springs from two fundamental sources of the mind; the first is the capacity of receiving representations (receptivity for impressions), the second is the power of knowing an object through these representations (spontaneity of concepts). Through the first an object is *given* to us, through the second the object is *thought* in relation to that representation (as mere determination of the mind. (A50/B74)

On the other hand, this way of characterizing the distinction between intuition and conceptualization seems to apply at most to what Kant calls "empirical" intuitions, namely those that involve sensation (A19–20/B34, A50/B74). Kant distinguishes between empirical and pure intuitions, and the latter do not involve sensation at all. A paradigm of pure intuition can be found in the representations of pure spatial forms to which a geometer appeals. (Kant also speaks of the geometer's representation of space as a "concept," from time to time, and not as an intuition. This seems to involve a broader use of the term than the one Kant officially defines.) The geometer, that is, abstracts from any "material" considerations about objects and merely considers their spatial forms. And in doing so the geometer is abstracting from what belongs properly to *sensation* in an intuition. Furthermore, the pure intuition thereby in question involves an active faculty of the knower:

> The imagination (facultas imaginandi), as a capacity for intuitions even without the presence of the object, is either *productive*, i.e., a capacity for original presentation [*Darstellung*] of the object (exhibitio originaria), which therefore precedes experience; or it is *reproductive*. . . . Pure intuitions of space and time belong to the former presentation; all the rest presuppose empirical intuition. . . . [8]

Sensory states often seem to be for Kant the primary example of empirical intuition. Thus seeing something appears to be a paradigmatic empirical intuition. The distinction between intuition and concept, then, would appear to involve a distinction between seeing something and the various possible ways in which one might recognize, or conceptualize, what one sees. Precisely what pure intuition would involve might still remain a mystery on this approach. But in any case it would seem to be something very different from a sensory state like seeing. As we have just seen, however, and as Kant also makes clear elsewhere (cf. B151–152), empirical (as opposed to "pure") *imagination* also provides an example of empirical intuition. Imagination does not seem to be a sensory state for Kant, though empirical imagination presumably does stand in some relation to sensory states sufficient for making them, unlike pure intuitions, a form of "empirical" consciousness.

It may seem, therefore, that when Kant speaks of intuition as the means by which objects are given to us, he is either speaking only about empirical intuition, and a special case of it at that (i.e., sense perceptions); or else the notion of givenness does not find its paradigmatic instance in the mere occurrence of sensory states at all. Perhaps, for example, Kant is using it in the more purely logical way that I suggested in connection with the notion of "immediacy," namely to indicate singular reference. In any case, in some passages Kant simply omits any reference to the notion of givenness in his definition of intuition.[9] In these passages the emphasis is primarily on the "singularity" of intuitions as contrasted with the generality of concepts (A320/B377).[10]

There are, then, two candidates for what Kant might mean by an empirical intuition, or at least by a sensory intuition. He might mean a sensory state like seeing or hearing, or he might mean one's actual *reference* to some object presented by means of such a state. The latter alternative is appealing on the ground that it might also be extended to both empirical and pure imagination. Thus the element of intuition in empirical imagination would be whatever is involved in our ability to refer to, or to attend to, things that we are merely imagining and not actually perceiving at some moment. Pure intuition, similarly, might involve our reference, in imagination, to the spatial and temporal forms of such objects.

There are other reasons one might offer for regarding the paradigmatic instance of sensory intuition as an instance of singular reference and not as a sensory state. For one thing, Kant explicitly distinguishes between sensory intuitions and mere sensations (A19–20/B33–34, A320/B376–377), the latter providing at most the "material" for the former. As we shall see more clearly later, however, this is compatible with regarding empirical intuitions as sensory states. An additional argument may stem from Kant's view of intuitions as components of judgments:

> With respect to its representative state my mind is either *active* and displays *capacity* [*Vermögen*] (*facultas*), or it is *passive* and consists of receptivity [*Empfänglichkeit*] (*receptivitas*). A *cognition* [*Erkenntnis*] contains both combined in itself [*verbunden in sich*]. . . .[11] For knowledge, two sorts of representations are required: (1) intuition, by means of which

an object is given, and (2) conception, by means of which an object is thought. To make a single cognition out of these two pieces, a further activity is required . . . .[12]

In these passages, to be sure, Kant speaks of concepts and intuitions as components of a "cognition" (*Erkenntnis*), not of a judgment. But it does seem clear that for Kant an *Erkenntnis* is a judgment.[13] In particular Kant connects intuition with the subject of a judgment and concepts with the predicate. The latter, he says, "as predicates of possible judgments, relate to some respresentation of a not *yet* determined object" (A69/B94). The "objects" of the former, correlatively, apart from the ways in which we conceptualize them, are "undetermined." Thus, he says, "The undetermined object of an empirical intuition is entitled *appearance*" (A20/B34). Also:

> No object is determined through a pure category in which abstraction is made of every condition of sensible intuition—the only kind of intuition possible to us. It then expresses only the thought of an object in general, according to different modes. Now the employment of a concept involves a function of judgment whereby an object is subsumed under the concept, and so involves at least the formal condition under which something can be given in intuition. (A247/B304)

It is of course natural to think of a judgment about some object as an act in which one employs a concept in combination with a reference to that object. But if our empirical judgments are referential in virtue of containing empirical intuitions, and if the paradigmatic empirical intuitions are actual instances of, say, seeing and hearing, then empirical judgments would not simply *refer* to objects presented by means of sensation; they would literally contain sensations as consitutents. In addition, concepts would not merely provide the means by which we predicate something of the things that we see and hear; they would literally be part of our seeing and hearing. These claims have seemed implausible to some people.[14]

It has been argued that even apparently general judgments, insofar as they express some real knowledge about the nature of things, involve intuitions functioning as subject terms.[15] Thus, Kant says,

> In every judgment there is a concept which holds of many representations, and among them of a given representation that is immediately related to an object. Thus in the judgment, 'all bodies are divisible', the concept of the divisible applies to various other concepts, but is here applied in particular to the concept of body, *and this concept again* [emphasis added] to certain intuitions that present themselves to us. (A68-69/B93)[16]

It might be supposed that Kant's point could be elucidated by means of a distinction between two ways of judging. First one might merely be judging, in effect, that anything that falls under the concept *body* also falls under the concept *divisible*. One merely judges in a general way that the proposition, or dictum, "that all bodies are divisible" is true. Hence this sort of judgment has been called judgment "de dicto." It does not, one might suppose, contain an intuition functioning as a subject term. But contrast this with a judgment in which we consciously *refer* our concepts to something. To be sure we are not referring, in a general judgment, to some particular object. Nevertheless, one might argue, we could still be referring to certain *sorts* of objects. Since we have now referred our concepts to something beyond the dictum in question, this kind of judgment has been called a judgment de re.[17]

If the judgment in question involves an intuition, it is of course difficult to see how that intuition could be playing a genuinely *referential* role in the judgment. What it would have to be referring to would be an entity of a nonparticular sort, and Kant does not seem sympathetic to the recognition of such entities. Certainly, his own explicit examples of singular reference, and of linguistic terms that express intuitions, do not involve such entities.[18] Furthermore, when Kant says that in the judgment that all bodies are divisible the concept *body* is applied to certain intuitions that present themselves to us, he might simply be taken to mean that in judging of bodies generally, that they are divisible, we are judging *that* the concept *body* applies to certain objects (namely objects of possible sense perception). He may not mean to imply that such reference is effected by combining, in a single judgmental act, some actual intuition with the concept in question. Or he might simply be saying that a necessary condition for that concept yielding *knowledge* in a judgment is at least the *possibility* of its being applied in intuition.

However Kant regarded the connection between general terms and intuitions, there remains the case of explicitly singular terms. Now with respect at least to so-called definite descriptions, Kant seems at first glance to rule out the possibility of regarding them as intuitions, or as expressing intuitions:

> The difference between a connection of representations in a concept and one in a judgment, for example, "the black man" and "the man *is* black" (in other words, "the man *who* is black" and "the man *is* black"), lies, I think, in this: in the first, one thinks of a concept as *determined*; in the second, one thinks of the *determining activity* of this concept . . . in the first, the man is merely *thought* as black (problematically represented), and in the second, he is recognized as black.[19]

Here Kant says that the singular expression 'the black man' expresses a *concept*. This may suggest a view about definite descriptions similar to Russell's.[20] According to Russell, the singular (or the apparently singular) reference of a definite description is purely a matter of certain general concepts (*black, man, giving a lecture*) combining in a judgment with the appropriate "logical form." For Russell this logical form involves a combination of what Kant would call "particular" (*some*) and "universal" (*all*) elements: *Some* man who (of *all* who are in question is the only one who) is black is giving a lecture. Kant himself does take pains to distinguish the logical form of a singular judgment from that of either the particular or the universal (A71/B96). These differences in logical form involve different ways in which the same elements might function to produce different judgments.

In the passage quoted, Kant's main point is not to deal with the nature of definite descriptions, but rather with the distinction between two kinds of "connection" of representations in our consciousness, namely one in which some assertion is made by means of that connection and one where no assertion is made. What Kant seems to do in dealing with this question is to introduce his distinction between assertoric and merely problematic judgments (A74–76/B100–101). Thus the mere "concept" of "the man who is black" is really a kind of judgment, albeit a merely problematic one, namely the judgment that the man might be black.[21] What distinguishes this from the judgment that the man really is black, then, is not the presence of judgmental form in the latter but the fact that the form is that of an assertoric judgment. Now this issue clearly concerns only the connection between our representation of "the man" (i.e., the man in question) and the concept *black*. In considering the issue Kant says nothing at all about our representation of *the man* in question.

That Kant would construe definite descriptions in something like Russell's manner (i.e., in terms of purely general, or "descriptive," terms) might appear evident from the following:

> . . . the question arises whether I can say without contradiction: the black man (who is black at a certain time) is white (that is, he is white, has paled, at another time). I answer no; for in this judgment I carry over the concept of black along with the concept of non-black, since the subject is thought as determined through the first. Consequently, since the subject would be both black and non-black at once, we would have an unavoidable contradiction. On the other hand, I can say of the same man, "*He is black*," and also, "*Just this man is not black*" (namely, at some other time, when he is bleached) . . . .[22]

Kant contrasts the judgment that "The black man is not (any longer) black" with the judgment, made *of* or in *reference* to the very man in question, that "Just *this* man is not black." The reason that the former, unlike the latter, involves a contradiction is that the singular term functions descriptively in the former. This may suggest something like a Russellian analysis of that judgment, namely "Some man who (of all in question is the only one who) is black is not black," which of course is self-contradictory.

However, all Kant has conceded in this passage is that, in using the expression 'the black man', I am using the term 'black' predicatively. The question remains whether I am not also referring it to some particular man, as opposed to using it as part of a judgment asserting *that* there is some particular man. That the term has some descriptive or predicative content is not incompatible with its being used referentially, and nothing in the passage implies that either 'the black man' or 'the man who is black' could not express an instance of genuine singular reference. Kant in fact seems to imply that it does. For in comparing the judgment that "The black man is not (any longer) black" with the judgment that "*He* is not (any longer) black," Kant supposes that the latter judgment is made *of the same man* as the former, and this seems to indicate that the former judgment did involve a genuine reference to the man in question. In that case, then, we would indeed have a case where not just a singular term but a genuinely singular reference gives expression to a *concept* (or a problematic judgment).

This may appear to blur the distinction between concepts and the "intuitions" supposedly responsible for singular reference. In any case, once we recognize that the so-called concept expressed by 'the black man' is really a kind of judgment (albeit a problematic one), the possibility must remain that such a judgment might at least *contain* an intuition. On some occasions, for example, what the expression gives voice to might precisely be the combination of some intuition with the concepts *black* and *man*. The latter concept, one might suppose, is assertorically connected with the intuition, insofar as the individual in question is represented as actually being a man. Insofar, on the other hand, as one is merely "thinking" him as black and not affirming his blackness, the former concept would be only problematically attached to the intuition. On some other occasion, of course, it might be assertorically, or both concepts indeed merely problematically, connected with some given intuition. Thus concepts themselves may be either what gets descriptively "attached" to an intuition, as in the representation of "this black man" (or of "the black man," when the latter is used referentially), or else the very *attachment* in question, at least when this occurs in a merely problematic manner.

Now in one sense, to be sure, all concepts are general on Kant's view: "It is a mere tautology to speak of general or common concepts;—a mistake which rests on an improper division of concepts into general, particular and singular. Not concepts themselves,—only their *use* can be so divided.[23] This is compatible with what I have said so far. For the "singular concept" is singular precisely in virtue of its judgmental *use*. Now part of the problem in assessing Kant's view is that he offers two accounts of singularity. First, singularity is provided by intuitions. Second, singularity may be provided by the "form" of a singular judgment. When Kant introduces the forms of judgment (A70/B95ff), he gives no indication that it is intuition that provides the form of a singular judgment. What is more, that supposition would seem to conflict with Kant's whole notion of judgmental form. For that is supposed to involve, not the "material" or the content that enters into a judgmental representation, but the way in which that content relates to our consciousness:

> To every judgment there belong, as essential components, *matter* and *form*.—The *matter* consists of the cognitions [*Erkenntnissen*] which are given and connected in the unity of consciousness;—the *form* of the judgment consists of the determination of the mode and manner in which the various representations, as such, belong to one consciousness.[24]

If the singularity of a singular judgment were a matter of the presence of an intuition in that judgment, then it would seem that the singular form was not a matter of form at all but of the material that enters into the judgment.

Perhaps the best way to deal with this problem is to suppose that the form of a singular judgment can be of two sorts. One involves the sort of case where a singular judgment is to be construed along something like Russell's lines. The other is where the singular judgment involves an intuition. Adopting this approach of course requires abandoning a simple equation of intuitions with singular representations. For on Kant's view judgments are kinds of representations (A68/B93), hence some singular representations (namely some singular judgments) would not contain intuitions. But while we might no longer equate intutitions with singular representations *simpliciter*, we might, to an extent, continue to equate them with instances of singular *reference*.[25] As for the difficulty posed by the fact that the form of a singular judgment is in some cases not a matter of mere form at all, in the sense that Kant specifies, perhaps the most that we can say is that at least the difference between the two kinds of singular judgments will *involve* a difference in form, even if it also involves a difference in content. For there will necessarily be a difference in the way in which whatever representations are in question are combined and brought into relation to the "unity of consciousness."

Kant himself does comment on the lack of a purely formal ground for distinguishing the singular from the other "quantitative" forms. In particular, he says, the singular is not strictly speaking formally distinct from the universal judgment:

> Logicians are justified in saying that, in the employment of judgments in syllogisms, singular judgments can be treated like those that are universal. For, since they have no extension at all, the predicate cannot relate to part only of that which is contained in the concept of the subject, and be excluded from the rest. . . . If, on the other hand, we compare a singular with a universal judgment, merely as knowledge, in respect of quantity, the singular stands to the universal as unity to infinity, and is therefore in itself essentially different from the universal. [In this respect] . . . it is certainly different from general judgments (*judicia communia*), and in a complete table of the moments of thought in general deserves a separate place—though not, indeed, in a logic limited to the use of judgments in reference to each other. (A71/B96)

The reason that Kant gives for saying that the singular is not really different from the universal judgment is that in both cases the predicate concept is predicated as holding over the entire "extension" (supposing there to be such) of the "concept of the subject" of the judgment. Nevertheless, Kant insists upon including the distinction as part of his presentation of the various forms of judgment.

Kant's attempt to draw the distinction is typically greeted as confused, or as at best based on a love for tripartite divisions. Sometimes the objection is offered that, introducing a special form for the singular judgment, one might as well introduce a special form for all of the "numerical" judgments, e.g., the judgment that exactly *two* men are giving a lecture. One could not defend Kant on this score by suggesting that what he was really discovering, albeit implicitly, is the formal difference between *any* specificially numerical judgment and the more "general" judgments (i.e., the universal and the "particular"). For it is clear that Kant has *singularity* and not just specific numericality in mind. However, it is worth remaining clear that Kant is at least correct in suggesting that the distinction between a judgment about something (*a* thing, *all* things, *some* things, or even *the* thing) of a certain sort de dicto and a judgment about something de re is a distinction that cannot even be drawn "in a logic limited to the use of judgments in reference to each other." Kant calls such a logic merely "general" logic and distinguishes it from "transcendental" logic. The latter alone raises the question about the possibility of relating our representations not simply to each other but to objects (A55/B79). It is of course in connection with the singular judgment, e.g., with the case of definite descriptions, that the distinction most naturally arises. It does not, for example, arise in connection with the judgment that *one*, or *two*, or *three* men are lecturing; but rather in connection with the judgment that *the* one, or *the* two, or *the* three men (in question) are lecturing. In any case it is important to see that while the distinction in question cannot be drawn in a purely formal way, it does nevertheless call for a distinct judgmental form. For it requires a distinction between two very different kinds of predication.

According to Kant, concepts always function in a predicative manner: "For, as stated above, the understanding is a faculty of thought. Thought is knowledge by means of concepts. But concepts, as predicates of possible judgments, relate to some representation of a not *yet* determined object." (A69/B94) In the case of a "singular" judgment, this claim might appear especially congenial to a Russellian approach. Thus the judgment that "the man is giving a lecture" would really be the judgment that *something that is* a man (and, among the things in question, the only one) is giving a lecture; or indeed, indifferently, that something that is giving a lecture is (among the things in question, uniquely) a man. In the following passage Kant confirms this point about the indifference of subject and predicate concepts in certain judgments. At the same time, however, Kant also distinguishes the logical content of any judgment of a given form from the logical content of a judgment of that "same" form, when that form has been determined by something *more* than "the merely logical employment of the understanding":

> [It is] concepts of an object in general, by means of which the intuition of an object is regarded as determined in respect of one of the logical functions of judgment. Thus the function of the categorical judgment is that of the relation of subject to predicate; for example, "all bodies are divisible." But as regards the merely logical employment of the understanding, it remains undetermined to which of the two concepts the function of the subject, and to which the function of predicate, is to be assigned. For we can also say, "Something divisible is a body." (B128–129)

Admittedly, this leaves us with something of an unclarity in Kant's position. When the universal judgment that all bodies are divisible is determined in a way that transcends "the merely logical employment of the understanding," we appear to have a case in which *intuition* is determined in some way. But as we have seen, it is not easy to understand how a universal judgment could contain an intuition, at least in the sense in which a singular judgment must.

In a genuinely referential singular judgment the order of concepts is not a matter of indifference. This may seem puzzling in the light of Kant's claim that concepts always function in a predicative manner. That claim might seem to imply that the judgment that, for example, "This man is giving a lecture" is of the same logical form as the judgment that "This is both a man and giving a lecture." That reading would, of course, leave it indifferent which concept comes first, and it would also make it clear, one might think, in what sense *neither* concept forms part of the subject of the judgment. That latter role would appear to be filled by a purely demonstrative element, expressed by the word 'this'. Consistency requires, however, that this not be supposed to be the logical form of such a judgment. On Kant's view, it seems clear, the subject of a singular judgment (at least of a genuinely referential one) is provided by an intuition and not by mere concepts. But this, Kant is now requiring us to concede, does not imply that concepts do not *also* function in the subject position, nor that it is a matter of indifference in any given case *which* concept is functioning in that position and which might instead be functioning (merely) as a predicate.[26]

Consider again the representation expressed by 'the man'. When this representation provides the subject of a genuinely referential judgment, we must suppose it to be a representation that is both an intuition and yet also contains a concept. Kant, as we know, regards such representations as a kind of judgment (perhaps "problematic"). But this might be regarded in two ways. First, we might suppose that the representation consists of two literal parts, one of which is the intuition in question and the other the concept *man*. This will be analogous to the case in which the expression 'this man' consists of two distinct components. The first of these, we might say, refers to the object of reference; the second expresses a certain descriptive characterization of that object. But there is a second way of regarding the relation between intuitive and conceptual elements in a representation that is referential as well as descriptive. This would be to regard the representation as analogous not to the concatenation of two distinct expressions but rather to the occurrence of a single expression in some semantically significant *way*. Suppose for example that we were to express the predication of the concept *green* of *this* thing not by saying "This is green" but simply by saying "This" in some particular way.[27] This would provide an analogue for the second of the two ways of regarding the relation between conceptual and intuitive aspects in a referential description. I shall say that, on this second way of looking at it, a concept *informs* the intuition in question. On the first, by contrast, the concept is merely externally attached to it.

I would suggest, then, that there are for Kant two different ways in which concepts might predicatively attach to an intuition, either externally or by actually "informing" that intuition. In a judgment most adequately expressed as the judgment that "This is both a man and giving a lecture," both the concepts *man* and *giving a lecture* would appear to attach externally to the intuition in question. In a judgment most adequately represented as the judgment that "This *man* is giving a lecture" rather than "This is both a man and giving a lecture," on the other hand, the concept *giving a lecture* would attach externally while the concept *man* would actually inform the intuition in question.

It is often assumed that on Kant's view intuitions are as such devoid of conceptual or descriptive content. This has led to the supposition that intuitions, as such, represent some sort of mysterious "bare" particulars.[28] It also leads in turn to puzzlement as to how a Kantian intuition could have any epistemological relevance.[29] But I see no reason for attributing this sort of view to Kant. To do so rests on the unjustified assumption that concepts at most attach externally to intuitions. Of course it remains a further question whether intuitions can also occur in the *absence* of conceptual informing. Kant is rather ambiguous on this point. He does say at times that they can: "For appearances can certainly be given in intuition independently of functions of the understanding" (A90/B122; cf. B67, 132). And intuitions are defined as forms of representation "with consciousness" (A320/B376). Yet he also says that apart from concepts intuitions are "blind" (A51/B75), "less even than a dream" (A112), could "not in any way concern us" (A119), and are "nothing to us" (A120); cf. also B132, A247/B304. I shall have more to say about this later.

One might object that Kant himself does not explicitly distinguish two kinds of predicative form in his treatment of the forms of judgment. He allows for a distinction, we might grant, between the kind of subject/predicate relation involved in a purely conceptual judgment and the kind of relation involved when concepts are predicated of an intuition. But he does not explicitly distinguish between two ways in which concepts might be predicated in relation to an intuition. But if we do not introduce the notion of "informing" predication, it seems to me, then we expose Kant to difficulties (e.g., concerning the epistemological role of intuitions) to which he presumably did not consider his own view subject. And if we do not distinguish informing from merely external predication, then I do not see how to make sense of the radical distinction that Kant wants to draw, with respect to the order-indifference of subject and predicate concepts, between judgments in which concepts are applied to objects and those in which they are merely related to one another and in which it is at most asserted *that* they apply to objects. Thus it is by no means a slip on Kant's part when he speaks of the "concept of the subject" of a singular judgment, even when the latter is a properly referential judgment.[30]

III. Intuitions as Modes of Awareness:
A Phenomenological Approach

The semantical notions of reference and predication obviously have an important place in Kant's theory. The distinction between a genuine reference to some particular thing (or things) and a merely general description of some state of affairs can indeed be used to elucidate the claim that intuitions but not concepts are singular representations, are the means by which objects are given to us, and are the mode of our immediate cognitive relationship with objects. Nonetheless, there are problems in the adoption of a purely logical or semantical approach to Kant's theory. As we have seen, after all, Kant appears to regard ordinary sense perceptions, as well as mere imaginings, as paradigm instances of intuition. But presumably we would want to distinguish the occurrence of a sense perception or a state of imaginative awareness from a reference *to* what some person is thereby perceiving or imagining. On the other hand it is clear that intuitions for Kant are literal components of judgmental representations but extremely unclear how a sense perception could be. At most it would seem that a judgment might contain some element which refers to a sense perception, or to the object of one (or at least to the object of a *possible* one). I shall return to this question after some preliminary remarks.

In a suitably broadened yet also restricted sense of the term, we might regard Kantian intuitions as certain sorts of *awareness* rather than as acts of quasi-semantical reference. To broaden the use of the term sufficiently, let us first of all agree to apply it to cases involving mere imagination. Then we should be permitted to say that, merely imagining my car, completely out of sight at this moment, I am in a certain sense aware of that car. This, I think, does not do any violence to ordinary language. For it is not uncommon to speak of imaginative awareness. On the other hand I want to restrict the notion so as to exclude those cases in which we would only speak of awareness *that* something is the case. We might speak, for example, of my awareness that the car is in its parking space. But if the only sense in which I am aware of my car at this moment is that I am aware that it is in its parking place, then I shall not say that I am at this moment intuitively representing the car to myself. This, we might say, is because I am not (even imaginatively) aware of the car at this moment but merely aware *that* something is the case concerning it. Of course one might be imaginatively aware of a certain object and also at the same moment aware that something is the case in regard to that object. I do not exclude that sort of case. I only exclude the case in which the *only sense* in which I am aware of something is that I am aware that something is the case concerning it.

I also want to exclude a presumption that is often made in connection with the notion of awareness. The presumption limits the employment of that notion to cases in which the awareness in question is a veridical one. I do not report my "awareness" that a car is in the parking lot if I do not think that a car really is in the parking lot. Now I have already excluded this particular case by excluding cases of (mere) awareness-*that*. But we tend to make a similar presumption with regard to awareness-*of*: to say that I am aware of a certain sort of object appears to imply that there really is such an object and that I am aware of it. This presumption, one might note, is also normally made in the case of sense perception but not always; and it is less frequently made in the case of purely imaginative awareness. Thus we do allow, though some might think qualification is in order, that someone might see a pink elephant, even it there really is no such thing to be seen. (For now I shall not attempt to elucidate the notion of "real" being in question.) And little qualification seems needed to legitimize the claim that I am at least imaginatively aware of pink elephants.

I am only excluding the *presumption* of veridicality in these cases. That is, sensory or imaginative awareness, in the sense I have in mind, may be sensory or imaginative awarenss of things that are not real at all (i.e., are at most real in the sense that there is such awareness of them, at the moment in question); or they may be awareness of something that is perfectly real (i.e., in something more than that minimal sense, if such be a sense of reality at all). This distinction, obviously, can be regarded as an extension of the distinction between representations de dicto and de re. At least so far as seems evident, though, nothing quite analogous to a dictum need be present. Instead, therefore, one might simply speak of intuitions considered purely "intentionally" or "phenomenologically." In that case, of course, one would not mean that some particular intuition does not involve the awareness of a really existing object. The point is simply to indicate that the notion of intuition is being applied in a case in which one is able to remain *neutral* with respect to questions concerning existence and non-existence. An intuition that is not in fact of any really existing thing might simply be called, e.g., a hallucination or a purely imaginary intuition.

This introduces a phenomenological element into the notion of intuition. In effect, though, we have encountered such an element already, in the distinction between informing and merely external predication. For on purely semantical grounds, there seems to be no reason why we should distinguish between the judgments, made of some particular man, that this individual is both a man and giving a lecture, that this *man* is giving a lecture, and that this *lecturer* happens to be a man. Nevertheless, as we have seen, Kant regards the introduction of a genuinely referential element as carrying with it the ground for such a distinction. From a phenomenological point of view this seems valid. There does seem to be a difference, with respect to the way a single state of affairs enters our *consciousness*, between representing some individual as a man who happens to be giving a lecture, or as a lecturer who happens to be a man, or simply as something that happens to be both a man and a lecturer.

Strictly speaking we could not say, without qualification, that Kantian intuitions are instances of either sensory or imaginative awareness. Or at least we could not say this so long as the sensory is limited to the five senses. As we shall see in more detail later, Kant distinguishes between what he calls "inner" and "outer" sense. Only the latter provides instances of what is normally taken to be sense perception. Furthermore, it is difficult to see the applicability to inner sense of our extension of the de re/de dicto distinction. However, I shall not try to say more about this now.

Kant also speaks of "pure" intuition. That he regards it as a kind of imagination at least in some cases seems appropriate. When the geometer constructs a figure in pure intuition, Kant says, he is indeed generating the imaginative awareness of some figure (A713/B741). (Why he calls such awareness "pure" is another question that I postpone for the present.) But Kant also says that our awareness of space itself (and also of time) is a pure intuition. It does seem odd to say that our awareness of pure space is a form of imaginative awareness. But neither of course is it a form of sensory awareness. Still it does not seem odd to say that we do at least have some sort of *awareness* of space (and of time) in a way that amounts to something more than our merely being aware that certain things are true of it. Or at least this seems to be what Kant wants to say. In any case the only forms of apparently nonsensory intuition for Kant are involved in our awareness of space and time as such and in the awareness of our own representational states.

The notions of the "given" and of "immediacy" are obviously applicable to intuition, in the sense suggested, in ways in which they do not apply to concepts. For even the most hallucinatory or purely imaginative awareness immediately presents us with some object (even if a totally imaginary one) to which various concepts might or might not be applied. This feature was guaranteed by our taking the notion of awareness as our paradigm and at the same time eliminating instances in which one is merely aware that something is the *case* concerning some object.

The singularity condition may seem to pose more of a problem. Of course all the cases that we have isolated will be cases in which one is aware either of *a* thing of a certain sort (even if a purely imaginary one) or *the* thing of a certain sort. But then, one might argue, we may also speak of purely conceptual representations of "a" thing of a certain sort, or even, through definite description, of "the" thing. Thus suppose that I merely happen to be thinking that there is some car, somewhere, in some parking lot. Then I am in a way entertaining a thought about "a" car. Moreover, it won't do any decisive good to reply that I am nonetheless not entertaining a thought about some *particular* car. For in the purely intentional case there is also a sense in which one's awareness of a car is not the awareness of a particular car. This may seem a decisive objection to the phenomenological approach. Kant after all does insist that no purely conceptual representation can be totally determined or specific in the way that an intuitive representation can. The mere concept *typewriter* leaves it undetermined, for example, what the color is of some particular object to which that concept applies, just as it leaves that object undetermined in infinitely many other respects. But the object itself to which the concept applies is presumably determined in all those respects. Therefore: "Since only singular things or individuals are thoroughly determined [*bestimmt*], there can also be thoroughly determined cognitions only as *intuitions*, but not as *concepts*. . . ."[31] However, this at most says that *only* intuitions can be completely determined, not that all in fact are.

In any case there is a sense in which intuitive representations, even when considered purely intentionally, are singular representations while purely conceptual representations are not. To see this we simply need to recall how the purely semantical approach was required to deal with the same problem. How after all on that approach does one deal with the obvious existence of "singular" representations that are purely conceptual? The difficulty posed by their existence is met, as we have seen, by claiming that such representations are not genuinely *referential*. An analogue of this same strategy can be applied on the phenomenological approach. Applying it, we see that even a purely imaginary awareness of some individual (i.e., one that is "of" an imaginary individual not simply in the sense that it is a mere imagining *that there is* such an individual) involves a kind of "reference" of whatever concepts are in question to that individual. These concepts are not merely related to one another in the judgment. In addition they are applied to some object that is present (even if only imaginatively) to the consciousness of the person so judging. To be sure, there is also a sense in which concepts may be applied to something in a purely conceptual cognition. They are so applied, for example, whenever one makes a judgment about some individual. But no purely conceptual cognition makes such an object *present* to one's consciousness in the way that imagination (and sense "perception" too) can make even complete unrealities present.

One might also adopt the following strategy with respect to the singularity of purely intentional intuitions. Suppose that we rejected the claim that an imaginative or sensory state, regarded in purely intentional terms, could be regarded as involving a reference to some particular object presented to consciousness. We might nevertheless say that the sensory or imaginative consciousness in question is a singular representation in the sense that it *would* involve the presentation of a particular object to consciousness if only certain purely external conditions are satisfied (i.e., conditions external to the phenomenological nature of the representations in question). If only, one might suppose, it happened to be the case that the representations in question were generated in an appropriate sort of way by some particular object, then the representations would in fact be the sensory or imaginative awareness of that object. To this one might of course respond that the same might be said about purely conceptual representations. Given the appropriate conditions linking the conceptual content of a certain *description* with some particular object, our judgment incorporating that description would be a judgment about that particular object. In fact there has been a good deal of interest recently in this sort of approach to an account of how beliefs and judgments succeed in referring to objects. As we shall see, Kant himself attached considerable importance to the role of causal relations in determining that intuitional representations are in fact representations of some particular object. But Kant's repeated emphasis on the "spontaneity" of purely conceptual representation makes it clear, I think, that he would not find such an approach congenial with respect to these kinds of representations. This point, incidentally, provides us with an additional reason for regarding the presence of sensuous content, or quasi-sensuous imaginative content,[32] as essential to the Kantian notion of intuition, or at least for denying that intuitions can be constituted out of purely conceptual ingredients.

So far as I can see there is no clear reason for supposing that the intuitive representations that Kant associates with "singular terms," or at least with those of them that are genuinely referential, are not in some cases intuitive precisely in virtue of involving a reference to the objects of empirical imagination. Of course some referential terms give expression to an instance of sense perception, e.g., when I judge that *this* man (whom I see) is giving a lecture. But in other cases, clearly, they do not give expression to sense perception, e.g., when I judge that Socrates was a philosopher. In the latter case, nevertheless we might suppose that the proper name gives expression to the fact that some individual is present to imagination.[33] At least we might suppose this is so when the name does not merely abbreviate, as of course it might, a purely conceptual description. In any case, if we do not require the presence of such phenomenological content in an intuitive representation, then the notion of empirical intuition would be an ambiguous one for Kant. For in some cases he clearly regards instances of imagination and sense perception as instances of intuitive representation. The only way to remove the ambiguity on the purely semantical approach would be to suppose that Kant did not really mean to be talking about instances of imagination and sense perception, but rather about instances of reference to their objects. It is difficult to believe that Kant was this confused.

As for the case of sense perception itself, the special difficulty that we encountered earlier stemmed, as we saw, from the seeming impossibility of regarding a sense perception, and hence sensations, as a literal component of a judgment and not merely as the means by which we come into contact with that to which some literal component of a judgment might refer. The appearance of this impossibility, I would now suggest, rests precisely on the failure to distinguish between genuinely informing and merely external predications. This in turn may stem from an even more general inadequacy with respect to the notion of mental representation as such.

As we shall see in more detail later, a sense perception is not the same as "sensation" for Kant. Nor is it simply a complex representation consisting of sensation together with some thought or judgment which that sensation happens to stimulate, and to which (or to the object of which) that thought or judgment might refer. At the very least a perception involves, over and above whatever element of sensation is in it, a specific determination of what Kant calls a "form" of intuition. A sensory intuition, that is, involves sensation plus intuitional form. In virtue of the sensation as such a representational state is a sensory one. But in virtue of sharing a common form with purely imaginative representation, a perception would also apprehend just the same spatial *Gestalt* that the latter apprehends imaginatively. Intuitional form, then, in virtue of informing a representation, constitutes it as the awareness, either sensory or merely imaginative, of an at least possibly real region of space. But it does not determine what is represented as *occupying* that region. Nor does it determine whether what is so represented is represented *as* occupying an at least possible (as opposed to an actual) region. This latter is a function of the "categories of modality," which are themselves a special sort of conceptual form.

Now suppose that we also regard concepts (in the primary sense of the term) as potentially informing representations. Consider the concept *tree*, for example, and suppose that it informs a sensory state that is also informed intuitionally. Then the presence of that concept accounts for that state's amounting to the perception of a (possibly hallucinatory) region of space as a tree. (The additional presence of the modal categories would be required, again, to provide for its representation precisely *as* either an actual or at least a possible one.) The same concept's informing an imaginative state would constitute the imaginative awareness of a tree. Thus it would distinguish that state from the imaginative awareness of some shape that someone *might* merely imagine as a tree. On the other hand, the informing presence of the concept *tree* in a representation that is neither sensory nor imaginative would constitute it as merely involving some thought or judgment about a tree, i.e., about *some* tree, or *all* trees, or *the* tree of some sort that might be in question. Finally, we need of course to distinguish between a case in which the concept *tree* informs a given intuition and a case in which it is only externally attached to one. It is important to note, however, that this is compatible with supposing that the concept in question must still function in the latter case by informing some representation. We might suppose, for example, that it informs a nonintuitive representation that is attached in the (quasi-)semantically appropriate way to some intuition. This may provide a ground for the phenomenological distinction between seeing something as a tree and seeing something that one merely *judges* (even if only problematically) to be a tree. Of course, this is also compatible with insisting that the intuition to which some concept externally attaches must at least be informed by *some* concept already.

On this sort of approach, we can indeed grant that sensations might be components of judgments and do not merely provide a contact with that to which the real components of a judgment might refer. For a judgment would be constituted by the mere fact of the informing presence of a concept in a sense perception. Such a judgment, in other words, would simply be that concept's *informing* the perception in question. Hence the perception would be as much a "constituent" of the judgment as the concept would. Indeed, since the concept itself is merely a "form" of some sort, one might say that the sense perception would itself *be* the judgment in question. Of course, this is not to say that all judgments involve sense perceptions in this way. In some, sensation will not be involved at all, and in others the total judgment in question will involve conceptual states merely externally attached to a given sense perception.[34]

This approach, furthermore, will allow us to grant the central role of intuitions in reference to the objects of judgment yet without requiring us to suppose that intuitions *are* as such references. Considered just as such, an intuition is merely the sensory or imaginative awareness of some (possible) spatial form. (I limit myself here to the case of outer intuitions.) It is not reasonable, therefore, to identify intuitions as such with instances of reference to the objects of possible awareness. But it is not unreasonable to identify an instance of reference to some object of awareness with the informing presence of a concept *in* some intuition. One might suppose, perhaps, that the field of consciousness is constituted of a vast variety of intuitional data to only part of which one actually attends at some moment (the rest remaining "blind" or "as good as nothing" for the time being). Attending to those elements might not unreasonably be regarded as a case of the perceptions in question receiving an appropriate conceptual form and thereby coming to constitute a judgment (though perhaps involving at best an extremely general or vague predication) in reference to those elements. This point can of course also be extended to the case of imaginative awareness, allowing for a distinction between the mere passing through one's mind of imaginary shapes and the actual *reference* to them in judgment.

It is important to remember, with respect to the claim that intuitions are "singular representations," that Kant does not think of linguistic symbols as the sorts of representations that are in question. They are at best our means for expressing the relevant sorts of representations. In the sentence "This is a tree" the referential component, the demonstrative pronoun, is clearly separable from the predicate. This may generate the illusion that since the pronoun expresses an instance of reference, while the predicate expresses the predication of some concept of the object thereby referred to, the total representation is really a conjunction of two distinct representations. By contrast, the suggested identification of sensory intuitions with sense perceptions might seem to imply that a sensory state, just as such, might constitute judgmental reference. Now there is a sense, on the present account, in which this is so. However, even if an intuition, or at least a conceptualized one, might be regarded as an instance of singular reference, its referential force would involve not its intuitional form as such, but the presence of conceptual form over and above whatever merely intuitional form is present. On the more purely semantical approach, intuitional form as such constitutes reference to the objects of sense perception. On the more phenomenological approach, it is at most a presupposition of such reference. It is what accounts for the fact that the concepts applied in judgment are referred not simply to something about which we have some general conception but of which we are immediately *aware* (either imaginatively or in sense perception). This, though, still allows that there may be no real awareness apart from concepts. For even if there were no awareness apart from at least rudimentary conceptualization, it might still be that awareness requires conjoining concepts with some preconceptual "forms of intuition." As I have already indicated, Kant himself seems ambivalent with respect to this issue.

The key to this attempt at unifying semantical and phenomenological elements into a single doctrine of intuitional reference rests, of course, on the notion of concepts "informing" sense perceptions and not merely attaching to them in some external way.[35] I shall have a great deal more to say about this notion. One might at least note, though, that failure to accommodate the possibility in question may in fact spring from a more general inadequacy with respect to the notion of representation as such. For if we fail to legitimize a notion of representation in which representational states are states possessed of representational quality, and we instead suppose that representations are *themselves* various representational qualities—i.e., the subject's various ways of representing—then the temptation is indeed great to assign distinct representational qualities to distinct cognitive states rather than to a single one. Thus one may be tempted to suppose that sensory quality, referential quality, and predicative quality must be a function of three distinct representational states rather than unifiable in a single Kantian intuition. In any case the Kantian view seems more accurate phenomenologically than the more purely semantical approach. For while it is necessary to agree with the latter that actual reference to the objects of sensory awareness is never precisely the same thing as sensory awareness itself, our primary references to such objects nevertheless seem more intimately conjoined than that account allows with the sensory ingredients involved.

Chapter 3

Matter and Form
in Intuition

KANTIAN EPISTEMOLOGY is at least to some degree "innatist." It rests, that is, on a distinction between contributions to knowledge that are received from "outside" the knower, or received from "experience," and contributions that the knowing mind somehow supplies from within itself:

> . . . though all our knowledge begins *with* experience, it does not follow that it all arises *out* of experience. For it may well be that even our empirical knowledge is made up of what we receive through impressions and of what our own faculty of knowledge (sensible impressions serving merely as the occasion) supplies from itself. (B1; cf. A86/B118)

But what do we mean by "experience" and by the suggestion that knowledge might or might not arise out of it? The question is really two. It might concern, first of all, what Locke called the "materials" of knowledge, i.e., "ideas."[1] However, when we attempt to say something about the "derivation" of judgments and beliefs from experience, there is something that may concern us but which does not concern us in the case of mere "ideas." What in experience, namely, *justifies* me in affirming the beliefs I do? Now in what Kant calls Transcendental Logic, he investigates the distinction between the materials of judgment, considered by themselves, and the judgments that we form from them. The materials are, as we have seen, concepts and intuitions. In the present chapter we are concerned with a distinction between matter and form *in* intuition. According to Kant, however, this has an important bearing on the justification of certain sorts of judgments.

As the *Critique*'s first sentences also reveal, there are at least two things one might mean by "experience":

> There can be no doubt that all our knowledge begins with experience. For how should our faculty of knowledge be awakened into action did not

objects affecting our senses partly of themselves produce representations, partly arouse the activity of our understanding to compare these representations, and, by combining or separating them, work up the raw material of the sensible impressions into that knowledge of objects which is entitled experience. (B1)

This passage begins with a fairly typical empiricist formulation. What the mind supplies from "within itself" is simply the capacity for combining and separating the ideas ("representations") produced by experience ("objects affecting our senses"). Yet at the same time Kant describes experience as that knowledge of objects that *arises* from such activity. The ambiguity might be removed by distinguishing experience in the sense of immediate acquaintance with objects affecting the senses and experience in the sense of knowledge formed from the materials thereby provided. In fact Kant generally speaks of experience (*Erfahrung*) only in this second way (cf. Bxvii, 218–219). But the ambiguity goes much deeper than this. For the notion of objects "affecting our senses" is ambiguous. The classical empiricist takes his start, say, from the perception of various colors and shapes presented in sensory experience. Building from our acquaintance with these, more complex ideas and judgments then are formed. But the point of Kant's Transcendental Aesthetic is that the empiricist's paradigm of acquaintance with objects affecting our senses (empirical intuition) already requires a distinction between merely empirical and a priori elements. If the merely empirical is what comes from "experience," then a third notion of experience is required. It is what Kant calls sensation (*Empfindung*).

I. Sensation as Material of Intuitions

Kant is never perfectly clear what sort of state sensation is supposed to be. Sometimes he seems to emphasize its relational nature: sensation is the "effect of an object upon the faculty of representation, *so far as we are affected by it*" (A19–20/B34; emphasis added). Other times Kant seems to imply that sensations are not affection relations but an effect produced within the perceiver via such relations. Thus "sensation relates solely to the subject as the modification of its state" (A320/B376). But this particular passage is ambiguous. It may mean not that sensations are internal states, narrowly considered, but simply that sensations are relations in which the subject's internal state is modified. In any case, even when it is clear that sensations are to be regarded as some sort of "*innerer Zustand*,"[2] there is an essential connection with one's awareness of the sense organs whose modifications lead, at least as we normally suppose, *to* it. The internal state is called "sensation" precisely in virtue of its ability to call our attention to the altered state of the sense organs: vision is to be regarded as the noblest of the senses because "its organ feels itself least affected"; consequently, vision "comes closer to a *pure intuition* (the immediate representation of the given object without any noticeable sensation mixed in)."[3]

In the *Anthropology* Kant does not appear to regard sensations as internal states capable of occurring in the absence of empirical intuition. In fact he often speaks of *Empfindung* precisely where he might otherwise have spoken of *Anschauung*. In the *Reflexionen* too Kant distinguishes two aspects of sensation when he might otherwise have distinguished between sensation and intuition,[4] and while he does say that certain sensations, namely, hearing, taste, and smell, involve no intuition at all,[5] he seems to mean what he elsewhere calls *outer* intuition. In the *Anthropology* itself Kant simply distinguishes between effects on our senses that are more or less "objective" or "subjective."[6] The latter are those that tend to call more attention to an effect upon our sense organs than to an external object, hence where the element of sensation tends to dominate over that of intuition. But even in those instances where the subjective element predominates, sensations do not cease to exhibit intuitional form. They simply convert from instances of outer to instances of inner intuition.[7] In any case, Kant never says that sensations themselves *are* modifications (i.e., modified states) of the sense organs. He either suggests that they are affection relations involving those organs or else that they are internal mental effects that are produced by such affections.

Now in the following passages Kant adumbrates that aspect of his innatist approach to the matter and the form of intuitions that has tended to inspire the severest criticism:

> In a representation of sense there is first of all something which you might call the *matter*, namely the *sensation*, and there is also something which can be called the *form*, namely the *specificity* [*species*] of the sensibles which arises according as the various things which affect the senses are coordinated by a certain natural law of the mind. . . . For objects do not strike the senses in virtue of their form or specificity [*per formam seu speciem objecta sensus non feriunt*]. So, for the various things in an object which affect the sense to coalesce into some representational whole [*in totum aliquod representationis*] there is needed an internal principle in the mind by which those various things may be clothed with a certain specificity [*speciem*] in accordance with stable and innate laws.[8]

> The effect of an object upon the faculty of representation, so far as we are affected by it, is *sensation*. . . . That in the appearance which corresponds to sensation I term its *matter*; but that which so determines the manifold of appearance that it allows of being ordered in certain relations, I term the *form* of appearance. That in which alone the sensations can be posited and ordered in a certain form, cannot itself be sensation; and therefore, while the matter of all appearance is given to us *a posteriori* only, its form must lie ready for them *a priori* in the mind. (A19–20/B34)

For it is not simply a matter of the character of the object of representation, but rather of that of the subject and its receptivity, upon which (no matter what sort the sensible intuition might be) the subject's thought (concept of the object) follows.—Now the formal character of this receptivity can not be derived from the senses, but rather must (as intuition) be given *a priori*. That is, there must be a sensible intuition which remains over when everything empirical (everything containing *sensation from the senses*) is removed . . . .[9]

In particular, Kant maintains, our representation of the spatial form of outer "appearances" is the a priori element in our perceptions of those objects:

The pure form of sensible intuitions in general, in which all the manifold of intuition is intuited in certain relations, must be found in the mind *a priori*. . . . Thus, if I take away from the representation of a body that which the understanding thinks in regard to it, substance, force, divisibility, etc., and likewise what belongs to sensation, impenetrability, hardness, colour, etc., something still remains over from this empirical intuition, which, even without any actual object of the senses or of sensation, exists in the mind *a priori* as a mere form of sensibility. (A20–21/B34–35)

On the surface of it this view is an absurd one. Kant defines the sensation which an empirical intuition involves as the effect that an object has upon our perceptual faculties. Then he says that in any perception the presentation of spatial form corresponds to an a priori element additional to the sensation it involves. This seems to imply that variations in perceptual stimuli might effect, for example, the colors that one sees on some occasion but not the visual shape or size of it; variations in the latter indicate not the effect of an object on a perceiver but some element added by the perceiver *to* that effect.

Sometimes an even more absurd view seems to be Kant's. He seems to hold, namely, not only that the mind imposes a form upon mere sensations, in virtue of which those sensations constitute perceptions of spatial appearances, but that the mind imposes a form in virtue of which sensations themselves *become* spatial appearances. Kant seems to hold, in other words, that sensation is not simply the "matter" of our perceptions of outer appearances, but it is the matter of outer appearances themselves:

Space is not an empirical concept which has been derived from outer experiences. For in order that certain sensations be referred to something outside me . . . and similarly in order that I may be able to represent them[!] as outside and alongside one another . . . the representation of space must be presupposed. (A23/B38)

Not only is it difficult to make sense of this view, but it also seems to contradict something else that Kant says, namely that we are not capable of perceiving our own "inner states" (and hence, presumably, sensations) in spatial locations and relations (A23/B36, A33–34/B49–50). On the other hand Kant himself holds that all outer appearances must, "as modifications of the mind, belong to inner sense" (A99) and exist "merely in us" (A129) and that things in space and time are mere "perceptions" (B147).

Commentators tend to adopt two lines with respect to Kant's pronouncements concerning matter and form in intuition. Some of them ascribe to Kant an extreme form of subjectivism according to which outer appearances are constructed by the mind out of our own sensations.[10] Others only suppose Kant to be saying that the nature of the mind predetermines that perceptions of outer appearances will be perceptions of objects in space. On this latter view the matter/form distinction is only secondarily drawn with respect to our perceptions of objects. It is primarily drawn with respect to the features of objects themselves. Those features whose perception is necessary, given the nature of the mind, are what belong to the formal aspect of appearances and hence to the perception *of* appearances.[11] On this view we do not need to suppose that a spatial perception arises only when the mind adds something to the effects received from objects. We simply need to suppose that spatial perceptions are *necessarily* the result of affection by objects, because of the nature of the faculty affected.

Both of these approaches tend to assimilate Kant's argument at A19–20/ B34 to the argument at A23/B38. With regard to the first, the primary internal difficulty is that the argument at A19–20 is a perfectly general one, demanding the presence of form in intuition on the ground that otherwise mere *sensation* would be present, not because that sensation would be nonspatial. For Kant spatiality is, along with time, only one of the two general forms of intuition. To account for the generality of the reasoning, then, one would need to suppose that the temporal counterpart of the argument at A23/B38 (namely, the argument at A30/B46) is at bottom the following: since sensations are as such nontemporal, the mind must impose a temporal form on them; otherwise in being aware of them we wouldn't be aware of anything temporal. But the passage does not in fact suggest that sensations become temporal in virtue of our imposing some sort of temporal form on a nontemporal material. Reality "in itself," and apart from the forms of our awareness of it, is indeed nontemporal and nonspatial for Kant (whatever those claims might turn out to mean). But Kant does not appear to regard that nonspatiotemporal reality as the "matter" of our sensory intuitions. Though Kant does often speak as if our intuitions clothe things in themselves with a spatiotemporal form, sensations are supposed to be effects upon, or within, a perceiver, whereas the "reality in itself" that is supposed to appear in a spatiotemporal guise is hardly so describable.

There is more to Kant's notion that the mind needs to add something to the sensations received from objects than either of these approaches allows. To see this we need to take notice that Kant's initial concern in the Transcendental Aesthetic is with what I have called empirical intuition de re. That is, Kant is dealing with conditions, with respect to some actual object, for obtaining perceptions *of that object*. Not all instances of empirical intuition are intuitions de re. For hallucinatory perceptions and mere imaginings are also empirical intuitions.[12] That Kant's initial concern is with intuitions de re is made clear by his emphasis on a point which Kemp Smith's translation obscures, namely, that empirical intuition takes place only insofar as the object *affects the mind* in a certain way (A19/B34). (Kemp Smith: "only in so far as the mind *is affected* in a certain way.") It is of course not unreasonable to suppose that a necessary condition for obtaining a sense perception of some (actual) object is that the perception be a state produced via a certain sort of effect (involving sense organs, presumably) by that object upon a subject's perceptual system. Merely hallucinatory objects cannot strictly speaking have such an effect or indeed any real effect on us. We might, speaking loosely, say that they do. But what we would mean is simply that the hallucinatory perceptions of those objects have an effect on us.

I would suggest that the apparently absurd view that Kant espouses in the passages in question is only a somewhat misleading way of making the following point. The relation of affection between some object and a sensory state is never identical with some perceiver's obtaining an empirical intuition of that object. That relation accounts, rather, for some thing's being the object of a sensory state only on an additional condition. The additional condition is that the state produced, in its intrinsic nature and quite apart from that relation, is already regardable as an empirical intuition. It must already be regardable, that is, as a perceptual awareness of something that (so far considered, at least) might or might not *turn out* to be some object to which one is thus related. Obviously empirical intuition, considered in this intrinsic manner, is intuition considered merely intentionally. Kant's claim then is twofold: (a) The affection relation is necessary for an empirical intuition de re but sufficient only on the assumption that the sensory state is as such an intuition; (b) the occurrence of the affection relation is irrelevant to a sensory state's *being* as such an intuition, which latter rather concerns the state's own intrinsic nature.[13]

It is not unusual, as we have seen, for Kant to regard sensations as affection relations with objects. But the interpretation that I have suggested is plausible even when we regard sensations as "internal states." For even so considered, what is peculiarly "sensational" about sensations is precisely their capacity for directing one's attention to the modification of a sense organ. So again Kant's point is the same: that some internal state has been produced via stimulation of sense organs by an object does not imply that the state consitutes *awareness* of that object (at least not in any sense of "awareness" relevant to cognition). A further condition needs to be satisfied, namely that the state so produced is describable, in its own intrinsic nature and apart from a concern with sense organs, as the awareness of something or other.

That the mind needs to "impose" an a priori form on mere sensation would then be just to say that representational quality derives in the first instance from the nature of one's own internal states. It is not in the first instance a matter of relations in which one happens to stand to some object. So affection relations provide at most the "material" for the establishment of genuinely representational, i.e., *cognitive* relations with objects. In fact as a passage quoted earlier (from the *Inaugural Dissertation*) shows, a whole *manifold* of such material is always in question. This reflects Kant's supposition that, whether or not corresponding distinctions can be drawn in one's *awareness*, a total sensory representation contains as its material a manifold of affection relations involving the parts, or parts of the surface of, its object.[14]

This might be put in a metaphor. Affection relations, hence sensation qua sensation, establish a kind of "inward" movement from objects to the subject. But representation of objects requires a kind of (metaphorical) "outward" movement. For genuine cognition, that is, internally received effects need to be referred *back* to objects, not simply in the quasi-semantical sense that judgmental "reference" is required but even more basically in the sense that what constitutes a "received" state as an awareness of some object to which one *might* refer judgmentally is its own internal intentional quality in the first place.

Leibniz, as we have seen, had a tendency to identify a manifold of affection relations (or rather a manifold of preestablished correspondences that might be, and according to Kant are better, regarded as affection relations) with a manifold of *representations*. Accordingly, he inferred from the fact that we stand in such "relations" with things in themselves that we have cognitive relations with them. According to Kant that would not follow at all. What we have genuinely cognitive relations with, as we shall see more clearly later, depends on the *intentional content* of the representations in question. These things Kant calls "appearances."

Perhaps Kant's more self-conscious critique at this point was with respect to his empiricist predecessors. Here indeed we encounter the paradigm of sensory representations, or ideas, "received" from outside into the knower. Thus Locke:

. . . our Senses, conversant about particular sensible objects, do convey into the mind several distinct perceptions of things, *according to those various ways wherein those objects do affect them* [emphasis added]. And thus we come by those *ideas* we have of *yellow, white, heat, cold, soft, hard, bitter, sweet,* and all those which we call sensible qualities; which when I say the senses convey into the mind, I mean, they from external objects convey into the mind what produces there those perceptions. This great source of most of the ideas we have, depending wholly upon our senses, and derived by them to the understanding, I call SENSATION.[15]

Kant himself, to be sure, emphasizes the receptive nature of sensory intuition (cf. A50/B74). This is because on Kant's view the "imposition" of intuitional form is on the whole automatic: it is part of the way in which the mind is by nature affected. It does not involve any of the special abilities, accordingly, typical of the conceptual elements that are mobilized when we form some *thought* about what the senses perceive. Nevertheless, Kantian "receptivity" is a far cry from the empiricist paradigm. For what the empiricists failed to see clearly, or clearly enough, is that sensory reception is not the reception of objects. It is at most the reception of an *effect* from objects. It is the business of the subject, then, that the sorts of effects of which it is receptive are those which possess intentional or (phenomenologically) referential quality. Admittedly this subjective business is a purely automatic one and no matter of any special talent or learning. Nonetheless, the shift in emphasis is monumental. For we now see more clearly than before that the ultimate epistemological problems are fundamentally those of *enriching* a referential quality already present in perception. This enrichment of course requires conceptualizing the perceptions in question. But once we are clear that what we are enriching is a mental "movement" from the subject *outward,* we cannot fail to recognize that even the most minimal conceptualization involves a process that cannot be receptive in anything like the way in which sensation is.

For the Lockean empiricist conceptual "enrichment" of sensory content is no more than its association with further content. Once clear, though, that conceptualization requires perfection of the subject's referential abilities, a more adequate acknowledgement of the spontaneity of concepts cannot fail to be forthcoming. We might put it this way: conceptualization requires conversion of merely phenomenological into quasi-*semantical* reference. Without, therefore, prior recognition of the (phenomenologically) referential nature of *what* the intellect needs to conceptualize, failure is inevitable with respect to any theory of conceptualization itself. The supposition that perception is receptive in the Lockean manner may foster the illusion that what one needs to enrich, conceptually, is merely some (mental) *object.* And how else to enrich it, in that case, than to associate it with other objects or to combine it with them in various ways?

The a priori formal features of intuition, then, are those that account for a state's being object-directed in the most basic sense of the term:

How, then, can there exist in the mind an outer intuition which precedes
the objects themselves, and in which the concept of these objects can be
determined *a priori*? Manifestly, not otherwise than insofar as the intuition
has its seat in the subject only as the formal character of the subject, in
virtue of which, in being affected by objects, it obtains *immediate representation*, that is, *intuition*, of them . . . . (A25/B41)

It is not in fact unnatural for Kant thus to have employed the notion of
perceptual "form." As we saw in Chapter One, he explicitly contrasts his
own notion of perceptual forms with the Scholastic account of perception
making use of that same term. The role of sensory "form" on the Scholastic
account is of course connected with its view of the "affection" condition.
The latter, on that account, is relevant to the obtaining of a perception of
some object only to the extent that it succeeds in delivering into the
perceiver's sensory apparatus the sensible form (*species*) of a perceptible
object. For Kant by contrast the conditions whereby the subject's state
becomes object-directed are not in any literal sense delivered into the
subject via an affection relation; nor are they, as on the Scholastic account,
"identical" with some form possessed by the affecting object itself.

There is one way in which we might attempt to meet Kant's argument.
We might call this the "comparative" approach to intentional intuition. On
this account to say that a generated state is the intuition, intentionally
considered, of a certain sort of object, say a roughly elliptical spatial
expanse, is just to say that the state *resembles*, in appropriate respects, the
sorts of states typically produced by (objects occupying) such expanses. We
might then grant that any instance of perception de re presupposes the
occurrence of perception considered intentionally. But that is simply
because perception de re involves the production of internal states that are
describable in terms of relations that they bear to standard perceptual
situations. The *production* of these states might constitute the means by
which whatever concepts they involve achieve a reference to some object.
Apart from that relation, however, those concepts yield no more than the
thought *that there is* (or seems to be, or might have been) an object of
such-and-such a description in such-and-such a relation to the perceiver.
Apart from an affection relation, accordingly, apparent reference to an
"object" of awareness reflects nothing more than recognition either that we
are thinking certain thoughts about an object or that certain similarity-
relations link the state in question with those typically produced via an
affection relation.

Were this objection sound, Kant would be bound to fail in his account of
mathematical cognition. For that attempt rests, as we shall see more
clearly presently, on Kant's view that "pure intuition" can explain how
mathematical knowledge (e.g., in geometry) can be both something more

than a set of generalizations derived from experience and yet also more than mere analysis of concepts. But on the comparative account any appeal to objects presented in "pure intuition," i.e., to what is imaginable or perceivable purely intentionally, would be either a purely conceptual matter or else secondary to an appeal to what is in fact possible in instances involving the affection relation. However, the comparative approach, so far as I can see, is implausible.[16] For it hardly seems plausible to suppose that the only sense in which one's internal states might be, apart from the conditions that generate them, the sensory awareness of some (at least possible) object or spatial expanse is that those states merely resemble some other states. Certainly they do resemble the sorts of states typically produced under certain specifiable conditions. But the only reason those conditions are regarded as generating *perceptual* states would seem to hinge precisely on the intrinsic quality of those states in the first place. If all that I was aware of in experiencing such a state were its resemblance to certain other states, and if none of those others was in its intrinsic nature the awareness of some object, then it is hard to see how my experience could involve the awareness of any (even merely *possible*) object. To be sure, my experience might include thoughts or judgments about some object, e.g. about the sorts of objects that typically produce the state in question. But that would make my "awareness" of the object a purely conceptual and not an intuitional one.

We are finally ready to connect the notion of intuitional form so far developed with Kant's claim that space is the a priori form of outer sense. At least part of the argument for that connection, we should now see, is presented at A20–21/B34–35. The argument is simply this. Intuitional form comprises those features in virtue of which an empirical intuition is, intrinsically considered, an awareness of some (possibly unreal) object. Now it is possible, Kant observes, to experience an intuitional state (namely in imagination) in which the object is simply a spatial expanse of some description. (Of course we might also *conceptualize* this object as being something more specific as well.) Hence the representation of spatial form is at least a sufficient condition for the occurrence of intuition:

> Thus, if I take away from the representation of a body that which the understanding thinks in regard to it, substance, force, divisibility, etc., and likewise what belongs to sensation, impenetrability, hardness, colour, etc., something still remains over from this empirical intuition, namely, extension and figure. (A20–21/B35)

Such purely imaginative form is of course insufficient for the occurrence of *sensory* intuition. But what is the difference between sensory awareness of some spatial expanse and a purely imaginative representation? The only difference, Kant seems to reason, is in the *way* in which that expanse presents itself. In the one case it presents itself in a sensory manner, in the other case not. In either case the same *object* is present, namely a (possible) region of space, hence a (possible) material object.[17] So the presence of sensory content is not essential for the object-directedness of the intuition in question, but only for constituting the difference between a sensory and a merely imaginative awareness of its object. Furthermore, the presence of sensory content is especially connected with the affection relation. For it is, except in rare cases, produced by means of that relation. Hence such qualities as sensory color are the correlates of "sensation" and part of the "material" aspect of perception. The spatiality of objects, on the other hand, is a correlate of intuitional "form" and independent of sensation.

None of these conclusions implies that the affection relation is incapable of generating a spatial perception or that it at most generates internal states upon which the representation of spatial form needs to be imposed. The relation in question is equally capable of generating an awareness of perceptual color as well as of perceptual shape. It is simply that the representation of the latter is a necessary and a sufficient condition for the kind of object-directedness that an internal state requires *when it is considered independently* of that relation. The representation of color is neither necessary (A20–21/B34–35) nor by itself sufficient (A22/B37ff.).

This approach reveals the inadequacy of a metaphor that is frequently used to elucidate Kant's theory:

> Space and time are thus sensible and yet *a priori* because they are derived not from particular sensations but from the general constitution of our nature in so far as we are adapted to receive sensations. . . . Because they are contributed by ourselves we can tell *a priori* that all objects which we experience will conform to them, just as when we use blue spectacles we can tell *a priori* that everything we see will look blue.[18]

> It is impossible to invent any exact parallel for this revolutionary doctrine, but if we looked at everything through blue spectacles, we could say that the blueness of things, as they appeared to us, was due, not to the things, but to our spectacles. In that case the spectacles offer a very rough analogy to human sensibility in Kant's doctrine.[19]

The inadequacy of the metaphor is simply that the use of blue spectacles can at most determine *how*, within limits, an object will appear; it does not provide the perceiver with an ability to receive appearances in the first place. But the forms of intuition are introduced precisely to account not just for the fact that objects appear in spatial form but that they appear at all. They are, that is, "the formal character of the subject, in virtue of which, in being affected by objects, it obtains *immediate representation,* that is, *intuition*" (B41–42) of objects. The blue spectacles analogy would be useful only if it were not at all problematic that sensations are able to provide an awareness of objects (or at least of regions of space) but only that they provide an awareness of the particular *sorts* of objects that are in question.

II. Pure Intuition and Knowledge a Priori

Kant's concern with the a priori is not, as already noted, limited to a preoccupation with the genesis of representations nor even with the genesis of knowledge claims based upon representations. The Kantian concern extends itself to, and is indeed primarily a concern with, the problem of *justifying* representations, i.e., of justifying knowledge claims involving one's representations.[20] Thus arises the problem of knowledge a priori. This problem, as Kant sees it, is the problem posed by knowledge claims that are justified "independently of experience." Here too Kant does not make it perfectly clear in what sense the a priori is independent of experience. But a necessary condition is at least this. Something that is known a priori cannot be something that is known on the basis of an appeal to the way things present or have presented themselves in sense perception.[21] What Kant regards as a clear and noncontroversial case would be one in which something is known simply on the basis of an appeal to the content of certain of our *concepts*. This would be the case when I know, for example, that triangles have three sides because I know what is contained in the concept of a triangle and not because I have examined triangular objects and have found that they, at least so far, all have three sides. Such knowledge is connected for Kant with attending to what we *mean* in judging that something is a triangle; it is also connected with what we would offer as a "definition" of the concept of a triangle. Certainly some judgments cannot be verified merely by appeal to the content of the concepts that they contain. Kant calls those that can be so verified analytic judgments; all others are synthetic.[22]

It has been argued that we cannot draw a clear line between cases in which our grasp of the mere concepts in a judgment is what entitles us to make that judgment and cases in which that entitlement arises from our observation of the objects to which those concepts are applicable.[23] However, I shall not pursue this issue. Kant's more important claims concern the possibility of nonobservational knowledge where the appeal to conceptual "containment" is not in question at all. Were our knowledge limited to analytic truths, according to Kant, then our judgments would not extend beyond the content of the concepts contained in them. In knowing for example that every triangle has three straight sides, I would at most know that the concept *having three straight sides* is contained in that concept of a

triangle upon which my judgment is based. Hence I would not be entitled
to affirm that those things to which I *refer* that concept have three straight
sides, but only that the concept in question is the concept *of* something
having three straight sides. Kant is not always clear on this point. Sometimes he suggests that the difference between an analytic judgment such as
that triangles have three straight sides and a synthetic judgment such as (in
Kant's opinion) that the shortest distance between two points is a straight
line or that triangles have internal angles totaling 180 degrees is that in the
analytic judgment I do not affirm anything that is not already contained in
the "subject concept" (*triangle*), whereas in the synthetic judgment I go
beyond that concept and attach to it something (a "predicate concept") not
already contained in it (A6–7/B10–11). Kant fails to make it clear, therefore, that the limitation of analytic judgments is not simply that they do not
take us outside of a subject concept but that they do not take us outside of
concepts altogether, to objects. Thus he also fails to make it clear that any
given analytic judgment must also have a synthetic counterpart containing
precisely the same concepts as subject and predicate. The judgment that
all triangles have three straight sides, for example, may be regarded
analytically as the judgment that anything that possesses the given *feature*
or *Merkmal* (i.e., triangularity) possesses the feature of having three
straight sides. But it may also be taken synthetically as the judgment
(knowable only a posteriori), made with respect to certain things to which
we have referred the concept in question, that *those* things possess the
feature of having three straight sides.[24]

Now some synthetic judgments that are knowable a priori are on Kant's
view in some way based wholly upon concepts, even though not based
upon the mere *analysis* of concepts. Just what this might involve is of
course extremely unclear, and Kant himself exhibits some ambivalence in
his statement of the point. Sometimes he characterizes "dogmatism" in
philosophy as the attempt to discover truths concerning the nature of
things on the basis of mere concepts (A184/B228, A216–217/B264). Other
times Kant defines philosophy precisely as the attempt to obtain such
knowledge through concepts (A724/B752, A736/B764; cf. A9/B13). What
Kant presumably means is that it is illegitimate to claim knowledge of a
proposition concerning the nature of things solely on the basis of examining
the concepts contained *in that proposition*. Thus in order to learn that
every event must be caused, Kant's "transcendental" procedure requires
that we consult some concept in addition to the concepts *event* and *cause*.
We must also consult the concept of a thinking subject who is in possession
of those concepts and able to apply them in concrete reference to objects.
Examination of that additional concept will allow us to conclude that, at
least when the judgment that some event has a cause is used in order to say
something about those things to which we apply the concept *event*, then

the judgment is necessarily true. To this of course it might be objected that the allegedly synthetic judgment then simply rests after all on the analytic judgment that anything to which we are able to refer the concept *event* has a cause. However, there is no reason to suppose that, when we are using the concept *event* not simply in a judgment that relates it to other concepts but precisely to refer to some object, then we are also really *using* the different concept of something to which I am *referring* as an event. So even if the ultimate ground for the necessity of the judgment in question is analytic, Kant might nevertheless be right in his claim that the ground in question is not the mere analysis of the concepts contained *in* that judgment.

Kant also holds that some synthetic truths can be known a priori by means of an appeal to something other than concepts altogether, namely to intuition. Of course the appeal in question is going to have to be to some kind of "pure" or a priori intuition. For empirical intuition could never provide a certainty of the highest possible kind. Furthermore, such knowledge would not be properly "philosophical" knowledge, though philosophy does tell us that such knowledge is possible. The clearest case of knowledge derived from pure intuition, in Kant's view, is that involved in our knowledge of arithmetic and geometry. The former somehow derives from our intuition of the temporal framework within which all instances of *counting* must occur, the latter from our intuition of the spatial framework to which all spatial concept must be applied.[25] I shall attend primarily to the latter.

Kant's claim that a pure intuition is the basis for the knowledge of truths in arithmetic and geometry is one that is easily misunderstood. Misunderstanding is facilitated by use of the English term 'intuition'. Something that is known by intuition, or intuitively, is something that one is said to know in some special yet inexplicable way. We speak in a similar manner about things that one just "sees" to be the case. However, insofar as pure intuition is a mode of knowledge for Kant, our capacity for it seems to be nothing more than our capacity for producing singular representations of spatial and temporal forms in imagination apart from the representation of any particular sort of "material" that might be thought to fill such forms. (On those occasions, on the other hand, where Kant speaks of pure intuition as identical with the form of *empirical* intuition, two things might be meant: first, a certain aspect of the total object of ordinary perceptual awareness; second, a certain aspect of one's awareness *of* such objects.) It is also reasonably clear that Kant's arguments concerning the intuitive character of our representation of space, in the Metaphysical Exposition, hinge on a distinction between the general concept of a spatial region (or of some particular sort of region) and that to which such concepts might be *applied*. The main point is that regions of space are to be numbered among the particulars to which we apply concepts. When I imagine some region of space, empty or full, I am no more merely imagining *that* something is the case than, when imagining some possible object, I am merely imagining that there is (or might be) such an object. In both cases, rather, I am imagining an *object*, not merely some possible state of affairs. Unfortunately, Kant's arguments to this effect in the Metaphysical Exposition are less than conclusive; they appear to be assertions rather than proofs of the point to be established.

Kant's first argument concerning the intuitional character of our representation of space is aimed against the suggestion that our awareness of space as a would-be object in its own right is simply the awareness of a system of possible relations among certain items:

> Space is not a discursive or, as we say, general concept of relations of things in general, but a pure intuition. For, in the first place, we can represent to ourselves only one space; and if we speak of diverse spaces, we mean thereby only parts of one and the same unique space. Secondly, these parts cannot precede the one all-embracing space, as being, as it were, constituents out of which it can be composed; on the contrary, they can be thought only as *in* it. (A24–25/B39)

As it stands, the main point of this argument is, I think, obscured. Kant leaves the impression that he and his hypothetical opponent are agreed in regarding regions of space as genuine particulars. The contention apparently distinguishing the two would then lie in Kant's insistence that the representation of any limited region presupposes that of some absolute whole in which that region is related to others; hence representation of a spatial whole cannot be regarded as reducible to the representation of relations among more limited spatial regions. In fact, however, Kant himself regards the primary opposition as stemming from those who regard the notion of a region of space as itself a kind of logical construction from that of spatial properties of, and relations among, possible *occupants* of such regions (A40/B56–57). According to this opposition, representation of the space extending beyond the boundaries of an object would be nothing more than representation of further *material*, or the possibility of such, located at a distance from those boundaries. The only particulars in question would be the bits of material extended "through" space, the regions of space which they might or might not occupy not being particulars in their own right at all, despite our treating them so grammatically. This is the main point of view that Kant is concerned to refute, not the rejection of space as an "absolute whole."[26]

From this point of view, the failure of Kant's pronouncements to constitute a genuine argument may appear more obvious than otherwise. The crucial question concerns the status of regions of space as genuine particulars, yet that status seems to be something that is taken for granted by Kant and something that Kant supposes his opponent to leave unchallenged. But we might reconstruct the following line of reasoning. (1) We are constrained to represent any region of space, either perceived or imagined, as bordering upon some adjacent region of space. (2) This constraint upon our powers of representation does not derive merely from what is contained in the *concept* of a region of space. For the bare concept of a region of space is merely the concept of a certain shape, and that permits no inference concerning our need to represent what might stand outside the boundaries of the objects happening to *instantiate* that shape. Or, if one prefers, the bare concept of a region of space is merely the representation of the possibility of matter existing in a set of locations defined by relations to other bits of matter, and that concept permits no inference concerning our need to represent an occupant of such a set of locations as (even so much as possibly) standing in relation to similar objects altogether outside of the originally instantiated situation. Consequently, (3) the constraint upon our power of representation must arise from our awareness not merely of the content of the concepts involved but rather from our awareness of those concepts *as applied in particular instances* (either in reality or merely imaginatively).

It must be as if that to which we apply a concept, either in reality or merely imaginatively, imposes certain constraints upon our representative capacities over and above whatever constraints are imposed by the content of the concept itself. But a mere set of relations, it seems clear, has no determinate content of its own over and above what is contained in our concept of it. Any additional content that we apprehend in some relational situation must derive from the content of the terms being related. If, accordingly, the representation of a relational situation constituting the possibility of a so-or-so shaped expanse is a representation that offers some determinate content to our representational faculty, this could only be because of our representation of those relations as *instantiated* in some (at least imaginary) medium. This medium, it seems reasonable to conclude, must be nothing other than the spatial region, real or merely imaginary, which those relations were mistakenly supposed to constitute in the first place.

It is important to be clear what role a priori imagination plays on this approach and how it relates to the claim that regions of space are particulars. It enters in, first of all, to the extent that nonanalytic knowledge of the necessary features of empirically real space is determinable by means of attempts at purely imaginative construction of spatial figures. This is part of Kant's claim, as I understand him, but not all of it. An equally crucial point is that the preconceptual object-directedness contained in any instance of imaginative construction involves a basic and irreducible kind of *inten-*

tionality. That the intentionality in question is basic and irreducible Kant regarded, I believe, as part of his demonstration of its a priori character. That it is preconceptual is of course the crux of his claims on behalf of its intuitive character. Without this additional feature of Kant's view, we could not properly speak of imaginative attempts at conceptualizing an *object* in pure imagination, and any constraints encountered in attempts at imaginative conceptualization could not properly be attributed to the nature of such an object. Of course, the "object" in any case would not be an object in the fullest possible sense of the term; that would require reference both to the "material" aspect of perception and to the conceptual conditions imposed by the categories of the understanding. Nevertheless, without the additional feature (and apart from the case where one's imaginative efforts are directed precisely toward some particular region of *real* space as such), we could properly speak of imaginative attempts at conceptualizing an "object" only in a derivative or merely "comparative" sense, by reference to the possibility of perceptions of real objects and of portions of empirically real space as such. That of course would undermine Kant's attempt to provide an a priori foundation for our geometrical judgments insofar as they are judgments about space. Apart from the assumption in question, all we have is the fact that our efforts at conceptualization seem to be subject to limits. There would be no real point to the claim that such facts are in turn founded a priori upon the nature of our representation of space (and hence on the nature of space itself, at least as an intentional object). Our "representation" of space in that case would simply be *defined* by the judgments that we are able to make concerning possible objects and constructions in it.

This reconstruction of Kant's argument may seem to blur the distinction between what Kant called the "metaphysical" and the "transcendental" expositions of our idea of space. It is Kant's intention, at least in the second edition of the *Critique*, to offer an independent argument for the claim that our representation of space is an intuition a priori and then to use that claim to explain our ability to make certain synthetic *knowledge* claims a priori. The former task would be accomplished by the metaphysical exposition, containing the argument in question; the latter by the transcendental exposition. On the suggested reading, by contrast, our whole reason for claiming that the representation of space is intuitive in the first place is that this alone could explain our ability to make certain sorts of knowledge claims a priori. Such for example would be the claim that any région of space is bounded by a region of space ad infinitum (or at least ad indefinitum). However, this should not surprise us. For one thing, in introducing the transcendental exposition, Kant in fact says only that it explains our representation of space "as a principle from which the possibility of *other* synthetic knowledge a priori can be understood" (B40). Thus Kant appears to concede that whatever argument has independently established the character of our representation of space is an argument that already involves the supposition that we are in possession of some knowledge a priori. The "other" knowledge, it appears, is knowledge that is more specifically geometrical, involving the notions of line and dimension, as opposed to the more general "metaphysical" knowledge that every region of space is bounded by some further region. Furthermore, immediately after offering his "independent" argument for the character of our representation of space, Kant proceeds to state that *for kindred reasons* geometrical propositions must be derived from an intuition a priori (A25/B39).

A similar point applies to Kant's arguments about our representation of time. To be sure Kant does point out in the transcendental exposition that one of the "metaphysical" arguments about time is really a "transcendental" one. The argument infers that our representation of time must be an intuition a priori, because only on that supposition can we explain the possibility of certain "apodeictic principles concerning the relations of time, or of axioms of time in general" (A31/B47). Such principles are that time has only one dimension, i.e., that different times must stand in an earlier/later-than relationship (rather than being simultaneous moments in two parallel time series). However, Kant also presents an argument about time that is parallel to the one about space which we have been considering. In this argument it is inferred that our representation of time is an intuition, because different times are necessarily represented as "parts of one and the same time" (A31–32/B47). On the surface, it may appear difficult to distinguish this argument, which Kant regards as properly part of a metaphysical exposition, from the argument based on appeal to the "axiom" of unidimensionality, which Kant claims to belong rather to a transcendental exposition. The difference, though, may be that the metaphysical argument (like the parallel argument about space) is meant to rest on no more than the assertion that representation of any particular temporal expanse (whether purely imaginatively or not) presupposes representation of it as bounded by some larger expanse, ad indefinitum. Acceptance of this principle, it seems clear, is not as such acceptance of the principle of unidimensionality. On this reading, then, Kant once again distinguishes between a metaphysical argument, which infers the intuitive character of our representation of time from the certainty of a synthetic principle concerning the inclusion of temporal parts within greater wholes, and a transcendental argument that then uses the fact of this intuitive (and a priori) character to explain the possibility of further synthetic principles a priori. Thus when Kant, immediately following the argument from time-boundaries, adds the assertion that "Moreover, the proposition that different times cannot be simultaneous is not to be derived from a general concept" (A32/B47), this may be taken as strictly parallel to his claim that "for kindred reasons" geometrical axioms require the intuitive character of our representation of space.

The advantage of this approach, of course, is that it does not require Kant to gain the reader's consent, as part of the argument for the intuitive character of the representations in question, to the certainty of any synthetic principles beyond those concerning time- and space-boundaries. Though Kant himself no doubt regarded such further synthetic principles as known with certainty a priori, his argument does not require the reader's agreement on this point. All his argument requires is agreement that the intuitive (and a priori) character of our representations of space and time shows how it is at least *possible* for such additional synthetic necessities to obtain. Perhaps, indeed, Kant might even have supposed something further, namely the necessity of at least *some* additional truths derivable from the intuitions of space and time. For Kant will have taken himself to have established that the representation (even in imagination) of some region of space or of time must be the representation of a genuine individual with an internal "nature" of its own. If this is the case, as we have seen him to reason, then it is necessary that our attempts to apply concepts to such regions must meet with a constraint imposed by the very nature of that to which we are attempting to apply those concepts. One such constraint is that involved in the necessity concerning our representation of regions as bounded by larger ones. But this constraint merely concerns the relation between some region and one outside of it. If the regions in question have natures of their own, independently of what is contained in the concepts that we apply to those regions (and of objects that might be represented as occupying them), then there ought to be some constraints that are more directly *internal* to those regions. Such, for example, might be the constraint expressed in a principle of dimensionality. Thus while Kant need not suppose the validity of any particular principle of dimensionality, he may not unreasonably have inferred (given his argument up to that point) the legitimacy of at least *seeking* such a principle solely by means of an attempt to apply concepts in imagination.

Admittedly, Kant conveys the impression that the intuitive character of our representation of space is supposed to be established in complete independence from our acceptance of synthetic principles a priori. In view of this, one might be tempted to return to an argument presented even before the metaphysical exposition of space and time. There (A20–21/B35) Kant asks us to imagine (or perceive) some particular object in space. Then he asks us to imagine away all of the properties specifically constituting that object as something that *occupies* a region of space (substance, force, hardness, color, etc.) What remains, Kant inquires? A region of space! That is to say, since the representation that we end up with as a result of the abstractive process is simply the original one shorn of certain accretions to it (namely those additional factors required for the representation of the region in question as filled in certain ways), that representation must indeed be that of a genuine *individual* (as the original was). One is not merely imagining that something is *the case* (e.g., that some object might exist in a certain complex of relations with other objects), but rather imagining some *thing* (namely, a region of at least imaginary space).

We might call this the "phenomenological" argument and distinguish it both from the metaphysical and transcendental arguments concerning space. In fact it appears not to be an argument at all so much as a bare assertion of what needs to be shown. In any case one might suppose Kant to have been antecedently convinced, by such phenomenological reflection, that awareness of a region of space is as much awareness of an individual as awareness of some occupant of it (and that the latter indeed involves no more than accretions to the former). We might suppose, further, that such antecedent conviction is precisely what led Kant to his own unclarity concerning the role of synthetic principles a priori in the metaphysical argument. On the one hand, pure phenomenology carries the conviction that a region of space is "essentially one" (A24/B39), i.e., a genuine individual that is not the mere logical construction out of a system of relations connecting what we ordinarily regard as its occupants. Pure phenomenology carries the conviction, therefore, that representation of the parts of some region is not merely representation of the possibility that objects might occupy those parts (i.e., stand in certain relations to the material situated elsewhere "in" the region or outside of it). On the other hand such reflection hardly amounts to an argument. To convert the reflections in question into an argument, then, Kant proceeds to offer a "metaphysical" argument resting (for example) on the acceptance of a synthetic truth concerning the relation between lesser and greater encompassing regions of space and of time. Since the distinction between the role of purely phenomenological conviction and that of argument based on the need to *explain* some conviction (e.g., that concerning the boundaries of spatial and temporal regions) may not have been perfectly clear in Kant's own mind, Kant may have been led to obscure the true relation between the metaphysical and transcendental expositions. In any case, as I have argued, there is still a significant difference.

It may have been Kant's at least implicit recognition of the need to preserve this much of a distance between the two expositions that led him to exclude from the argument of the *Critique* a consideration to which he elsewhere attaches considerable weight. This is the argument from "incongruous counterparts" which he presents in an essay of 1768, in the *Inaugural Dissertation*, and again in the *Prolegomena*.[27] Roughly, the argument is this. We are immediately aware of the impossibility of moving a left-handed glove through space so as to make it coincide, in occupied volume, with a counterpart glove exactly alike except for right-handedness. (The point, obviously, applies to any three-dimensional counterparts of the sort in question.) This distinguishes our awareness of the possibilities of motion with respect to a three-dimensional object from our awareness of such possibilities with respect to two-dimensional figures. For we are immediately aware of the possibility of moving any two-dimensional counterparts (alike except for handedness) so as to achieve coincidence. Now the difference in our awareness in these instances clearly concerns differences in what *motions* are possible for the objects in question, as opposed to any differences in their internal characteristics. For were we aware of the possibility of causing the two gloves to coincide, then we would ipso facto not be prepared to claim to have detected any internal differences in the objects. In this case, in other words, our judgment concerning an internal difference between the two occupants of space is secondary to our awareness of what motions are possible *through* space. But this, Kant concludes, appears to require that we have an immediate awareness not merely of the occupants of space but also of the space that they occupy. It requires, further, that any attempt to conceptualize what we discover to occupy that space be subject to constraints arising not merely from concepts themselves but from the very nature of that to which we are attempting to apply concepts. Now there is a simple reason, I think, why we would not find such an argument as this in Kant's metaphysical exposition. It is, namely, an argument that appeals to a rather specific synthetic truth about movements through space. The *Critique* takes no such truths for granted as valid, as part of the attempt to establish the intuitive character of our representation of space.

Now it might be argued that, as reconstructed, the argument concerning "constraints" upon the imaginative conceptualization of space neglects a certain alternative, namely that the constraints in question stem not from the nature necessarily represented, intuitively, in the region to which we are attempting to apply some concept, but simply from the weakness of our own imaginative powers. Of course, as we shall see more clearly later, the "objects" with which we are concerned are precisely *supposed* to be objects that are defined (at least in part) by our own representational powers. For the objects in question are in the first instance the intentional objects of awareness. These, as we shall see more clearly, are closely related to the objects that Kant calls "appearances" and to which all our knowledge claims must be limited. Intentional objects, of course, are precisely as they are intended by consciousness (though we shall see that Kant's distinction between actual and "possible" consciousness leaves room for a distinction between "real" and merely illusory intentional objects). In this case, then, at least certain limitations upon our representational faculty will ipso facto amount to limitations with respect to whatever reality is presented as an *object* to that faculty. Nonetheless, even Kant will have to grant that there is some distinction between limitations imposed by the very factors setting up an intentional reference to some object in the first place and additional limitations that may beset our attempts to add on to that orginally constituted representation. Put in "realistic" terms, as opposed to the intentionalistic counterpart in Kant's transcendental ideal-ism, we would speak of a distinction between limitations due to the nature of the individual to which we are attempting to apply some concept and limitations due simply to our imaginative weakness when attempting to make some judgment about that individual. Translating into the more intentionalistic vocabulary, we are distinguishing between the internal constitution of an intuition that *sets up* our mental reference to some object, as potential subject for conceptualization, and merely external factors involved in our attempts to conceptualize that intuition. Granting that, since any intuition must have an internal constitution, there will be some constraints on conceptualizing activity presented just by that intui-tion itself, the question remains of knowing when we've found them.

This criticism, I think, is telling to the extent that it shows that the metaphysical exposition concerning the intuitivity of space, at least as reconstructed, is in a certain way question-begging. It is question-begging insofar as it assumes our possession of nonanalytic knowledge, such as that concerning boundaries in space, that nevertheless reflects something more than subjective limitations concerning our ability to make *suppositions* about space. For it thereby presumes the limitations in question to be reflections of the nature of regions of space themselves, at least as inten-tional objects. That is precisely what is at issue: whether, even as "inten-tional objects," there is reason to suppose there to be such things as regions of space. If it is not question-begging, on the other hand, Kant's exposition simply seems irrelevant to the notion of intuition supposedly in question. As noted earlier, it then amounts to no more than the assertion that all spatial objects are interrelatable in a single spatial system. One might of course attempt a more general argument based simply on the need to distinguish between particulars, on the one hand, and the concepts de-scriptive of them on the other. But that would still leave unestablished the need to regard *regions of space* as particulars in their own right. In addition, we would still lack a reason for supposing that the regions of space that we merely *imagine*, when imagining figures in space, are not merely (quasi-)linguistic correlates of our ability to imagine *that* certain things are the case concerning the construction of figures in real space.

These considerations seem to me to compel recognition of the genuine, if implicit, priority in Kant's thought of what I have called the "phe-nomenological reflection." According to this reflection, it is simply phe-nomenologically *evident* that, "stripping away" mere sensory clothing from

our representation of bodies in space, we arrive at a kind of pure imagination of spatial regions that, however we may conceptualize them, serve as
genuine objects for conceptualization in a sense resistant to naturalistic
reduction. The considerations in question also require us to avoid ascribing
to Kant a view of geometrical knowledge as based upon the "inspection" of
a constructed object in order to *discover* in it various traits that are not
derivable from mere inspection of the concepts in question. This view faces
an immediate objection. It leaves unexplained, namely, our alleged ability
to distinguish, on the basis of inspection of the constructed figure, those
features that arise from constraints imposed by the (perhaps imaginary)
region of space in which the figure is constructed and those merely due to
contingent aspects of the figure constructed in that region. One obviously
needs, for example, to be able to abstract from those properties of an
imagined triangle that depend upon the fact that one is imagining (or has
drawn) an instance that happens to be scalene. What we need to remember, however, is that Kant is not calling upon us to construct a triangle for
the purpose of *inspecting* it. The process of construction is of concern only
with respect to the constraints encountered in *applying a given concept* to
it. It is the concept that is crucial, and the activity of applying that concept
to some imagined region, rather than what is discovered *in* that region:

> The single figure which we draw is empirical, and yet it serves to express
> the concept, without impairing its universality. For in this empirical intui-
> tion *we consider only the act* whereby we construct the concept and
> abstract from the many determinations (for instance, the magnitude of the
> sides and of the angles), which are quite indifferent, as not altering the
> concept 'triangle'. (A714/B742; emphasis added)

Thus some feature that we discover in some imagined (or sketched)
figure may indeed be due neither to the nature of space itself nor to the
concept involved, but merely to the way one happens to have imagined (or
sketched) an instance of that concept. However, what we are concerned
with is not what features are discovered in the constructed figure, but
rather what constraints we encounter when we *imagine that this figure is a
triangle*. Imagining that some figure is a triangle is of course not the same
thing as imagining that it is a scalene triangle, even if in both cases the
region does present the "appearance" of a scalene figure.[28]

It will be useful, finally, to add a few words concerning the second of
Kant's "metaphysical" considerations regarding the intuitive character of
our representation of space. Like the first, this may appear to rest on an
assumption that Kant elsewhere rejects, namely that we are able to represent space "as an infinite *given* magnitude" (B39; cf. A25). However, as we
observed earlier, conceding that the whole of space is not indeed pre-

sented as an object "given" to our cognitive faculty (whether intuitively or in some other manner) is perfectly compatible with insisting that any particular region of space is presented as a genuine object in its own right. In addition, Kant maintains that there is a sense in which infinitely many subregions are indeed "given" in our awareness of a given spatial region. This, according to Kant, is precisely what distinguishes the sense in which we are given infinitely many regions beyond any given region, insofar as we are given the ever-present task of *seeking* beyond any region, and the sense in which we are given infinitely many regions *within* a region. The difference, on Kant's view, allows us to describe the former as a mere progress *in indefinitum* and the latter as a genuine progress (or regress) *in infinitum* (A523–524/B551–552). On the other hand, obviously, it is no more the case that we are actually able to *discriminate* infinitely many regions within any given region than we are actually to encounter infinitely many beyond any one. So what, one may wonder, really is the point of the distinction?

The point, we must suppose, is nothing other than this. Even if we concede that the discrimination of ever more minute subregions within some region is merely given as a task that one might endeavor to carry out, nevertheless any such region thereby discriminated must be viewed as something that was a genuine *part* of the original region all along. The claim that infinitely many regions are initially "given" with the whole containing them is, in other words, nothing more than the assertion that we are not merely given the possibility of *marking out* more minute regions within any given region, but that any such more minute region, along (therefore) with the whole containing it, is a genuine object in its own right. This has the advantage of removing apparent inconsistency, but leaves us unclear where any argument is to be found. Kant now appears to assume what was to have been proved, namely that regions of space (even merely imagined ones) are as genuine subjects for conceptualization as any material body. All that he offers as an argument is that while space is presented as an infinite given magnitude and while a concept may represent infinitely many instances that "fall under" it, no concept can actually contain infinitude within itself. Surely it is possible, on Kant's view, to *represent* something infinitely divisible merely by means of concepts. In addition, what could it possibly mean to suppose that an *intuition* might contain an infinitude within itself? Presumably, all it can mean is that the attempt to conceptualize any intuitive *awareness* of a region of space inevitably meets with a constraint requiring the supposition that the region in question contains a subregion. Once again, therefore, though there is indeed a significant logical movement within Kant's argument, it is different from what might at first be apparent. As in the other of Kant's "metaphysical" arguments, the movement is from the presence of some constraint imposed upon our attempts to conceptualize a region of space to the postulation of some preconceptual content *in* that to which we are applying the concept. In the first of Kant's arguments, the emphasis was upon the region of space itself as the constraining factor. In the argument from infinitude, Kant appears to waver between a constraint stemming from the intrinsic character of a represented region and one that arises from the character of our awareness *of* that region. This ambiguity should of course not surprise us, since the regions of space with which Kant is concerned are regions of space considered merely qua represented, i.e. regions of space considered as merely intentional objects.

Chapter 4

Pure Intuition and
Transcendental Idealism

I. Several Kantian Claims

KANT DRAWS an important conclusion based upon the fact that we are capable of intuition a priori with respect to space and time. The conclusion, part of his "transcendental idealism," is that space and time are "nothing but" (A26/B42, B49) forms of "appearances" and that they do not pertain to "things in themselves" (*Dinge an sich*: A26/B42), or to things as they might in fact *be* "in themselves" (*wie sie an sich selbst sein mögen*: A34/B51). Space and time necessarily pertain to appearances, or to the way things appear to us. But they do not pertain to things (as they might be) considered in abstraction from the way they appear to us.

On the surface Kant's argument to this effect seems invalid. With respect to space, for example, he appears to reason in the following way. I am capable of discovering a priori certain features pertaining to the spatial structure in which I am able to locate objects and events. But it is impossible to discover a priori limitations that apply to things as they are "in themselves." Furthermore, even if we could discover such limitations, it would only be possible to do so in an analytic manner. If it followed from the concept of a thing existing in some spatial location, for example, that the thing must be subject to certain limitations, then we could be said to know that the thing is indeed subject to those limitations. But our knowledge about spatial structures is not of the purely analytic sort. It therefore requires an appeal to what is actually presented in intuition, and it does not derive merely from an appeal to what is contained in certain concepts. Now, no appeal to intuition can possibly establish how things are "in themselves." For intuition is a way in which things are *presented* to us, but how things may be in themselves is a question about how they are even apart from the ways in which they are presented to us. Of course one might infer from an observation regarding what is presented in intuition to some conclusion about the ways things "must be" apart from that intuition. Thus we might infer that a certain object must really be red even when we are not looking at it, on the ground that it presents itself as red when we look at it. But this sort of judgment is obviously not one that can be made on an a priori basis. By contrast we are capable of judging in an a priori manner, and without bothering to generalize from our observations of objects that are presented in sense perception, concerning features of the spatial framework in which we locate such objects. Hence we are able to obtain, on the basis of an intuition a priori, information concerning the structure of a certain framework. Since no such information can be obtained a priori concerning things as they are in themselves, Kant seems to say, the framework in question must not *pertain* to things as they are in themselves:

> Space does not represent any property of things in themselves, nor does it represent them in their relation to one another. That is to say, space does not represent any determination that attaches to the objects themselves, and which remains even when abstraction has been made of all the subjective conditions of intuition. For no determinations, whether absolute or relative, can be intuited prior to the existence of the things to which they belong, and none, therefore, can be intuited *a priori*. (A26/B42)

The argument appears to involve two major claims, for neither of which Kant might be supposed to have provided adequate support. The first is the claim that we do indeed have knowledge a priori concerning the objects that we locate in space. (Since the argument concerning time parallels that of space, I ignore it here.) Specifically, we have such knowledge concerning the very *spatiality* of those objects. It might appear that even if we grant the claims considered in the preceding chapter Kant has failed to support this thesis. There we considered Kant's argument that our awareness of regions of space must be the awareness of genuine particulars. This argument was based upon our discovery of limitations and conditions with respect to imaginable possibilities concerning regions of space. Here, one might claim, lies the downfall of Kant's own argument. For the most that we would then appear entitled to suppose is that we have some kind of knowledge a priori concerning the structure of imagined space. The conclusion that Kant draws, however, is that we have knowledge a priori, through pure intuition, of a set of conditions upon *bodies* in space, hence of a set of conditions imposed by the structure of real and not merely of imagined space. Apart from this problem Kant's argument may appear invalid for another reason as well. Rather than allowing the inference that the spatial framework about which we have some knowledge a priori does not really pertain to things as they are in themselves, Kant's argument would seem at most to permit the inference that this framework cannot be *known* (or at least known a priori) to pertain to things as they are in themselves. That I can know on the basis of an intuition a priori that objects as they present themselves conform to a certain limiting structure, but can never know a priori that things as they are in themselves are limited by that structure, hardly seems to imply that the latter are not subject to the limitations of that structure. At most it seems to imply that they cannot be known (a priori) to be so.

There are also two distinct issues raised by Kant's claim that we are capable of knowledge a priori concerning the structure of real space, and it is not unlikely that Kant failed to distinguish them as clearly as he might have. One concerns our ability to acquire insight into those features of space that are *invariable*. As seems obvious, Kant's "transcendental idealism" fails to provide any help with respect to this concern. [1] The other issue concerns the legitimacy of *inferences* from the structure of imagined space to that of real space. Both of these issues might be put in terms of what is "necessarily" the case. If, for example, we are entitled a priori to apply to real space propositions that describe the structure of imagined space, then, given our insight into the structure of the latter, bodies necessarily *must* behave in such-and-such a fashion. However, in saying that bodies must so behave we do not imply that they have necessarily always so behaved or that they always will. All we are saying is that, given the origin of our geometrical insights in pure intuition, those insights must also apply to bodies presented in empirical intuition. That is, pure intuition is also the "form" of empirical intuition (A20/B34). It would of course be a significant achievement to legitimize an inference from imagined to real space. With that sort of license, then even if we might be wrong in *supposing* that something in fact pertains to the former, as opposed to reflecting some extraneous limitation upon attempts to conceptualize imagined space, it would at least remain no less legitimate to base a *judgment* concerning real space on the upshot of such attempts than it would to base it on the observation of bodies in space. Indeed, the purely imaginative methodology might in some ways be the preferable one, since when one is attempting to discover conditions imposed by the structure of space itself, precisely what one needs to do is to abstract from features that merely happen to stem from the specific nature of the bodies encountered in it.

Unfortunately Kant himself appears to conflate these issues. He appears to move, that is, from the legitimacy of applying to real space, in an a priori manner, the results of reflection in pure imagination, to the supposition that we are in possession of an a priori methodology of a specially infallible sort or at least of a sort designed to legitimize claims concerning invariable structures of real space. In any case I shall not pursue these issues. My primary concern is with Kant's twofold move from imagined to real space in the first place and then to the nonspatiality of things in themselves. Before we can pursue this further, however, we need to get clearer about the general distinction between things in themselves and appearances. [2]

At least some general supposition concerning the purport of Kant's distinction presumably underlies the suspicion that Kant's reasoning may have gone awry in his affirmation that things are not spatial in themselves. Those who think it has gone awry, in particular, would appear to suppose that Kant is distinguishing between what pertains to certain things so far as we are capable of experiencing them, and what in *fact* pertains to things (independently of how we are capable of experiencing them). If of course Kant had some other sort of distinction in mind, then our suspicion might be allayed. For example, Kant might simply mean by things considered "in themselves" things considered in abstraction from those specific features that are necessary conditions for our obtaining knowledge of them in the first place.[3] Since space and time are such necessary conditions, it would follow that things in themselves are not in space and time, and this conclusion would no longer carry the paradoxical force that it first seemed to carry. The apparently negative claim would in fact be a roundabout way of saying something positive about human knowledge.

It seems to me implausible to attempt to minimize Kant's assertions in this manner. If we do so, for one thing, it would then be difficult to see why Kant would have presented the conclusion that things in themselves are not in space and time as a "conclusion" from the metaphysical and transcendental argumentation preceding. Second, Kant frequently says not simply that space and time are conditions of our knowledge of things, or conditions of "appearances," but also that they are *nothing but* such conditions. It would be difficult to see what the point could be of adding this further assertion, and yet the whole thrust of Kant's argument seems to be precisely to provide a justification for it. Third, Kant accuses certain thinkers, in the chapter on the Antinomy of Pure Reason, of offering arguments based upon the mistaken supposition that objects presented in space and time are things in themselves (A491/B519 ff.). It is clear that Kant does not take the objectionable supposition in these arguments to be the supposition that space and time are necessary conditions for our knowledge of things. Rather the alleged error seems to be much more like denying that the characterization of objects by means of spatial and temporal predicates is nothing more than a characterization of our cognitive relations with objects. That the *spatiotemporality* of things is nothing more than some kind of relation in which things stand to our knowledge of them therefore appears to be the view that Kant himself is espousing, and that is much stronger than the view that space and time are necessary conditions for our knowledge of things.

There are other approaches that also attempt to dispel the seeming paradox of Kant's claims. When Kant says that things in themselves are not in space and time, or that space and time do not (or would not) pertain to things when (and if) they are considered in themselves, he might simply mean that all spatial and temporal *concepts* involve the concept of some relation between a (potential) knower and the thing to which the concept would be applicable.[4] Thus, for example, one might hold (as Kant in fact seems to) that the concept of a rectangle is merely the concept of an object whose form might be generated by a construction according to a certain rule. That is just part of what we mean by a rectangle. Consequently the very concept of a rectangle involves the concept of objects in relation to certain of our own activities and judgments. Or again one might hold (as Kant also appears to) that the concept of a group as consisting of a certain number of members is the concept of a group whose members can be counted in accordance with a certain rule. Thus again the very concept of a group as containing a certain number of members involves the concept of objects in relation to our own (possible) activities and judgments. It is undeniable that one of Kant's main endeavors, in the Transcendental Analytic, is to regard concepts as rules or at least as essentially involving rules for the carrying out of certain operations in relation to our faculty of judgment. Therefore it may not appear implausible to suppose that something like the suggested approach is in fact adequate for capturing the import of Kant's distinction between things in themselves and appearances. To say that things are not spatial or temporal "in themselves" would then not imply that things are only experienced as spatial and temporal but in fact are not. Rather it would simply be a way of telling us that spatial and temporal concepts involve the conception of objects as *related* to us in certain ways.[5]

There are, I think, serious problems with this line of interpretation. On this approach, Kant's point is that spatial and temporal concepts refer to possible relations between ourselves and objects, and therefore, obviously, they do not represent objects as they are "in themselves," i.e., in abstraction from their relations to us. But Kant does not simply tell us that spatial and temporal concepts fail to represent objects as they are in themselves. He also takes pains to insist that our spatial and temporal *intuitions* fail to represent objects as they are in themselves:[6]

> What we have meant to say is that all our *intuition* is nothing but the representation of appearance; that the things which we intuit are not in themselves what we *intuit* them as being, nor their relations so constituted in themselves as they *appear* to us. . . . (A42/B59; emphasis added)

Furthermore, Kant's *inference* to the desired conclusion rests on the argument that we are able to obtain, in an a priori manner, knowledge concerning limitations upon the objects that we locate within a spatial or temporal framework. So had Kant intended this conclusion as nothing more than the view that spatial and temporal concepts represent objects only with respect to their (possible) relations to ourselves, then we would have to suppose that on Kant's view the knowledge in question is something that can be obtained in a purely analytic manner, by the examination of *concepts*. Kant's argument would presumably be that since we are able to know about such features of possible objects independently of generalization from objects actually observed to exist (i.e., independently of sense perception), something follows *about* the concepts that are thereby applied to objects. But were that the whole of the story, then it would be difficult to see how Kant's view that the knowledge in question is *synthetic* knowledge could play as central a role in the argument as he himself assigns to it.

These have of course been negative points in regard to certain suggested, relatively "minimal" interpretations of Kant's distinction between things in themselves and appearances. But the primary and more positive consideration, from my own point of view, is that quite a different approach emerges from the line of interpretation already undertaken in the preceding chapters. This will turn on the notion that appearances are "intentional objects" and, in a sense to be clarified, that they have a merely intentional or "phenomenal" existence. This line of interpretation offers what seems to me a more plausible account than the alternatives do of Kant's conception that geometrical judgments rest on an irreducible "form of intuition" accounting for their synthetic and their a priori character. The first part of the argument has been presented in Chapter Three. Before presenting the remainder, I shall attend to a consideration that seems to require precisely some form of the more minimal approach.

II. The Double Aspect vs. the
Double Existence View

Most of the time Kant writes as if the objects that we perceive as appearances must also be supposed to have an existence "in themselves," so long as they are regarded as empirically or materially real. Thus most of the time Kant seems to adopt a "double aspect" approach to appearances. What appears in space and time is a single thing that can be considered in two different ways or from two points of view. We might consider it with respect to how, specifically, it is capable of (and knowable as) appearing in space and time. But it might also be considered, though perhaps not by us, in some other way altogether. Of course it is not initially clear what sort of consideration Kant has in mind in the latter case. As we have seen, it might even be supposed to be a purely negative consideration, whose real point is only to be found in the contrast with its opposite.[7] But what may at least seem clear is that when Kant talks about things "in themselves" he does not mean to be talking about entities that are really distinct from appearances:

> In dealing with those *concepts* or *principles* which we adopt *a priori*, all that
> we can do is to contrive that they be used for viewing the same objects from
> two different points of view—on the one hand, in connection with experi-
> ence, as objects of the senses and of the understanding, and on the other
> hand, for the isolated reason that strives to transcend all limits of experi-
> ence, as objects which are thought merely. (Bxviii, n.)

> [A]ppearance . . . always has two sides, the one by which the object is
> viewed in and by itself (without regard to the mode of intuiting it—its
> nature therefore remaining always problematic), the other by which the
> form of the intuition of this object is taken into account. (A38/B55)[8]

In other passages Kant seems plainly to speak of the need for regarding
immediately perceivable spatiotemporal things as things that have an
existence "in themselves."[9]

Particular support for the double aspect view has been offered by Gerold
Prauss. Despite the impression engendered by translation, he shows, the
expressions '*Ding an sich*' and '*Sache an sich*' are rare in Kant's writings.
What is by far more common is the longer '*Ding an sich selbst*.' We are
tempted to regard expressions of the former sort as complete substantival
terms. In that case '*an sich*' would seem to function as an adjective. It tells
us what *sort* of thing we are supposed to be considering, namely a thing "in
itself" (a thing-in-itself). This one may easily suppose to be a different sort
of thing from what is usually contrasted with it, namely "appearances." But
the longer German expression is not most naturally regarded in this
fashion. The longer expression is best regarded as containing an adverbial
phrase with a completion not yet provided. Accordingly, we should not
think of a thing *an sich selbst* as a distinctive sort of thing; we should only
think of it as a thing that is capable of doing something, or having something
done in regard to it, in a distinctive sort of *way*. This thing may then be no
different from what Kant calls "appearances."[10]

It is true that Kant often employs longer expressions in which the
adverbial phrase appears to receive its proper completion. Thus he often
speaks of a thing that is *considered* or *regarded* (*betrachtet*) "in itself." This
of course suggests the double aspect approach. On that approach we are
only dealing with one sort of thing and with two ways of "considering" it.
On the other hand, even this longer expression might still be incomplete.
This in fact is the suggestion that I think is the correct one. The primary
distinction between appearances and what exists in itself is not, I agree,
between two sorts of things. Rather it is between two ways of *existing*. To
exist as an appearance is to exist in what I shall call a "phenomenalistic"
sense; it is to exist, in a certain sense, merely "intentionally." To exist in
itself, on the other hand, is to exist in a non-phenomenalistic sense.
Naturally, if this is the primary distinction, then it is perfectly in order to

speak of a thing that may be considered *as* existing in one or the other of these senses. As I shall argue, however, it is not strictly speaking possible to suppose that the very same thing might exist in both of the senses in question. Of course, it will then be necessary to explain the predominance of double aspect language, which is something I shall in fact try to do in the last section of this chapter.

There are, it seems to me, more passages in which the expressions '*an sich*' and '*an sich selbst*' are intended to modify some term other than a verb of consideration or regard. Thus Kant says in the Antinomies chapter that antinomies arise when we attempt to regard the world *als an sich selbst bestimmt* with respect to size—either as finite or as infinite. When we do this, he says, we are illegitimately attaching one of these determinations to the world *als einem an sich selbst wirklichen Dinge* (A504/B532). Here the problematic expression modifies a form of the verb 'to determine' and the adjective 'actual'. We might of course try to avoid this by supposing the tacit presence of a verb of consideration or regard. Then Kant's point would be that the error leading to antithetic results consists in attempting to see the world *regarded in itself* as determined (*als an sich selbst betrachtet bestimmt*) with respect to one of the predicates 'infinite' or 'finite'. However, this would misplace Kant's actual concern in the Antinomies chapter. If antithetic results spring from attempting to attach these predicates to the world "regarded in itself," it is so precisely because the "world" (as Kant uses the term) is not *anything* regarded in itself. The world, as Kant uses the term, designates the sum-total (*Inbegriff*) of appearances. If, Kant concedes, this sum-total of appearances *were* a whole existing in itself (*ein an sich existierendes Ganzes*), then it would indeed be either finite or infinite (A506/B534). Of course in some sense the world is indeed a whole. For it is after all an *Inbegriff*. The antithetic results arise precisely because it is not a whole *existing in itself* (A506–507/B535). Hence as Kant immediately concludes, appearances *in general (Erscheinungen überhaupt)* are nothing outside of our own representations (*ausser unseren Vorstellungen nichts sind*).

Kant does maintain that we cannot legitimately regard the world, as sum-total of "appearances," as either finite or infinite. However, the primary consideration is that the world does not exist in a way that is *compatible* with that kind of regard. This is confirmed by the following consideration. Surely Kant does not deny, on a double aspect reading, that appearances, considered in themselves, are something actual or existent. As proponents of the double-aspect view themselves insist, appearances are perfectly real and actual "in themselves." Their point is only that if one should *consider* those appearances as they are in themselves, one would not be considering them as appearances any more (or at least not as mere appearances). However, Kant is emphatic that appearances do not exist in themselves (*nicht an sich existieren*), but only relatively to the subject of perceptions (B164). Assuming this does not mean that appearances, *considered* in themselves, do not exist, Kant must mean that appearances do not *exist* in themselves; the notion of the "in itself" primarily modifies that of existence, not that of a certain sort of consideration or regard. Many other passages support this reading.[11]

With respect to the Antinomies chapter in particular, it might of course be argued that when Kant says that the world of appearances is nothing in itself, this at most implies that by 'world' Kant simply means the sum total of things considered as they *appear*. Given this, it would be quite impossible to attribute some predicate to the "world" considered in itself. For this would involve the contradiction of considering things, considered precisely as they appear, *not* as they appear. However if this were Kant's point, then his claim that the world is not a whole existing in itself would turn out to be a trivial one, whereas Kant himself presents it as a significant claim, a claim that is controversial but nonetheless required to avoid the apparent paradox of equally plausible antithetic arguments (A506/B534). A similar point applies to Kant's distinction between "transcendental idealism" and the "transcendental realism" that leads to the antithetical results in the first place:

> We have sufficiently proved in the Transcendental Aesthetic that everything intuited in space or time, and therefore all objects of any experience possible to us, are nothing but appearances, that is, mere representations, which, in the manner in which they are represented, as extended being, or as series of alterations, have no independent existence [*keine an sich gegründete Existenz*] outside our thoughts. This doctrine I entitle *transcendental idealism*. The realist in the transcendental meaning of this term, treats these modifications of our sensibility as self-subsistent things [*an sich subsistierende Dinge*], that is, treats *mere representations* as things in themselves [*Sachen an sich selbst*]. (A490–491/B518–519)

Surely Kant does not mean that the transcendental realist makes the error of considering things considered in one way *not* in that way. If the transcendental realist makes the mistake of considering things in two incompatible ways, this could not be a function solely of the two ways of *considering* those things. Otherwise the error would appear to be a trivial one and not an error that requires the extended argument of the Transcendental Aesthetic (or the Antinomies chapter) in order to expose it. Rather the incompatibility between the two ways of considering things must itself stem from some fact about those things themselves. It seems clear what that basic incompatibility involves. The transcendental realist makes the error of supposing that objects in space and time are in themselves *real*, or are things that *exist* in themselves.

A number of passages seem to show that appearances are things that exist only in the sense that they are perceivable (i.e., necessarily would be perceived under the appropriate conditions):[12]

> For though [the concept of a thing] may be so complete that nothing which is required for thinking the thing with all its inner determinations is lacking to it, yet existence has nothing to do with all this, but only with the question whether such a thing be so given us that the perception of it can, if need be, precede the concept. (A225/B272)

> For the appearances, as mere representation, are in themselves real only in perception. To call an appearance a real thing prior to our perceiving it, either means that in the advance of experience we must meet with such a perception, or it means nothing at all. For if we were speaking of a thing in itself, we could indeed say that it exists in itself apart from all relation to our senses and possible experiences. (A493/B521–522)[13]

> Whatever, therefore, and however much, our concept of an object may contain, we must go outside it, if we are to ascribe existence to the object. In the case of objects of the senses, this takes place through their connection with some one of our perceptions, in accordance with empirical laws. But in dealing with objects of pure thought, we have no means whatsoever of knowing their existence . . . any existence outside this field [of possible experience], while not indeed such as we can declare to be absolutely impossible, is of the nature of an assumption which we can never be in a position to justify. (A601/B629; cf. A104–105, A108–109, A189/B234ff.)

Appearances qua appearances exist in the sense that certain perceptions are possible or necessary. Things in themselves are things that exist in something more than this sense.

One might suppose that just as one thing can be considered in two different ways or from two points of view, so one and the same thing might be considered to *exist* in two quite different senses of the term. Things might be supposed to exist "in themselves" and yet also to exist in the sense that they are perceivable, i.e., in the sense that they are capable of appearing and being known in sense perception. However, if we suppose that considering something as an appearance is considering something that exists in itself not *as* existing in itself but as it "appears" to us, then we are committed to a view that Kant could not consistently accept. We are committed to holding that considering something as an appearance presupposes judging that a particular thing (existing) in itself is having a causal effect upon us. We are committed to this because, presumably, the claim that something is "appearing" to us would simply *mean*, at least in part, that it is having a certain sort of effect upon our sense organs. However, Kant is emphatic in maintaining that if we are ever in a position to use a category such as that of "cause and effect" in order to assert something about specifically indicable or identifiable[14] objects, then we are never in that position with regard to anything *other* than things considered as appearances (cf. A235/B294ff.). Accordingly, one should never be in a position to assert, of some specifically indicable or identifiable object, that *it* is a thing that both exists in itself and has a causal effect upon us.

This difficulty does not attach to every form of the double aspect view. It only arises on that version which takes the distinction between things in themselves and appearances as a distinction between two ways in which one and the same thing might be supposed to *exist*, namely "as it appears (or is capable of appearing)" and as it is apart from the ways it appears. We have seen that there are other forms of a double aspect view. On one of them, for example, the point is that the concepts by which we are able to describe things all involve some sort of reference to ourselves and to our possible judgmental or perceptual activities. Nothing on that view implies that considering something as an appearance entails considering it as a thing that both exists "in itself" and also *appears* to us in certain ways. All that is implied, on the view in question, is that things are being considered (and must be) with respect to certain sorts of *concepts*. Similarly on a second sort of view already considered. On that approach, regarding something as an appearance is simply regarding it with respect to the necessary conditions required for obtaining *knowledge* of a thing of that sort. The notion of a thing "in itself," accordingly, is simply that of the possibility (perhaps not open to ourselves) of regarding things in abstraction from those conditions. The distinction, then, is between things considered with respect to, and in abstraction from, a certain set of considerations. It is not concerned with things considerable in one way that also happen to *appear* in some (perhaps different) way. In any case, I have offered some reason for supposing that the distinction between appearances and things in themselves does involve a distinction between two notions of existence, and also noted a difficulty in the attempt to combine that distinction with a double aspect approach.

III. Four Kinds of Phenomenalism

Kant's claim that the spatiotemporal objects of our acquaintance are mere appearances, and his claim that space and time do not apply to things in themselves, seem to me to lead most naturally to a phenomenalistic reading. However, more than one kind of phenomenalistic view might be supposed to represent the point of Kant's "transcendental idealism." It is important to distinguish at least four of these with some care.

One form of phenomenalistic interpretation might be called "predicate phenomenalism." This is because it does not focus on the existence of the things that appear to us in space and time and which we attempt to describe through ordinary judgments and knowledge claims. It focuses instead on the predicates that enter into those judgments. In effect, it says, Kant is defending a phenomenalistic analysis of such predicates. He is not claiming that the objects that present themselves in space and time exist only in the sense that certain perceptions are possible (or necessary). But the only things we are able to *judge* concerning these objects relate to the various ways in which they are able to appear to us in perception. The predicates that we attach to such objects tell us only how they are capable of appearing, not how they are in themselves. They are all "phenomenalistic" predicates, one might say, even though the things to which they attach are supposed to be things that exist in more than a phenomenalistic sense. Of course these things are also characterized by nonphenomenalistic predicates. However, we are unable to know the truth of judgments containing such predicates; perhaps we are not even able to understand what they say. That is the whole point of Kant's claim that we are not able to know anything about things in themselves.[15]

It is evident that predicate phenomenalism is a form of the double aspect approach.[16] It is therefore one that takes at least something of the edge off of Kant's denial that things are not spatial (or temporal) in themselves. (On the view in question that denial is still compatible with conceding that things that exist "in themselves" are as really spatial as they are anything else: they are as truly things that appear to us in spatial form as they are anything else.) Obviously, some of the difficulty already considered with respect to forms of the double aspect view will apply to this theory. For one thing, it is a form of the theory that takes Kant's claims about "mere appearances" to be claims about the proper analysis of the *concepts* by which we are capable of describing objects of intuition. In addition, we have noted a difficulty stemming from the need to construe the notion of a way in which something, existing in itself, *appears* in terms that involve a causal relation with things that exist in themselves. On the predicate phenomenalist view this difficulty becomes even more severe. It is not simply that the view commits us to recognizing the possibility of judgments apparently disallowed by Kant himself, namely judgments about causal relations with particular things existing in themselves. Rather, the predicate phenomenalist view appears to contradict itself. On that view all empirical predicates rest upon the notion of a way in which things are capable of affecting a perceiver. What consistency would require, therefore, is that this notion in turn be phenomenalistically construable. Since, however, on the account in question a predicate is phenomenalistically construable insofar as it describes the way in which something appears or is capable of appearing in sense perception, the notion of a causal relation between a perceiver and some object of perception would be phenomenalistically construable only on pain of a vicious circularity in the analysis.

The issues that we are considering are complicated by the uncertainty whether to ascribe to Kant some form of a "sense datum" theory. On a sense datum approach (as I shall employ the terminology), to say that an (empirically real) object is appearing in sense perception is to say that it is presenting itself via an entity that *is* the "appearance" of it. It presents itself, that is, via a sense datum (or a complex of such entities). So on the view in question the entities that are presented as the immediate objects of sense perception are not entities that are identifiable as those to which we ordinarily attach empirical predicates. In some cases, of course, such entities might present themselves in the absence of any objects of the latter sort altogether (e.g., in the case of hallucination). The doctrine of predicate phenomenalism, then, might attempt to elucidate the notion of a thing that, existing in itself, also "appears" to us in certain ways, by appealing to some relation between such a thing and the various sense data through which the thing appears to us. It might, on the other hand, take the notion of "appearing" in a nonontological way, without the introduction of further entities that are themselves "appearances." Appearances, on such a view, would (at least insofar as they are being contrasted with "things in themselves" according to a *transcendental* rather than an *empirical* distinction)[17] simply be the very objects to which we ordinarily apply empirical predicates—considered insofar as they appear or are capable of appearing to us.

The first of these views involves what has been called the "theory of appearances" and the second the "theory of appearing."[18] The two together, insofar as they are taken in connection with the doctrine of predicate phenomenalism, constitute two of the kinds of phenomenalistic doctrine that one might care to distinguish. In addition, of course, a sense datum approach might be offered as an alternative to predicate phenomenalism and a double aspect view altogether. It might, for example, regard ordinary material objects as complexes or sequences of (actual and perhaps possible) sense data. These objects might then be said to have a reality "in themselves" simply in order to contrast them, as "logical constructs" out of sense data, from any particular *instances* of the data in question.

The primary reason for rejecting any form of the sense datum approach is that there is only one candidate, in Kant's system, for what the account in question is forced to regard as the immediate objects of sense perception. On such an account, it would seem, we could only suppose that these entities are the perceiver's own sensations, somehow projected and externalized by means of the imposition of spatial form. There is some textual evidence for this view, though in some cases it is in fact generated by translators' decisions. I have discussed this issue elsewhere.[19] Here I would simply observe that even should there be passages in which Kant implies that *Empfindung* is the material aspect of appearances, this in itself offers no reason for supposing that on Kant's view our own sensory states provide the material of appearances. As we have already observed, it is not uncommon practice among philosophers to use certain terms for cognitive states or aspects of those states to stand also for the *objects* of those states. This might of course merely indicate that the objects of one's cognitive states are to be considered only with respect to their status *as* such objects. In that case it would not be at all odd to speak of the objects of our own *Vorstellungen* as themselves *Vorstellungen* (A30/B45, B147). More specifically, it would be perfectly in order for Kant to refer to the objects of sense perception as themselves *Anschauungen* (e.g., A163/B204, B207, A168/B209) without supposing that they are really just our own perceptual states. Now suppose, finally, that within the object of sense perception we distinguish between two aspects, one of which *corresponds* to the presence of sensation in a perceptual state. Then it would be perfectly in order for Kant to refer to that element as itself "sensation." In fact Kant himself introduces the "matter of appearances" as what "corresponds" to sensation in the object of intuition (A20/B34; cf. A168/B209).[20]

Apart from this issue, were Kant committed to the sense datum theory, then it is difficult to see how he could have considered as obvious the move from pure intuition to empirical reality. That move requires the supposition that the spatial structure revealed in pure intuition is a structure to which empirical reality must conform. Now on the sense datum interpretation of Kant, the spatial form "imposed" by cognitive faculties a priori upon received sensation is the form revealed in pure intuition. Thus we are aware of that one form in two different ways, once as a structure revealed in the pure imagination of spatial forms and once as the actual structure of data presented in sense perception. However, this could not suffice to account for the judgments that we make about spatial reality. For while on that account sense data are themselves a part of reality, they are in no instance identifiable with the spatial realities that are judged to appear through them. The latter realities need not, of course, be something that the sense datum account regards as things existing "in themselves." They may simply be "logical constructions" out of sense data (including facts about the possibilities and necessities involved in apprehending them in the first place). In any case, it would make no sense to suppose that the spatial boundary of some particular datum apprehended perceptually *is* at the same time the boundary of a physical object. Nor could we suppose that the space "occupied" by perceived data is the same space as that which we judge to be occupied by physical realities. It seems to follow, therefore, that even if the spatial structure revealed in pure intuition were identical with that of the data immediately presented in perception, it would not be identical with the spatial structure of physical reality. So judgments that we make concerning the possibilities of movement and measurement through physical space could not be immediately inferred from judgments that we make concerning the possibilities of "movement" and measurement within and among sense data.

An alternative approach, as I have suggested, is the "intentional object" approach. Here we also need to allow, as on the sense datum theory, the apprehension of spatially characterizable objects other than physical realities. For example, we sometimes perceive merely *hallucinated* objects. However, we do not now suppose that the apprehension of a merely hallucinated object is the apprehension of some *entity* related to the perceiver in some way. The object of such a perceptual state is a merely intentional object, and merely intentional objects, considered precisely *as* such, are something that do not exist at all. On the other hand, this does not preclude the possibility of *identifying* such an object with (or as) a genuine physical reality: any pure hallucination *might* have been the apprehension of a physical reality. In that sense, we might say, the object of a pure hallucination is a *possible* physical object (in an instance, of course, in which that possibility has not been actualized).

The distinction that we have drawn can now be extended to cases of ordinary perception. To do this we simply need to recognize the legitimacy of describing a case of veridical perception as one in which some possible object that happens to be apprehended *also* happens to be an actual one. Of course one might question the legitimacy of this. Consider for example a case in which one perceives an object that is really cubical, but the object appears to be spherical in shape.[21] Then considered purely as an intentional object (and apart from the possibility of *conceptualizing* the intuition in question by means of the concept of a cube) the object is something spherical: we are presented with a spherical "appearance." Considered as a physical reality the object is cubical. How can these be the *same* object? How can something spherical be identified with (i.e., *as*) something cubical? The answer must of course be that the notion of "identity" that is in question is simply not the same as our notion when we identify one and the same *entity* as something that presents itself to us, let us say, under two distinct descriptions. In the purely intentional sense, "appearances" are not entities at all. Precisely how this notion of identity is then to be explicated will therefore remain a question.[22] In any case, insofar as the immediate objects of perception are regarded not as entities but as "possible physical objects," it would seem legitimate to maintain at least that the general conditions determining the *possibilities* (and necessities) involved in our apprehension of such objects must also be applicable to actual physical objects. Even if the spherical "datum" is not any sort of *entity* identifiable with a real physical thing, it would at least be correct, on the intentional object approach, to describe it as a possible physical *sphere*. (Furthermore, the actual physical cube with which we "identify" that sphere is *also* a possible sphere, though that particular possibility is not one that has been actualized.)

One might of course wonder what it could possibly mean to allege that a presented "appearance" is in fact a spherical one, in a case in which we are supposedly abstracting both from identification of that appearance as some actual spherical thing and from questions concerning the concepts that are being used to conceptualize it. Whether or not some presented object actually is spherical, so long as it is being conceptualized *as* spherical one might concede that the apprehension in question is "of" something spherical. What about a case in which it is not so conceptualized? The most that we can say in that case is that the apprehension is "of" something spherical in the sense that it is an awareness of a region whose shape is *connected* in a special way with the concept of a sphere. This relation is of course not easy to define. I presume, though, that it is the relation that Kant has in mind in speaking of the manifold of appearances that are "synthesized" by a given concept. In one way this gives a certain priority to concepts over intuitions but in another way not. On this view the concept of a intuition as an intuition of an object so-or-so describable is derivative from the concept of the very relation *between* some particular concept and that intuition. Thus to say something about the specific object of an intuition (considered purely intentionally) is precisely to say something about some concept in whose "manifold" that intuition is "synthesized." In this sense, as Kant puts it (A51/B75), "intuitions without concepts are blind"; their objects are indeterminate.

This, it is crucial to see, is not to concede that the representational quality of intuitions is totally (though obviously it is partially) derived from the presence of conceptual elements in them. At most it is to say that what the object of an intuition is (considered purely intentionally) concerns what concepts *might*, in some normative sense of that term, be present in it. The position in question is compatible with granting that an intuition that *is* conceptualized involves an unanalyzable and primitive sort of "object-directedness" that does not derive merely from the concept in question, but precisely from the fact that the concept is being applied to a special sort of representational state, namely an intuition. That there are, and must be, states possessed of this primitive sort of representational force is perfectly compatible with holding that it is indeterminate specifically *what* the object of an intuition is (regarded purely intentionally) so long as we are abstracting from considerations concerning concepts altogether.

IV. Pure Intuition, Transcendental Idealism, and Phenomenalism

One of the advantages of the suggested interpretation is that it allows us to see how crucial a role is in fact played in Kant's reasoning by the insistence that pure intuition is a kind of intuition. This insistence, as I have emphasized, amounts to regarding the imagining of spatial forms as a mode of presentation with particulars of a spatial sort, namely imagined regions of space. Thus what is crucial about Kant's account of pure intuition is that on that account pure intuition always involves a genuine activation of the referential capacities of our cognitive nature. For whatever conceptual or predicative elements might be present in some instance of pure intuition, they could only be functioning as part of our attempt to conceptualize some imagined *object* presented in that intuition. So there is an object-directed element in every sensory awareness that is already ingredient in the internal "form" of that awareness, quite apart from external considerations concerning mind-independent reality (e.g., apart from reference to other *possible* perceptions) and over and above whatever intentional elements are introduced by the particular concepts in question.

This interpretation is of course designed to account for Kant's view that limitations encountered when we attempt to apply concepts to merely imagined objects are at least in some cases due to the positive *content* of the representation in question and not to whatever concepts might be involved. The point may be formulated, as we have seen, with two different emphases. From the perspective of the intentional object, we may put it by saying that concepts applied to instances of imaginative representation are always applied in order to conceptualize some imagined region of space. This imagined region of space must therefore possess a content whose presence is not wholly a function of those concepts themselves. But insofar as we are abstracting from the mind-independent reality of objects, an imagined region of space is of course merely a phenomenological correlate of the act of imagining it. From this perspective, then, the point is simply that intuitive *representations* always contain intrinsic yet nonconceptual features helping to determine their object-directed character. If they didn't, then we could never account for the phenomenological fact that attachment of concepts to an intuition serves precisely to conceptualize some (at least possible) object presented *in* that intuition. Of course in some cases "imagination" does not involve intuition at all. In such cases as these, when one is supposed to imagine something or other, what one is doing is merely supposing or imagining that something is the case. This might be a purely conceptual matter. However, supposing or imagining that something is the case is not the only kind of supposing or imagining. For there are also cases in which concepts are introduced not merely in order to suppose or imagine that something is the case but precisely in order to suppose something about an at least possible *object* that one is imagining. With respect to this sort of imagining, the suggested account is able to explain at least one part of Kant's conviction that the intuitive character of purely imaginative representations provides a ground for the possibility of synthetic judgments a priori concerning objects in space.

Now from this we may proceed, I think, to explain the other part of Kant's conviction, namely that discoveries made in pure intuition are indeed applicable to real objects in space and not *merely* to imagined (or hallucinated) objects. This involves seeing that, once Kant has adopted the view so far presented, it will be natural for him to continue reasoning in the following manner. If pure imagination, first of all, already involves the reference to some at least possible region of space, then the only additional capacity that a *sensory* intuition would seem to involve is our capacity for being affected in a distinctive way through our sense organs. Apart from that additional feature and whatever it brings along with it (namely that regions of space are now presented "in a sensory manner"), our capacity for becoming aware of some object, at least purely intentionally, via sensory affection must involve the very same features as are already involved in our pure intuitions of spatial expanses: the form of pure intuition is something that would "remain over" if we abstracted both from what is due to sensation and from what is due to the concepts that we happen to be employing (A20–21/B35).

With respect to this assertion, I have so far argued only that whatever "apriorism" it might involve does not imply extreme subjectivism. Thus it does not involve the notion of our mind imposing forms upon mere sensations in order to generate perceptual objects with those sensations as their material. Now we might make an additional point. For if Kant is right in saying that our pure imagination of spatial expanses is not merely a way of thinking about regions of space, but rather a way of attending to (possible) regions *about* which we might think, then it seems at least *reasonable* to agree that the only general difference between pure and empirical intuition involves the presence of sensation in the latter. One might of course think all sorts of thoughts about regions of space that conform in no way to the space of empirical intuition. In this sense, admittedly, one might also "imagine" all sorts of misguided things. However, we are not now talking about merely imagining that something is so; we are talking rather about imagining something *about* which something is imagined to be so, namely a possible region of space.

Given that our pure imagination of regions of space does involve a genuine activation of the mind's referential capacities, it would indeed be purely arbitrary to suppose that sensory intuition adds anything to that intuition over and beyond the fact that the objects now presented are presented in a sensuous way rather than in a purely imaginative one. Maintaining such a view would be tantamount to supposing, for no apparent reason, that we are not even *capable* of presenting, in pure intuition, the very same forms as we might apprehend in sensuous intuition. If we do not suppose that the forms of pure intuition are also those of empirical intuition, then we must suppose that the referential capacities actualized in the latter are different from those actualized in the former case. If that is so, then we are in possession of two sorts of referential capacities, only one of which is supposedly operable in pure intuition. Once however we have granted in principal that at least some primitive referential capacities do also function on a purely imaginative level, it would seem wholly arbitrary to suppose that those of empirical intuition may not do so as well. If they indeed do so, Kant might reasonably argue, and if in addition they do not conform to certain *other* capacities that are also to be found in pure imagination, then this should be something that manifests itself in the sort of internal contradiction in pure imagination that we simply fail to encounter.

We may also look at this same issue in another way, in relation to what we might call "impure" imagination. While Kant argues, as we have seen, that a certain sort of intuitive element is involved in geometrical imagination, we should recognize that the additional presence of geometrical *concepts*, and the absence of any others (at least by way of actually characterizing or "informing" that imagination), is also part of its status as a "pure" imagining of the sort that Kant has in mind. Now there is, one should note, no reason in principle why an imagined expanse, represented in the absence of sensation, might not be conceptualized in impure terms as well. While a "catlike" region of space might be conceptualized in purely geometrical terms, for example, it might also be conceptualized in imagination precisely as a *cat*, even as one of some fairly definite color, pose, and temperament. Surely, after all, we do sometimes imagine a cat by means of a representational state involving no actual sensation, and in at least some such cases we are not merely imagining or supposing that something is or might be the case. Kant's account provides us with an analysis of such situations. On that account we have simply to deal with precisely the same sort of intuitional "form" in virtue of which we are able to perceive catlike regions of space through sensation, yet in this case in the absence of actual sensation. In this respect imagining a cat is like experiencing a pure intuition for Kant, though there is also a difference. The difference is that the former involves concepts that are not purely formal (e.g., that of a cat). Now if there is no alternative account of impure imagination that is clearly superior to this one, given that (as Kant has argued) we will in any case need to account for *pure* imagination, then the Kantian account will obviously be one that needs to be taken seriously. For my own part I do not see that anyone has suggested an account of empirical imagination that is in fact clearly superior. Kant's theory thus provides an account of empirical imagination that is at the very least a reasonable one, and it does so without appealing to any terms beyond those that are required for the possibility of the pure imagination which his metaphysical and transcendental expositions demand in any case.

To be sure, there are two respects in which the forms of pure intuition could not possibly account, even when combined with actual sensation, for the "referential character" of our perceptual states. The first applies when perception is considered as the awareness of objects de re, that is, as the apprehension of objects that exist in something more than the sense that there is some apprehension of them. Though he is not always consistent, it is the objects of perceptual states considered in this manner, as objects comprising empirical *reality*,[23] that Kant often officially designates as genuine "objects" of perception. Kant also makes it clear that a necessary condition for regarding some such object as the object of a sensory intuition is that the object be regarded as playing a causal role in the production of that intuition: "intuition takes place only in so far as the object . . . affects the mind in a certain way [*das Gemüt auf gewisse Weise affiziere*]" (A19/ B33). Obviously, the truth of the judgment that an object plays such a role must be a function of more than the intrinsic character of the perception in question. There is also a second respect in which mere forms of intuition could not by themselves account for the "referential character" of a perceptual state. This is a sense that is independent of the distinction between perceptual states considered purely intentionally and de re. The point in this case is simply that the "object" of one's perceptual state is also determined, to some extent at least, by the way in which that state has been *conceptualized*. This raises questions to be further pursued later.

It is important to keep a number of things in mind with respect to the first of these points. We need to be clear, first of all, that Kant's resolution to speak only of "actual" objects as the *Gegenstände* of intuitions is perfectly compatible with his holding that perceptual states might also be regarded as object-directed even when considered purely intentionally, i.e., as awarenesses of objects that might or might *not* be anything actual. Obviously we are simply dealing with two uses of the term 'object'. Secondly, the attempt to distinguish between the objects of perceptual states considered purely intentionally and the actual objects comprising empirical reality is still compatible with a phenomenalistic view regarding the latter. One might for example hold that our judgment that the object of a perceptual state is in fact a part of empirical reality (and does not exist merely *as* the object of that state) is simply the judgment that the object of that state, considered purely intentionally, is connected in accordance with certain rules with a whole set of other such objects that necessarily *would* be perceived if the predictions implicit in such a judgment were in fact to be tested. Roughly, we might say, empirical reality (as opposed to merely intentional or "phenomenological" reality) is defined in terms of relations among the members of whole *sets* of the objects of perception, considered purely intentionally: the reality of appearances in one sense of the term is defined in relation to that of appearances taken in another. Indeed, a phenomenalistic definition of empirical reality is not incompatible with the supposition that some object whose existence is so defined plays a causal role in the *production* of the perception of it. Consistency merely requires that the meaning of the judgment that an object plays that sort of role must itself be spelled out in terms of predictions leading from one set of immediate objects of perception to others. Finally one should not assume without further argument that something whose existence is not definable phenomenalistically might not *also* play a role in the causal generation of a perceptual state. Consistency merely requires that there be some sense in speaking of causal relations in nonphenomenalistic terms; it also requires conceding that any such causal agent would not be the *object* of a perceptual state in anything like the sense in which empirically real objects are.[24]

In any case we need to acknowledge an additional step in Kant's reasoning. The first was the step from regions of space regarded as the objects of pure intuition to regions of space regarded as objects of sense perception considered purely intentionally. The additional step is now from the latter to regions of space (i.e., actual bodies) regarded as objects of perception considered de re. Kant himself hardly regarded this as an additional step at all. An advantage of the approach that I have suggested is that it explains why this might have been so. Given that the objects of sense perception, considered apart from questions of empirical reality, could be nothing other than *possible* empirical realities, it follows either that none of the objects in question is actual or else that in at least some cases our judgments concerning physical reality are judgments in which we take some immediately apprehended intentional object precisely *as* actual (and hence not to be a *merely* intentional object). Surely the first hypothesis is unreasonable. Furthermore Kant offers an argument, in the Refutation of Idealism (B274ff.), to the conclusion that some physical realities *must* be among the immediate objects of sense perception. So at least some physical reality is "identifiable" with the immediate objects of perception (or perhaps better, some immediate objects of perception are identifiable *as* physical realities). The only way, then, in which physical reality could fail to conform to pure intuition's limitations upon the regions of space that we apprehend perceptually would be in the case that it contained *other* objects that could not in principle be identified with the immediate objects of a possible sense perception. However, if physical reality were regarded as containing elements that are not in principle identifiable with the immediate objects of sense perception, then in what sense could such reality even be supposed to be the object *of* sense perception? Only one construal could be placed upon the supposition. The claim that such entities are the objects of sense perception could amount to nothing more than the claim that they play a certain sort of causal role in generating perceptions. We could then suppose Kant to have reasoned in the following way. Even if there are such entities, they could not be the objects of sense perception in the same sense as those that are *identifiable* with the immediate objects of sense perception. In that case, therefore, they could not even be supposed to be "perceived" by us, in the sense of the term that is properly applicable to the other sorts of entities. However, nothing is more reasonable, Kant might claim, than the supposition that objects that are in principle imperceptible are objects about which there could not possibly be any empirical knowledge. Therefore they could not comprise part of what we mean by empirical reality.

While it is a necessary condition for something's being the object of a perceptual state (de re) that it play a causal role in the production of that state, this cannot be a sufficient condition. What else is required? On Kant's view the further condition involves *identification* of the object with the "immediate object" of the state in question. Now we have already seen that, on an intentional object approach, the identification of the immediate object of a perceptual state with an empirically real entity differs in one way from what we often mean by a judgment of identity. In particular we are not now considering the identity of a single *entity* with respect to two distinct descriptions that might be given of it. For insofar as objects are considered merely intentionally, they are not being considered as entities at all. It might be argued, therefore, that we are faced even on Kant's view with the necessity of *specifying* a sense in which some empirically real entity might be identified with the immediate object of a perceptual state. What is to prevent us from specifying that an entity will be "identical" with the immediate object of perception just in case it plays the right sort of causal role in the generation of that perception?

Kant may simply have considered it obvious that if the only sense in which some entity could be regarded as identical with the immediate object of a perceptual state was that it played a causal role in relation to that state, then such an entity could not really be regarded as one that we immediately perceive. For though we could say that we immediately perceive the entity, all that we would mean is that the entity plays some causal role in *relation* to our perceptions. Therefore Kant may have considered it obvious that such could not be what we mean when identifying an entity with the immediate object of a perceptual state. This of course leaves the question as to just what we do mean when we identify the immediate object of a sense perception as an actual physical entity.

Perhaps the strongest support for the intentional object approach to Kant is that it shows how the most natural answer to this question could at the same time be regarded as leading to the conclusion that things are not spatial "in themselves." This of course was the problem with which we began the present chapter: how could Kant have considered it to follow directly from the fact that the forms of pure intuition are conditions upon empirical reality that those forms do not also apply to reality considered in itself? We may simply suppose Kant to have reasoned in the following way. The same defect that is apparent in our above attempt to specify a sense in which some entity is identical with an immediate object of sense perception will apply in the case of *any* entity considered as existing "in itself." It will apply, that is, in the case of any entity that would be an independent term of a perceptual relation in some sense of independence that is not definable phenomenalistically. Insofar as we are dealing with that sort of "independence," we could never be dealing with anything other than some external relation between one entity, the supposed empirically real object of perception, and the perception itself with its own immediate object. In any such case, therefore, we could never take seriously the supposition that the entity in question is "identifiable" with the immediate object of perception. It will simply be a matter of a relation between *two* entities. To be sure in any instance of perception de re, precisely what we want is a relation between two entities, namely between the perception of some object and some object perceived. However, so long as the existence of the latter is not definable in phenomenalistic terms, and hence precisely in relation to the former, then it will bear much too external a relation to the perception of it to be supposed to be the *object* of that perception.

In short, rather than possessing an absolute identity on its own and then being supposed to enter into such relations as allow for its identification with the immediate objects of perception, the very identity of the object that is to be identified in the manner in question must itself be a *function* of its identifiability with the immediate objects of perceptual states. That is to say, by the object in question we cannot mean anything other than what, should we undertake to confirm the predictions implicit in our empirical judgments, would necessarily be apprehended as the immediate objects of perceptions. We can only mean what is defined in terms of whole sets (or "manifolds") of perceptual states, regarded purely intentionally:

> We have stated above that appearances are themselves nothing but sensi-
> ble representations, which, as such and in themselves, must not be taken as
> objects capable of existing outside our power of representation. What,
> then, is to be understood when we speak of an object corresponding to, and
> consequently also distinct from, our knowledge? . . . it is clear that, since we
> have to deal only with the manifold of our representations, and since that x
> (the object) which corresponds to them is nothing to us—being, as it is,
> something that has to be distinct from all our representations—the unity
> which the object makes necessary can be nothing else than the formal unity
> of consciousness in the synthesis of the manifold of representations. (A104–
> 105)

Appearances are the sole objects which can be given to us immediately, and that in them which relates immediately to the object is called intuition. But these appearances are not things in themselves; they are only representations, which in turn have their object. . . . The pure concept of this transcendental object, which in reality throughout all our knowledge is always one and the same, is what can alone confer upon all our empirical concepts in general relation to an object, that is, objective reality. This concept cannot contain any determinate intuition, and therefore refers only to that unity which must be met with in any manifold of knowledge which stands in relation to an object. This relation is nothing but the necessary unity of consciousness, and therefore also of the synthesis of the manifold. . . . (A108–109)

Everything, every representation even, in so far as we are conscious of it, may be entitled object. But it is a question for deeper enquiry what the word 'object' ought to signify in respect of appearances when these are viewed not in so far as they are (as representations) objects, but only in so far as they stand for an object. The appearances, in so far as they are objects of consciousness simply in virtue of being representations, are not in any way distinct from their apprehension . . . . (A189–190/B234–235) [A]ppearance, in contradistinction to the representations of apprehension, can be represented as an object distinct from them only if it stands under a rule which distinguishes it from every other apprehension and necessitates some one particular mode of connection of the manifold. (A191/B236)

Before seeing now how the nonspatiality of things in themselves follows from this move, we need to note an ambiguity in the claim itself. One thing that might be meant applies to those things that are identifiable with the immediate objects of sense perception, namely that they are spatial realities only in a sense that is phenomenalistically definable. It should now be clear how this conclusion is supposed to follow from the doctrine of pure intuition. Kant appears to have reasoned in the following way. (1) Pure imagination involves the imaginative presentation of particulars, i.e., possible regions of space; therefore (2) any given sense perception (considered intrinsically and apart from its external relations) must be the apprehension of an object that might or might not be identifiable as a physically real one; therefore (3) since judgments concerning physical reality involve nothing more than the ways we identify immediate objects of sense perception *as* physical realities, the latter must be definable phenomenalistically, i.e., precisely in terms of the immediate intentional objects of sense perception.

On other occasions, Kant's insistence upon the nonspatiality of things in themselves seems meant to include even those things (assuming there to be such) that are *not* identifiable with the immediate objects of sense perception but that might nonetheless be supposed to be real. Kant's conclusion would then simply be that nothing that exists in such a nonphe-nomenalistic sense could possibly be a spatial entity. Now so long as by a spatial entity we mean anything that is spatial in the sense in which immediately perceivable objects are spatial, then Kant's conclusion does follow. While things in themselves might be spatial, for example, in the sense that they play a certain role in the production of *perceptions* whose immediate objects are spatial, that of course would be different from the sense in which the latter might be regarded as spatial. The latter are (at least when regarded as empirical realities) spatial in the sense that certain perceptions are possible (or necessary). The former would at most be spatial in the sense that they provide some *ground* for the possibilities (or the necessities) in question. The fact that some entity provides a ground for perceptions, the immediate objects of which are spatial, of course hardly implies in any ordinary sense of the term that the entity is in itself spatial.

The alternatives seem unable to explain Kant's convictions on these various points. This was already shown with regard to a sense datum approach. It was shown, that is, with respect to accounts that see the immediate objects of sensory awareness as entities and not merely as *possible* entities. On any such view one may well grant that sensory awareness involves some object-directedness over and above what con-cepts might impart to it. However, no such view could justify Kant's inference that limitations encountered in attempts at pure imagination have a legitimate bearing on objects regarded as real in space. One might attempt such a justification by supposing that the reality of objects in space lies wholly in the various ways in which they are able to appear to us via sense data. Then with the additional supposition that the "forms" of merely imagined data are also those of actually sensed data, one might conclude that principles derived from reflection on the former are indeed applicable to objects regarded as real in space. However, this would totally reverse Kant's actual procedure. As we have seen, Kant does not first suppose that objects in space are mere appearances in order to justify his account of pure intuition and geometry. Rather he concludes *from* his account of the latter that the objects in question are mere appearances. In any case the sense datum approach is objectionable on independent grounds.

What is left to see is that the remaining alternative is equally deficient with respect to Kant's inferences. There are, it seems, three alternatives in all: the immediate objects of sensory awareness are possibilities that might or might not be materially actual; or they are actualities (sense data) that are never as such material in the first place; or they are themselves material actualities. The third alternative may be labelled the "direct transcenden-tal realist" approach. I have already rejected it in one of its forms, insofar as the doctrine of "predicate phenomenalism" is a form of such realism (so long as it does not rest on the introduction of sense data). Any such interpretation must of course explain what Kant means by denying that we perceive and know things in themselves. The predicate phenomenalist explains this by supposing Kant to mean that while the objects that we directly perceive do exist in themselves, we perceive and know them only through phenomenalistic predicates. However, there might also be non-phenomenalistic accounts.

Obviously, a direct transcendental realist might grant that a perceptual state does possess an element of object-directedness quite independently of the character of whatever material reality is its object. For example, one might always grant that, from the phenomenological point of view, *concepts* that enter into perceptions help to determine what the "objects" of those perceptions are. In this sense, for example, if I conceptually take what I see to be a tree in the distance, then whether or not it really is, "the object" of my perception can be said to be a tree. However, on the approach in question there is no *other* element of genuine object-directedness present in a perceptual state besides the two just mentioned. The whole point of that approach is to maintain that directly perceived material objects are the only objects to which concepts are *applied* in a perception.

As we saw earlier, one might always introduce a kind of "comparative" object-directedness, defined neither by the actual material reality present in perception nor by the concepts that enter into it. So one might maintain that a sensory state is object-directed in a third sense without having recourse either to intentional objects or to sense data. One might say, for example, that a perception is a perception "of" an object of some description simply if it is the sort of state typically involved *when* an object of that description is materially present to the senses. Obviously the direct realist could grant that in this sense perceptual states involve an object-directedness that is a function neither of actually presented physical reality nor of purely conceptualizing factors. Equally obviously such a concession would be of no help to Kant. It would be of no help precisely because it does not appeal to an *intrinsic feature* of a perceptual (or imaginative) state. It appeals to a feature definable only in terms of its relation to states in which material realities are presented. Hence the feature in question can be of no use when we are seeking to ground an a priori methodology with respect to the geometry of those very realities.

V. The Double Aspect View: Final Reflections

What remains is to offer an explanation for the pervasive presence of the double aspect language in Kant's writings, as well as to consider some special difficulties that seem to favor the double aspect approach. Part of the reason for the double aspect language, I think, in those passages implying that phenomena must also have a reality in themselves, is simply to express the feeling that phenomenalistic existence must have a nonphenomenalistic underpinning. For something to exist phenomenalistically is for certain perceptions to be possible (i.e., under the appropriate conditions necessary). The immediate object of any such perception is an object that might or might not be (empirically, "materially") real; to regard it as real is simply to suppose that this perception can be connected with a manifold of others in accordance with the guidance offered by the concept of the sort of object supposed to be in question. Now Kant seems clearly to have supposed that, while the existence of appearances is a matter of what is (or must be) perceivable, there must be something whose existence is not merely such a matter and whose existence is what ultimately *accounts* for what is perceivable. Appearances would then most naturally be regarded as appearances "of" such things and could not inappropriately be described as *being* those very things "as they appear," even if they are not in fact literally identical with them.

What we need especially to bear in mind, with regard to the prevalence of double aspect language, is the specific and highly unique character of Kantian phenomenalism. This character derives from the role of intentional objects in Kant's philosophy. On Kant's view it is not the case that perceptions of material reality are really perceptions of entities of a different sort (sensations, e.g., or sense data) that we judge to be connected into those systems or collections that we call material objects. That would be more like Berkeleyian idealism, where material objects are mere "collections of ideas." When Kant says that empirical reality, and all of material nature, is merely our own *Vorstellungen*, he does not have any such doctrine in mind. On that sort of doctrine what we perceive in sense perception could never be identified as a material object; at most it is a *constituent* of those systems or collections that we call material objects. On Kant's view, by contrast, the immediate object of sense perception might or might not itself *be* a material object. Also, on the sense datum approach, when the immediate object of sense perception does not in fact happen to comprise part of material reality (in the case of hallucination, for example) it is nonetheless still a reality in its own right. It is just as much a sense datum as it ever could have been. On Kant's view, if a possible object apprehended in sense perception should prove not to be identifiable as an actual material reality, then it simply cannot be regarded as a reality at all; it remains a mere possibility. Now this consideration may explain, I think, the prevalence of double aspect language in Kant. This is because, to the extent to which Kant might suggest that we are *not* dealing with one set of entities, considered from two points of view, most readers would naturally suppose that we are therefore dealing with *two* sets: reality in itself and the immediate objects of sense perception. Since this is precisely the suggestion that Kant wants to avoid, choice of the double aspect language might have appeared to him the lesser of two evils.

At times Kant does not simply use double aspect language. He not only writes as if he supposes that appearances, in addition to being appearances, have a reality in themselves, but he also seems to insist that there would be a contradiction in any other supposition. At least he seems to think there is a contradiction in denying that appearances are appearances "of" something that, existing in itself, appears through them:

> But our further contention must also be duly born in mind, namely that though we cannot *know* these objects as things in themselves, we must yet be in position at least to *think* them as things in themselves; otherwise we should be landed in the absurd conclusion that there can be appearance without anything that appears. (Bxxvi)

> The sensibility . . . does not have to do with things in themselves but only with the mode in which, owing to our subjective constitution, they appear. The Transcendental Aesthetic, in all its teaching, has led to this conclusion; and the same conclusion follows from the concept of an appearance in general; namely, that something which is not in itself appearance must correspond to it. For appearance can be nothing by itself, outside our mode of representation. Unless, therefore, we are to move constantly in a circle, the word appearance must be recognized as already indicating a relation to something . . . in itself, that is, an object independent of sensibility. (A251–252)

> At the same time, if we entitle certain objects, as appearances, sensible entities (phenomena), then since we thus distinguish the mode in which we intuit them from the nature that belongs to them in themselves, it is implied in this distinction that we place the latter, considered in their own nature, although we do not so intuit them, or that we place other possible things, which are not objects of our senses but are thought as objects merely through the understanding, in opposition to the former. . . . (B306)

If the relation between appearances and things existing in themselves is merely that the existence of the latter is supposed to provide some ground or explanation for the former, it is difficult to see why there would be a logical *contradiction* involved in denying the existence of the latter altogether. There seems to be no logical contradiction in supposing that all that exists are perceivers and the various ways in which those perceivers happen to perceive. The supposition may be a groundless or even a foolish one, but it hardly seems to involve a logical impossibility. If, on the other hand, what we mean by "appearance" is simply the ways in which things that exist in themselves *appear* to us, then there would be a contradiction in supposing the reality of appearances while denying that of things existing in themselves.

It is important to see that Kant does not quite say that a logical contradiction is in question here. What he says is that the notion of an appearance in
some sense requires that of reality existing in itself and that it would be
"absurd" to deny the latter. We also need to remember that for Kant the
reality of appearances does not simply amount, on a phenomenalistic
approach, to the fact that certain perceptions happen to occur. Rather what
is the case is that (A104–105) appearances are to be judged real only to the
extent that some *necessity* is found in their occurrence. It is a notoriously
difficult problem to explain what sort of necessity Kant could have in mind
here. Clearly it is the kind of necessity that attaches to specific causal laws
in nature. This would seem to be neither the necessity of a synthetic
judgment a priori nor of an analytic judgment. In any case it is part of our
concept of an empirically real object that we regard our perceptions of it as
constrained by that kind of necessity. In whatever way Kant understands
this sort of necessity, then, he may well have supposed that it requires a
grounding in something that exists in itself. There "must," that is, be some
explanation as to why perceptions occur with the necessity with which they
do occur, that is, with precisely those necessities that define empirical
reality for us. Obviously to attempt such an explanation by appeal to
appearances themselves would be "to move constantly in a circle."

Kant does at least make it clear that in whatever sense there "must" be
things existing in themselves so long as there are appearances, this sense is
one involving the need for explanation or "grounding":

> If, on the other hand, appearances are not taken for more than they actually
> are; if they are viewed not as things in themselves, but merely as repre-
> sentations, connected according to empirical laws [i.e., necessities], they
> must themselves have grounds which are not appearances. The effects of
> such an intelligible cause appear, and accordingly can be determined
> through other appearances, but its causality is not so determined. (A537/
> B566)

> For the existence of appearances, which is never self-grounded but always
> conditioned, requires us to look around for something different from all
> appearances, that is, for an intelligible object in which this contingency may
> terminate (A566/B594).[25]

This is of course compatible with the double aspect view, but it is also
compatible with its denial. That the reality of appearances qua appearances
"must" be grounded in that of some reality in itself is compatible with
holding that appearances literally also *have* a reality in themselves. The
point might simply be that their reality as appearances concerns the ways
in which they appear to us, which in turn involves their ability to have a
causal effect upon our sense organs. However, the position is also compati-

ble with supposing that the reality of appearances is a matter of what perceptions are possible (or "necessary") and that such matters must always have an explanation involving things existing in themselves. In any case there is no reason to suppose, even on the basis of the passages quoted, that on Kant's view what we *mean* by an appearance is the way in which a thing, existing in itself, appears to us.[26]

It is of course possible that terminological confusion has obscured Kant's real point. As we have seen, there are two different senses in which appearances might be supposed to have an existence in themselves. Taken one way it simply means that the existence of appearances is grounded in that of reality in itself, which is compatible with appearances themselves existing merely phenomenalistically. Taken in the other way the claim implies that appearances do *not* exist merely phenomenalistically. Perhaps Kant tended to confuse these two senses. Certainly not a few commentators hold Kant the victim of confusion when he argues that the concept of appearance "requires" the admission of things in themselves. One of the strengths of the present approach is that it offers a way to explain such confusion. Let us restrict our attention to contexts in which empirically real appearances are in question. These after all are what Kant usually reserves the term 'object' in order to designate, even though, as I have argued, the term has a broader use in reference to objects that might or might *not* be empirical realities. In this broader sense we are dealing with appearances in a purely phenomenological or intentional sense. For simplicity one might speak of "phenomenological appearances" as contrasted with "objectively real appearances." But of course we need to bear in mind that any phenomenological appearance might in fact happen to *be* objectively real. Consider then some objectively real appearance O; for example this piece of paper. Also consider the present phenomenological appearance O_1 that I happen to be apprehending in the course of apprehending O. Given then that we are dealing with a case of objective and *not* merely of phenomenological apprehension (though of course we are also dealing with the latter), the following propositions obtain:

(1) O_1 is the appearance of something that appears *through* it; it is a "way in which" something (namely a piece of paper) is appearing on this occasion.[27]

(2) O_1 is "identical" with O, a piece of paper in front of me.

From these two propositions, one might suppose Kant was led to conclude that O, being "identical" with O_1, must like O_1 be the appearance of something that appears through it. That is, an ordinary piece of paper is *itself* a "way in which" something appears to us. This something of course could only be a thing that exists "in itself."

There is a second difficulty that needs to be considered. This concerns Kant's views about human agency. According to Kant the judgments that we make concerning human agency require regarding a person, or at least supposing that a person can be regarded, from two points of view.[28] The person of course appears as an object of perception both to itself and others. In addition the person, as free moral agent, must be supposed to be something existing in itself. This appears to require a double aspect approach to persons. If phenomena and things in themselves were not just the same entities considered from two points of view, then we would apparently have to deny that the same person could satisfy both of the sets of descriptions that Kant is attempting to apply to any morally responsible member of the phenomenal world. On that view, it might be argued, we could at most speak of a sensuously determined but unfree and nonresponsible phenomenal subject on the one hand and a being, on the other hand, that acts solely in accordance with rational moral principles.

This reasoning seems to me to rest on an error. The error lies in the supposition that a phenomenal being, purely qua phenomenal, can be regarded as a person. If the "phenomenal self," purely qua appearance, were a person capable of action, then the objection would hold. In that case we would, on a two-object interpretation, be dealing with two persons capable of action, one phenomenal (and capable of acting only as determined by sensuous inclination) and one existing in itself (and capable of acting only in a purely rational manner). However, it is compatible with the two-object interpretation to deny that a phenomenal person is identifiable with a particular phenomenal object or appearance. A phenomenal *person* (as opposed to other sorts of appearances) might better be regarded as a subject, existing in itself, regarded as the "ground" of at least some of the behavior exhibited by some particular phenomenal object.[29] This may suggest acceptance of the double aspect approach after all. It seems to grant the identity of the phenomenal subject with something that has an existence in itself. However, this is not what the suggestion is meant to imply. What is meant is rather that a phenomenal person is a certain sort of composite: it is a composite of a subject, existing in itself, and a particular phenomenal object. Thus while the two-object interpretation might well grant that the phenomenal self and the self as it is in itself are really just two aspects of a single *self*, namely of a phenomenal person, this is compatible with denying that the phenomenal self is merely qua phenomenon a self at all. It is also compatible with denying that the two "aspects" in question are strictly speaking the same entity regarded in two ways. The two aspects may be regarded as aspects of a phenomenal person simply in the sense that they are the necessary *constitutents* of any phenomenal person's existence.

There may appear to be insurmountable difficulties in this view. For one thing, objection may be raised to the notion of a composite constituted out of one thing that supposedly exists only as an intentional object of perceptions and another thing that is supposed to exist nonphenomenalistically. We can perhaps make sense of a theory according to which an ordinary person is a composite of two distinct "subjects." Consider for example the Cartesian view of persons as composites of mind and body. However, on that view at least both of the constituents in question are regarded as equally real. There might seem to be a logical mistake in attempting to construct a composite out of a pair of entities that do not even satisfy this initial condition. It makes sense, for example, to say that Arthur Conan Doyle was on the streets of London on a certain date. It also makes sense to say (at least with respect to the relevant intentional context) that Sherlock Holmes was on the streets of London on a certain date. It would seem to make little sense to suppose that the two were on the streets *together* on some occasion.

It is not necessary to take the notion of a composite as literally as this objection supposes. A phenomenal person may be regarded as a composite of a subject existing in itself and a phenomenal object simply in the sense that all propositions about a phenomenal person (qua person) are analyzable into *propositions* about (or "about") both something existing in itself and something that is an appearance. Thus the claim that some phenomenal person has performed a certain action may be regarded as a claim about a decision made by a subject existing in itself and some behavior supposedly *explained* by that decision, as exhibited by a certain phenomenal object (that is, some behavior that exists only in the sense that it is perceivable in accordance with the conditions of empirical intuition). In this sense, if Conan Doyle's walking the streets were indeed a systematically determining ground of Sherlock Holmes at least being *perceived* to walk the streets, then one might in fact say that both the real Conan Doyle and the merely perceived Sherlock Holmes constitute parts of a single "phenomenon." We could do this without supposing that the merely perceived Sherlock Holmes is merely the way in which we perceive Conan Doyle *himself* walking the streets. Of course the notion of "ground" or "explanation" that is in question may remain obscure. However, as we have seen, Kant himself does appeal to that notion in order to indicate the need for a distinction between appearance and reality in itself in the first place.[30]

I turn to a final argument in behalf of the double aspect approach. On the account I have proposed, things existing in themselves could not literally be the same things as phenomenal objects or appearances. However, it might be argued that Kantian principles exclude the possibility of judgments concerning anything other than a phenomenal object. If we are able to think intelligibly about things other than appearances, then we would have to do so by means of concepts from which conditions of reference to possible objects of experience have been dropped. These are what Kant calls "unschematized categories." We would have to be able to make use, for example, of the unschematized categories of quantity and modality in order to speak of distinct *particulars* (i.e., one or more of them) enjoying a real *existence*. We would also have to admit the intelligibility of supposing such particulars to exert a real *causal* influence of some sort, at least with respect to one another. Yet Kant maintains that apart from schematization of our categorial concepts, we retain only "pure forms of the understanding's employment through which alone no object can be thought" (*ohne doch durch sie allein irgendein Objekt denken . . . zu können*: A248/B305).

At the very least Kant himself was ambivalent with respect to the question whether categorial concepts, in abstraction from conditions determining their reference to objects of experience, retain a conceptual "content" sufficient for the formation of intelligible judgments. Kant did maintain that unschematized categories are in some sense meaningless. However, he was also prepared to grant that they possess a meaning sufficient for the formation of "thoughts" by means of such concepts, even if not for the obtaining of any *knowledge*. At one point Kant wrote that "The pure concepts can find no object, and can acquire no meaning which might yield a concept of some object" (A147/B186). Later, however, he altered the passage so as to assert merely that pure (unschematized) concepts "can acquire no meaning which might yield a *knowledge* [my emphasis] of some object." At the same time, similarly, that he asserts that "the merely transcendental employment of the categories is, therefore, really no employment at all, and has no determinate object, not even one that is determinable in its mere form" (A247/B304), Kant also maintains that a "pure category in which abstraction is made of every condition of sensible intuition . . . then expresses only the thought of an object in general, according to different modes." In addition Kant later altered the first of these passages so as to say merely that a purely "transcendental employment" of categories is no employment "for the *knowing* [emphasis added] of anything": *kein Gebrauch, um etwas zu erkennen*.[31]

The supposition that Kant's theories preclude intelligible judgments about things in themselves as distinct particulars may stem from a failure to realize that the primary distinction between things in themselves and appearances is merely between two kinds of existence claims, not between two sorts of *things*. On this approach the formation of judgments about things in themselves would simply be the formation of judgments asserting that something exists in a nonphenomenalistic sense. The fact that determinate reference to and knowledge of such objects is impossible does not imply that those judgments are unintelligible. The supposition that they are unintelligible may be due to Kant's insistence that what such judgments are "about" would have to be entities of a nonspatial and nontemporal sort. This may suggest that the primary notion is of a certain sort of object. As I have argued, however, it is not part of the *concept* of a "thing in itself" that it lack spatiality and temporality. That is a conclusion Kant draws only after the argument presented in the Transcendental Aesthetic.

Any interpretation of Kant's views concerning existence will have to recognize that his treatment of this category differs from his treatment of the other modal categories (necessity and possibility). In the latter case Kant allows for a difference between what appears to be a schematized and an unschematized form of the category in question. Thus he distinguishes what is "logically" (analytically) necessary from what is necessary "in accordance with universal conditions of experience (A226/B279), and he distinguishes what is "logically" (analytically) possible from what is possible compatibly with the "formal conditions of experience" (A219/B266). He does not make a parallel distinction in the case of existence. However, Kant was perhaps a bit unclear concerning his own position with respect to the modal categories. We cannot take it for granted, I think, that the formal ("logical") notions of necessity and possibility, characterized in terms of analytic relations among concepts, in fact define the (unschematized) modalities of possibility and necessity for him. Kant seems to offer two distinct ways of viewing these modalities. In the "Postulates of Empirical Thought" (A218/B265ff.) he characterizes formal possibility and necessity in terms of logical relations among *concepts* and real (material or empirical) possibility and necessity in terms of logical relations between concepts and the "conditions of experience." In the "Schematism" chapter (A137/B176ff.) his approach is rather different. Here for example schematized necessity is defined as "existence (*Dasein*) of an object at all times," and schematized existence ("actuality" or *Wirklichkeit*) as "existence (*Dasein*) in some determinate time" (A145/B184). Thus the relation between our concepts of necessity and actuality is quite different from that presented in the Postulates chapter. Furthermore Kant here seems to operate with two distinct concepts of actuality, *Dasein* and *Wirklichkeit*. One could of course argue that this is merely provisional and that Kant attempts a significant definition of the modalities only later. However, Kant later makes no attempt to define *Dasein*. He also asserts that "in this treatise, I purposely omit the definitions of the categories" (A82–83/B108).

It seems to me that the most reasonable approach is to regard Kant's characterizations of formal or logical possibility and necessity in the Postulates chapter not as definitions of the unschematized categories of possibility and necessity but merely as *criteria* for the application of those modalities in judgment. He then is simply able to offer no corresponding criterion for the unschematized modality of existence. This is not to say that Kant says nothing at all about the matter. He attempts to explain it in terms derived from descriptions of the logical forms of judgment:

'Being' [*Sein*] is obviously not a real predicate. . . . It is merely the positing of a thing, or of certain determinations, as existing in themselves [*die Position eines Dinges, oder gewisser Bestimmungen an sich selbst*]. Logically, it is merely the copula of a judgment . . . . [W]e attach no new predicate to the concept of God, but only posit the subject in itself with all its predicates [*setze ich kein neues Prädikat zum Begriffe von Gott, sondern nur das Subjekt an sich selbst mit allen seinen Prädikaten*], and indeed posit it as being an *object* that stands in relation to my *concept*. (A598–599/ B626–627)

Yet, Kant acknowledges, it is impossible to say just what is being done when we "posit" a thing as instantiating a concept (i.e., when we judge that there is such a thing):

Were we dealing with an object of the senses, we could not confound the existence of the thing with the mere concept of it. For through the concept the object is thought only as conforming to the *universal conditions* of possible empirical knowledge in general, whereas through its existence it is thought as belonging to the context of experience as a whole. . . . It is not, therefore, surprising that, if we attempt to think existence through the pure category alone, we cannot specify a single mark distinguishing it from mere possibility. (A601/B629)

We can say what is involved in phenomenal existence (i.e., perceivability in accordance with the demands of categorially structured intuitions). We cannot say what would be involved in existence "in itself." Nevertheless we have some comprehension of it, insofar as we are able to perform the requisite ("logical") *acts*, namely acts of "positing." Hence Kant by no means concludes that there is no distinction between the two sorts of existence claims in question. He merely observes that we lack any criteria for determining the truth of one of these sorts of claims:

Whatever, therefore, and however much, our concept of an object may contain, we must go outside it, if we are to ascribe existence to the object. In the case of objects of the senses, this takes place through their connection with some one of our perceptions, in accordance with empirical laws. But in dealing with objects of pure thought, we have no means whatsoever of knowing their existence, since it would have to be known in a completely *a priori* manner . . . [a]ny existence outside this field, while not indeed such as we can declare to be absolutely impossible, is of the nature of an assumption which we can never be in a position to justify. (A601/B629)

I shall have more to say about the logical forms of judgment in the next chapter and how Kant attempts to distinguish them from the determinate concepts that enter into judgments of the various possible forms. In any case one may want to object to the obscurantism involved in introducing a notion for which no criteria of application are forthcoming. However, we do need to remember something. Whatever notion Kant has in mind when considering things as "existing" in themselves, it can be no different from what we all have in mind when we do not operate with a phenomenalistic notion of existence. Most people, I presume, are not phenomenalists. They think that judgments about what is perceived or perceivable provide criteria, and perhaps the only legitimate ones, for the formation of existential judgments, but they do not suppose that all that one *means*, in asserting that something exists, is that certain perceptions are possible (or even under the appropriate conditions necessary). What one supposes, rather, is that the truth of those judgments about perception is in its own turn grounded in the fact that certain things exist. It is simply that our only *evidence* for the existence of those things lies in our judgments about what is perceived or perceivable. Now Kant of course holds that what most people regard as mere "criteria" for existential judgments is in fact, in the case of judgments concerning objects of possible perception, the very *content* of those judgments. So of course there is a substantial disagreement between Kant and most people. At the same time, such people would have to be the last to object that the notion of "existence in itself" is unintelligible, since precisely what they themselves suppose is that the objects of ordinary human knowledge have such an existence. Kant does not say that such judgments are unintelligible. He only tries to argue that they must be false.

Chapter 5

Concepts and Judgments

I. Concepts and Rules

KANT SAYS that intuitions are useless without concepts:

> Thoughts without content are empty, intuitions without concepts are blind. It is, therefore, just as necessary to make our concepts sensible, that is, to add the object to them in intuition, as to make our intuitions intelligible, that is, to bring them under concepts. (A51/B75)

As the passage indicates, there is also a sense in which concepts are nothing wihout intuitions. Now Kant classifies concepts as representations (A320/ B377). This suggests that they are a kind of mental entity, a special kind of "introspectible particular."[1] One might conclude that any instance of genuine knowledge involves combining two different kinds of mental entity: intuitions, or "sensuous" ideas, with concepts, or "intellectual" ones. These would then form a concrete judgment about some object. But this appears impossible. It appears to contradict the claim that intuitions are "blind" apart from concepts. If a concept is at best something externally combined with an intuition, then the intrinsic identity of the latter would be independent of the former.[2] Furthermore, the approach seems to involve a doctrine of "bare particulars."[3] Intuitions provide our references to particulars; concepts provide the means by which they are classified as certain *sorts* of particulars, in terms of the various characteristics or *Merkmale* that they exhibit. It seems to follow that by themselves intuitions refer to something characterless. Not only does this appear nonsensical, but it contradicts Kant's claim that it is the form of intuition itself by which concrete spatial and temporal characteristics are presented for possible conceptualization in the first place.

   The suggestion that concepts are a kind of "representation" may seem a holdover from a more Cartesian point of view.[4] The means of escape from that point of view is supposedly provided by Kant himself,[5] when he characterizes concepts as rules: "But a concept is always, as regards its form, something universal which serves as a rule" (A106). It has been tempting to attach some sort of behavioristic meaning to this claim. Strictly speaking, there are no such entities as concepts; instead there is merely that condition of an organism by which it is describable as "possessing" one. And this is to be regarded in purely dispositional terms: to possess a concept is to be able, and under the appropriate circumstances disposed, to engage in certain sorts of behavior. The relevant behavior for Kant is the forming of judgments. So knowledge does not involve combining mental entities but simply the making of judgments in the right sets of circumstances. The judgments will then involve two features. First they must be made in connection with a certain kind of sensory input (or, in cases of indirect knowledge, at least be judgments that refer to the *possibility* of such input). Second, they must arise from the right kind of disposition. They cannot merely be judgments that I happen to have made on some particularly appropriate occasion. They must be judgments whose formation involves my being subject to *rules* appropriate to the occasion. On this approach intuitions apart from the judgments based on them are mere sensations and to that extent "blind." And concepts are simply capacities and dispositions for forming judgments in accordance with rules governing such "behavior."

We have already seen that a number of things might be meant when a philosopher speaks of internal "ideas," or mental "representations." One of these is of course a notion commonly attributed to Descartes and Locke: an idea is an entity, internal to the perceiver, that is the "immediate object" of its cognitive activities. On this approach, what we are immediately aware of are our own ideas about reality, and knowledge depends on the extent to which they are adequate representations of that reality. Though some commentators take Kant's conception of "appearance" to reflect this approach, it is especially difficult to square it with his theory of concepts. Far from being immediate objects, they appear to be nothing other than the rules or patterns governing our intelligent *responses* to objects. But there is something else that might be meant by an idea or representation. Descartes may have had it in mind when he spoke of ideas as the "forms" of one's thoughts about objects. These would not be any sort of immediate objects of awareness. Instead they would be certain features or aspects of awareness. They would be those in virtue of which an awareness is *of* whatever it is an awareness of. But we would then need to adopt an intentional or phenomenological perspective. For it is only from that perspective that some internal feature or aspect of a cognitive state could be responsible for its being an awareness of one thing (or state of affairs) rather than another.

So long as objects are regarded purely intentionally, of course, we might introduce still another notion of representation. In this sense, representations are the objects of a subject's cognitive states, regarded purely as *intentional* objects, i.e., precisely as whatever is represented *as* an object to the subject. As we have seen, Kant employs this notion. He does so when he speaks of the whole material world as mere representations. He must also have the notion in mind when he says that concepts are *Merk-male*, or the general features or characters of the things we classify in judgments.[6] But this notion is always secondary. Material objects are representations in relation to certain of our own cognitive states, which are in turn representations in a more primary sense. Similarly, the general characters or features of objects are "concepts" only in the sense that they are the phenomenological correlates of certain of our own cognitive states, or aspects of those states. It is the latter that are concepts in a primary sense.

The criticism mentioned earlier supposes that a "representationalist" regards concepts as some sort of internal entity or introspectible item within the mind. There is no reason to suppose this. Concepts function as representations insofar as they are certain features or aspects of mental activity itself, not a peculiar sort of object. This is what we ought to expect, given Kant's insistence that concepts function as "predicates of possible judgments" (A69/B94). As we saw in Chapter Two, it is also suggested by his claim that concepts are merely "partial" representations, functioning as a mere *part* of a whole judgment. In our earlier discussion we already saw the advantage of regarding the predicative role of concepts in terms of their constituting an aspect of a representational state. Thus consider when one sees something and recognizes it as a tree. This of course involves a state with the form of an intuition. Its object is (at least) a spatial form of a certain sort. In addition, though, the intuition may be supposed to be "informed" by still another representational feature, namely, the concept in virtue of which it is the awareness not simply of a treelike form, but of a form that is in fact *recognized* as a treelike one. Were this concept not an actual aspect or feature of the intuition, then we could not comprehend how it is supposed to be referred precisely to that spatial region that is its *object*. Regarding the concept as part of the very form of the intuition (but not of course of its purely "intuitional" form) we can see its predicative role: the intuition, as a total representation embodying the concept, constitutes singular reference to an at least imaginary region of space of which the concept is (at least "problematically") predicated.

The possession of a concept for Kant is no doubt best construed disposi-tionally, not in terms of the literal presence of something within, but rather in terms of abilities and dispositions of the knower. If a concept is primarily the sort of thing that one might possess, then no doubt there really are no such things as concepts. There is only such a thing as "possessing" one, that is, various sorts of abilities and dispositions to act and react in more or less intelligent ways. But we need to remember that the primary actualization of a conceptual disposition is the making of a *judgment* for Kant: "Now the only use which the understanding can make of these concepts is to judge by means of them" (A68/B93). A judgment is a kind of representation (A68/B93), and concepts are (possible) predicates of judgments. Unless we are to suppose, therefore, that the primary actualizations of conceptual abilities are mere patterns of behavior (the uttering of sentences, for example), we cannot avoid supposing that those internal states that are the primary actualizations in question contain some *feature* in virtue of which they are so. These of course could not be regarded as the sort of thing one might be said to "possess" in the way that one possesses a concept. Nevertheless, they are what Kant is calling concepts. This may seem contrary to the claim that concepts serve as rules. But we shall see that this is not so.

Kant's discussion of the "threefold synthesis" in the first edition Transcendental Deduction confirms this approach. This is particularly so with regard to the synthesis of recognition in a concept" (A103). There is less room for controversy concerning Kant's argument at this stage than with respect to the two stages, or aspects, of synthesis preceding it. So I shall first comment briefly on those. Here is what Kant says about the "synthesis of apprehension in intuition":

> Every intuition contains in itself a manifold which can be represented as a manifold only in so far as the mind distinguishes the time in the sequence of one impression upon another; for each representation, *in so far as it is contained in a single moment*, can never be anything but absolute unity. In order that unity of intuition may arise out of this manifold (as is required in the representation of space) it must first be run through, and held together. This act I name *the synthesis of apprehension*, because it is directed immediately upon intuition, which does indeed offer a manifold, but a manifold which can never be represented as a manifold, and as contained *in a single representation*, save in virtue of such a synthesis. (A99)

It is sometimes supposed that Kant maintains that the apprehension of anything manifold must always arise out of an act whereby the mind puts a manifold of discrete items (sensations?) together into a whole. Since we are not conscious of any such act, and in ordinary experience are already presented with spatial wholes to be conceptualized in various ways, it is also tempting to suppose that the acts in question must occur on some deeper, pre-empirical (noumenal?) level.[7] The same may seem implied by the claim that "all combination—be we conscious of it or not, be it a combination of the manifold of intuition, empirical or non-empirical, or of various concepts—is an act of the understanding. . . . [W]e cannot represent to ourselves anything as combined in the object which we have not ourselves previously combined . . . (B130).

There is no need to adopt this line. What we need to remember is that Kant is undertaking an explanation of the application of concepts to intuitions. He is concerned, that is, with whatever conditions are involved in *recognition* of the spatial (and temporal) forms with which we are presented. In that context, when Kant claims that a certain kind of "synthesis" is involved in the representation of anything manifold, he can only be talking about conditions involved in the conceptualization or recognition of something as a manifold. There is no need to suppose an activity whereby a whole is generated out of parts; at most we are dealing with an activity whereby a whole is recognized as having parts. This is made more obvious later: "We cannot *think* [emphasis added] a line without *drawing* it in *thought* [emphasis added], or a circle without *describing* it" (B154); "I cannot represent to myself a line, however small, without drawing it in thought, that is, generating from a point all its parts one after another. Only in this way can the intuition be obtained. Similarly with all times, however small. In these I *think* [emphasis added] to myself only that successive advance from one moment to another . . ." (A162–163/B203). Kant is only contending that recognition of a whole as a whole must in some way involve thinking about the act of proceeding through the manifold of discriminable parts of that whole. This does not mean that we must in fact literally proceed, or have proceeded, through such a manifold.

This may seem to contradict Kant's involvement of the faculty of imagination in his doctrine of synthesis. He claims that all synthesis is due to the imagination (A78–79/B103–104). As we have seen, of course, Kant distinguishes pure from a merely empirical imagination. As we have so far considered the former, it seemed to involve either of two things: (a) imaginative awareness of a possible region of space or time; (b) imaginative awareness of something that might occupy a region of space or time, but without regard to any of the factors essential for distinguishing that region from what might be occupying it. We then thought of empirical imagination, negatively, as the calling up of "images" in all cases where the conditions for a pure imagination are absent. In the Transcendental Analytic, Kant connects the notion of impure imagination more directly with "reproduction." Though he appears to slip and concedes the possibility of an a priori or a "transcendental" form of reproductive imagination (A102),[8] he is generally clear that only the "productive" is part of the transcendental aspect of knowledge (cf. A118, B152). It is not perfectly clear what this is supposed to be. But the fact that Kant rests his theory on the notion may seem to imply that, contrary to my own suggestion, the representation of a manifold as a manifold must indeed involve an act of running through something. For it must at least involve running through a manifold in imagination.

This conclusion is unwarranted. It is perfectly possible to imagine the act of running through a manifold wthout running through anything at all, even in imagination. The notion of running through something in imagination is ambiguous. It might mean that I run through a manifold by separately imagining things, one after another. But it might also mean that I am not representing various things one after another at all, but merely *imagining* representing them that way. Naturally, it is difficult to say what is involved in this case and how to distinguish it from the other. The mystery is no doubt responsible for Kant's referring to the faculty of "schematism," which he connects closely with imagination, as "an art concealed in the depths of the human soul, whose real modes of activity nature is hardly likely ever to allow us to discover, and to have open to our gaze" (A141/ B180–181). I shall have more to say about schematism later. In any case it seems clear that *actually* representing in imagination a manifold of items one after another is paradigmatic of what Kant means by merely "reproductive" imagination (A101–102).

Kant is clear, in the second edition, that productive imagination involves an "action of the understanding on the sensibility" (B152). So any complete understanding of it must involve attention to the function of concepts as such. Such attention allows us to see why Kant might have felt a need to introduce imagination in the first place. As we have already seen, on Kant's view there must be some sense in which one "imagines" the activity of running through a manifold of items, whenever one applies a concept to an intuition. But this is not sufficient. For why wouldn't we be as well off saying that one necessarily *thinks* of oneself as running through a manifold of items, when applying a concept in intuition? Why insist on imagination? I would offer the following suggestion. What Kant insists upon most forcefully is that imagination (even pure imagination) involves *intuition*. The reason he does so is this. The application of a concept to an intuition involves, as we have seen, in some sense "thinking" the possibility of running through a manifold of items not actually present as such to the mind. But if the contribution that a concept makes to an intuition were that of a purely intellectual (or even an imaginative) *attachment* to it, then it would not do anything to enter, as it were, into the very fabric of the intuition in question. It would be as if we had a mere thought or image externally connected (or "associated") with an intuition:

> *Imagination* is the faculty of representing in intuition an object that is *not itself present*. Now since all our intuition is sensible, the imagination, owing to the subjective condition under which alone it can give to the concepts of understanding a corresponding intuition, belongs to *sensibility*. But to the extent to which its synthesis is an expression of spontaneity, which is determinative and not, like sense, determinable merely, and which is therefore *able to determine sense a priori in respect of its form*

[emphasis added] in accordance with the unity of apperception, imagination is to that extent a faculty which determines the sensibility *a priori*; and its synthesis of intuitions, conforming as it does to the *categories*, must be the transcendental synthesis of *imagination*. This synthesis is *an action of the understanding on the sensibility*. . . . In so far as imagination is spontaneity, I sometimes also entitle it the *productive* imagination, to distinguish it from the *reproductive* imagination, whose synthesis is entirely subject to empirical laws, the laws, namely, of association. . . . (B151–152)

What Kant wants to insist upon is that the spontaneous factors involved in conceptualizing an intuition enter *into* that intuition. You *see* something different, depending upon the ways in which you conceptualize what you see.[9] It is not simply that, necessarily attached to your seeing what you see, there are additional things that you also think or imagine. Whatever role thinking or imagining plays in connection with intuitions, it is a role they play by actually entering into what one sees, actually "informing" the intuition in question. That is why Kant speaks of an "action of the understanding on the sensibility." It is also why he says that this action is productive of an *image*: "imagination has to bring the manifold of intuition into the form of an image" (A120; cf. A141–142/B180–181). It is not that a manifold of items must first be brought together into some whole by imagination in order to form an "image." The point is simply that what the appearances you are apprehending are appearances *of* (thus, phenomenologically considered, what you are apprehending in the first place) depends not simply upon the "form of intuition" but also on the way that form is conceptualized. You see something different, depending upon the concept involved, and this involves a concept actually entering into an intuition and not remaining merely externally attached to it. No doubt Kant had a good deal of trouble finding the vocabulary for making this point. For it embodies an insight that was contrary to the theories of mental representation preceding his work.

Now let us return to the threefold synthesis. Kant distinguishes the synthesis of "apprehension in intuition" from a synthesis of "reproduction in imagination" (A100ff.), even though he concedes that the former involves an "action" of the imagination (and hence, as the second edition Deduction makes clearer, the understanding) upon perceptions (A120). In effect, the real point of the first edition distinction was to call our attention to two different cases in which we have to deal with a "manifold" of intuitions to be run through in imagination. The case focused on first is where one might imagine running through the parts of some perceived whole, e.g., the parts of a perceived line or circle. This is essential, on Kant's view, to all geometrical concepts. The concept of a plane figure, for example, in some sense is just the concept of the possibility of proceeding along the edge of a possible object in accordance with certain rules; or, alternatively, for drawing such a figure in the first place. In the section on "reproduction," Kant introduces a different but related notion. Here we are dealing with the set of paradigmatic appearances associated with a certain sort of object. Thus there are certain appearances characteristically associated with the stone cinnabar. But as Kant makes clear, this is no mere matter of association. Rather, reference to that manifold of appearances is part of the very concept of a stone of that sort. Kant also makes another point clear. This is that it is also part of the concept of a certain sort of object that the appearances associated with that object may be anticipated in accordance with certain *rules*. For example, the color red is associated with cinnabar, but this hardly implies that cinnabar always presents a red appearance. Part of the concept of cinnabar involves some notion of the conditions under which one would *reasonably expect* a red appearance, assuming we are dealing with cinnabar. In case one is not now actually apprehending such an appearance, it would therefore involve an idea of how to proceed from what one is apprehending *to* a red appearance. In some respects, then, we are dealing with notions already introduced in connection with geometrical synthesis. In both cases recognition of something as of a certain sort (as a circle, for example, or as cinnabar) involves "reference" to, or "imagining," the possibility of running through a manifold of items presentable in intuition in accordance with rules for getting from one to the next. In the one case running through those items would amount to apprehending connections among discriminable parts of the originally presented object. In the other case, though we are dealing with a manifold of items (appearances) synthesized into a unity by a concept, the object itself (say a piece of cinnabar) cannot literally be regarded as containing those items as discriminable parts. As earlier argued, what is rather the case is that the *existence* of the object (as opposed to its being merely hallucinated or imagined) is simply a matter of the possibility of actually proceeding through that manifold, in accordance with the right rules. In this sense, but only in this sense, can some object of perception be regarded as made up of a manifold of appearances.

We are ready to turn to the argument concerning "synthesis of recognition in a concept" (A103ff.). Its point, I think, is precisely what I have suggested. Recognition of an appearance, by means of applying a concept to it, cannot be accounted for wholly in terms of one's capacity or disposition, upon apprehending it, to connect it with other appearances that are not at the moment apprehended but that are at least reproduced in imagination. Any such account would be circular, Kant argues. For reference to additional appearances would be relevant to conceptualization of an originally given one only on the supposition that we are able to recognize *those* appearances as falling under the same concept as the first:

> If we were not conscious that what we think is the same as what we thought a moment before, all reproduction in the series of representations would be useless. For it would in its present state be a new representation which would not in any way belong to the act whereby it was to be gradually [*nach und nach*] generated. The manifold of the representation would never, therefore, form a whole, since it would lack that unity *which only consciousness can impart to it* [emphasis added]. . . . The word 'concept' might of itself suggest this remark. For this *unitary consciousness* [emphasis added] is what combines the manifold, successively intuited, and thereupon also reproduced, into one representation. This consciousness may often be only faint, so that we do not connect it with the act itself, that is, not in any direct manner with the *generation* of the representation, but only with the effect [*Wirkung*]. But notwithstanding these variations, such consciousness, however indistinct, must always be present; without it, concepts, and therewith knowledge of objects, are altogether impossible.(A103–104)

Kant does not deny that recognizing any given appearances involves the capacity, ability, or disposition to generate further representations connected with it. He puts the point in terms of the generation of representations because he is thinking that conceptualization of an appearance involves at least imagining the possibility of running through, in accordance with the appropriate rules, a manifold of other appearances. So these other appearances are, at least loosely speaking, "generated" in our imagination. Presumably Kant would also have been prepared to put his point in terms of a more dispositional approach. In that case the primary emphasis is not on one's capacities for generating anything in imagination. The emphasis is on capacities and dispositions for applying a concept to other perceptions *or* images, should they in fact arise and whether they are generated or not. To recognize this appearance as a such-and-such is to be prepared to respond in certain more or less predictable ways to other perceptions in other possible circumstances. Whether the latter are in fact imagined or not is irrelevant. (On a behavioristic approach, of course, the responses in question would have to be construed in terms of concrete behavior, for example the application of a word.)

Kant could as easily have put his point in these terms as in terms of the generation of representations in imagination. Part of the reason for his procedure stems from the fact that the Humean account of the conceptualization process proceeds by appeal to some sort of faculty for reproduction and association in imagination. Kant was often specifically concerned with a refutation of Hume.[10] In any case, he does not deny that a necessary part of the application of a concept to an intuition involves capacities and dispositions for responding in rule-governed ways with respect to a manifold of other intuitions (both properly perceptual and merely imaginative). This is what he tries to capture with the notion of the "act" whereby further representations are generated. In fact he defines concepts in terms of the "unity of the act of bringing various representations under one common representation" (A68/B93). This is obviously connected with the fact that a single conceptual ability involves a capacity for rule-governed response to a manifold of representations beyond whatever particular one might be in question at the moment. This will be so, presumably, whether those further representations are perceptions one happens to perceive, images that associate themselves with a given perception, or perceptions or images deliberately generated in accordance with a rule, i.e., with the very *same* rule as is embodied in the original act of conceptualization. In all these cases, the point is the same. No such notions can explicate the unity of *consciousness* that obtains when one apprehends a manifold of appearances as falling under a concept. They may be part of the explanation, but they cannot be all of it. In each case there must be some actual difference in the consciousness in question at that moment (that is, in the "effect" [*Wirkung*] of the act of "generation") that constitutes the needed element of recognition.

Unfortunately, this sort of approach might appear to undercut any attempt to regard forms of intuition as nonconceptual. Kant, as I have argued, regards concepts as features or aspects of possible representations. As we have considered the doctrine so far, this means that concepts are features or aspects of possible intuitions. That at least is their primary role. Concepts, then, are those features in virtue of which an intuition is not simply an "awareness" of a possible region of space or time, but involves some particular way of recognizing that region, some particular *judgment* about it. It follows that both concepts and forms of intuition are in a certain sense something "universal." They are both features or aspects of possible mental states. Hence, just as more than one state might instantiate the same form of intuition, more than one might instantiate the same concept. This might suggest that forms of intuition must be a certain sort of concept, namely a basic spatial or temporal concept.[11] If so, then the distinction between the Transcendental Aesthetic and the Transcendental Analytic would be destroyed. More importantly, Kant's attempt to account for the synthetic a priori character of mathematics would be undercut. In fact, though, Kant himself sometimes blurs the distinction between forms of intuition and concepts. Thus he speaks in the Aesthetic of *concepts* of space and time precisely at points where he means to be arguing for the intuitive character of spatial and temporal representations. The following passage from the Analytic seems to make the point even more evident:

We are already in possession of concepts which are of two quite different kinds, and which yet agree in that they relate to objects in a completely *a priori* manner, namely, the concepts of space and time as forms of sensibility, and the categories as concepts of the understanding. (A85/B118)

The distinction between forms of intuition and concepts is presumably connected with the notion of concepts as rules for the synthesis of intuitions. Insofar as we think of concepts as rules for the synthesis of intuitions, we cannot think of them as those features in virtue of which intuitions are intuitions in the first place. Rather we must suppose that intuitions possess some internal form of their own and that concepts serve as "rules" for the synthesis of sets of representations possessing precisely that form. However, there is no incompatibility between regarding concepts as features or aspects of possible internal states of the perceiver and as "something universal which serves as a rule."[12] Kant's theory appears to be this. While there must be some aspect of a perceptual state that consitutes the specific recognitional content of that state, this feature could provide it with a specific recognitional content only in virtue of being connected in a lawlike manner with a whole set of other possible states. In principle, of course, any such feature might be found in any sort of intuition. But it is one thing for a feature to happen to be present in a perceptual state and quite another for that feature to be connected with it in a lawlike manner. It is quite another matter for there to exist a "rule" connecting the feature with that state. In addition, we need to remember, the rules in question will always connect a concept with particular sorts of perceptual states only in correlation with a whole set of such states. Thus any number of concepts might be connected, through a rule of the appropriate sort, with a particular sort of perception. But one of these concepts might be distinguished from the others in virtue of rules concerning the other perceptions with which it is connected, and particular ways of getting from one to the other, i.e., of "generating" the perceptions in question.

This is analogous to the fact that the representational capacity of any *linguistic* item (a word, for example, or a sentence) is a function of that item's instantiating particular features, for example the shape or sound of a particular word. But the shape or sound of a particular word does not by itself determine representational significance. In addition we need to consider rules bearing upon the sorts of situations in which *use* of words of that shape or sound are paradigmatically appropriate or inappropriate.[13] (Included in our specification of the "sorts" of situations will be conditions concerning the way in which they were "generated" in the first place.) Given that, we may then be fully justified in using a word of a given shape or sound in any number of other situations as well; the justification need not *always* be part of the system of "rules" determining the significance of the word in the first place. Kant's theory seems to be that concepts function in much the same way as such features of linguistic items, where what instantiates the analogous features in the case of concepts is not a linguistic entity, but one of the perceiver's own perceptual states. (I limit consideration here to representations that are not *purely* conceptual.) In this sense we might say that concepts are "second-order" features of perceptual states: it is in virtue of a feature *of a feature* of a perceptual state that the state constitutes the recognition of some object as of a particular sort. It is this second-order feature that determines representational significance. Further, it is presumably only of this feature that we are in any way "aware," when we are aware of the recognitional component of our own mental activity. Unlike the first-order feature of some linguistic item, like the shape or sound of a word, we are simply not aware, in introspection, of the corresponding feature of our own perceptual states. To us they are merely those features (whatever they are) that constitute our awareness as of a specific recognitional content. Perhaps Kant thought of them as part of a "noumenal" description of our psyches that is simply unavailable to us.

To some extent it might appear that a "behavioristic" approach is justified. For the representational significance of a concept is not determined by any immediate (first-order) feature of internal mental activity. But two points need to be borne in mind. First, this could hardly support a doctrine attempting to relegate all representational content to purely "external" factors. The representational significance of concepts lies in the system of rules governing their instantiation in possible intuitions, and the latter are internal states whose contribution to knowledge lies precisely in their intrinsic character. The conceptual content of a perceptual state must always be regarded as an enrichment of a state whose total object-directed character is (at least phenomenologically) also a function of purely internal factors. Further, there is no reason to suppose that Kant himself thought that the constitution of the relevant system of rules is to be analyzed solely in terms of the *dispositions* of the perceiver. The cognitive significance of a concept is of course a function of its rule-governed connection with perceptual states other than whatever state happens to be instantiating it at the moment. It is tempting to suppose that this connection is wholly a matter of how the perceiver is disposed to respond to those perceptual states, i.e., whether or not by conceptualizing them in some particular manner or other. Nothing indicates that this was Kant's own supposition. All he says is that conceptual content is a matter of the obtaining and recognition of rules. He offers no theory concerning the analysis of this notion. In any case it is no doubt the role played by our recognition of rules and norms, i.e., by our recognition of what *ought* to be the case[14] and not simply what is or will be the case, that accounts for Kant's insistence upon distinguishing concepts from intuitions in terms of the presence or absence of "spontaneity" in such representations:

> Our knowledge springs from two fundamental sources of the mind; the first is the capacity of receiving representations (receptivity for impressions), the second is the power of knowing an object through these representations (spontaneity of concepts). Through the first an object is *given* to us, through the second the object is *thought* in relation to that representation. (A50/B74)[15]

The following passage may appear to contradict this approach:

> Space, represented as *object* (as we are required to do in geometry), contains more than mere form of intuition; it also contains *combination* of the manifold, given according to the form of sensibility, in an *intuitive* representation, so that the *form of intuition* gives only a manifold, the *formal intuition* gives unity of representation. In the Aesthetic I have treated this unity as belonging merely to sensibility, simply in order to emphasize that it precedes any concept, although, as a matter of fact, it presupposes a synthesis which does not belong to the senses but through which all concepts of space and time first become possible. For since by its means (in that the understanding determines the sensibility) space and time are first *given* as intuitions, the unity of this *a priori* intuition belongs to space and time, and not to the concept of the understanding. (B160, note)

This passage may appear to imply that the representation of particular regions of space is accomplished only by the introduction of concepts into perceptions. If so, then abstracting from such concepts, intuitions would be reduced to mere sensations, and they would no longer possess any intrinsic intuitional form. Or if any sort of intuitional form does remain, as Kant insists it does, then it could not be a form in virtue of which any object-directed character of a representation is in question. Only a manifold *for* the representation of a possible object is at hand. Of course if this were Kant's view then his own theory of geometrical knowledge would fall to the ground.

The question that this passage raises is, I think, simply whether a cognitively relevant "representation" is possible in abstraction from concepts. Can one, for example, be "aware," whether perceptually or in imagination, of some region of space without conceptualizing that region in some way? In the present passage, it seems, Kant denies the possibility. Two points are worth noting, however. First, Kant appeared to waver with respect to his own answer to the question. Second, even if one denied the possibility of awareness of regions of space apart from their conceptualization, it still would not follow that, in any perceptual or imaginative state in which some region of space is conceptualized, the (intentional) *object* presented by means of that state does not contain intrinsic features over and above whatever is due to the concept in question (and also beyond what is due to the specific sensations involved). Of course, that the content of a perception does indeed contain such additional features is precisely one of the points that Kant himself makes in the passage we are considering.

In some passages Kant explicitly acknowledges the possibility of unconceptualized intuitions: "For appearances can certainly be given in intuition independently of functions of the understanding" (A90/B122).[16] On the other hand Kant also appears to say the contrary: "There can be in us no modes of knowledge, no connection or unity of one mode of knowledge with another, without that unity of consciousness which precedes all data of intuitions, and by relation to which representation of objects is alone possible" (A107). However, we need to remember that all such passages occur in a context in which Kant is attempting to distinguish mere awareness of regions of space from awareness of objects that occupy those regions. This appears to be the whole point of the distinction between the Transcendental Aesthetic and the Analytic. Thus we have to deal, as already noted, with an ambiguity in the notion of an "object" of intuition. The same goes for the notion of an "appearance." Kant says at one point that "only by means of these fundamental concepts can appearances belong to knowledge or even to our consciousness, and so to ourselves" (A125). Yet elsewhere he says that "appearances might, indeed, constitute intuition without thought, but not knowledge; and consequently be for us as good as nothing" (A111) and that apart from understanding, sensibility "though indeed yielding appearances, would supply no objects of empirical knowledge, and consequently no experience" (A124). Kant himself, we need to remember, defines intuition as a form of representation *with consciousness* (A320/B376–377). He also defines appearances as the "undetermined object" of (impure) intuition (A20/B34). The undetermined character of the object in question presumably relates to Kant's attempt to consider what is presented to cognition independently of the understanding's ability to "determine" sensibility. In any case there is an ambiguity in the notion of an "appearance." Sometimes Kant clearly speaks of ordinary material objects as appearances, and it is obvious that concepts are required for the representation of appearances in this sense. Other times, though, Kant speaks of the appearances *of* material objects. These, as I have argued, are the intentional objects of sense perception regarded prior to any question concerning their identification as actual material objects. It remains an open question whether such objects might be presented in intuition independently of conceptualizing activity.

Even if it is not possible for an intuition to present a region of (possible) space apart from conceptualization, it would still not follow that the object-directed character of conceptualized intuitions does not involve some unique and irreducible form of intuition. If such a form is involved, of course, it would seem to be logically possible for a perceptual state to lack conceptualization and yet to contain a specific instance of it. However, all this means is that a state might occur such that, were it conceptualized in some way, the result would not simply be a thought about some possible region of space but an intuitive "awareness" of one. The result, that is, would be a state in which an at least possible *object* is conceptualized in some way. From the phenomenological point of view, therefore, conceptualization of the state in question would be analogous to the illumination of some pre-existing object. It would be as if one's concepts served to illuminate or elucidate an object that, apart from them, would simply have remained in the dark, outside the realm of genuine consciousness. Given this point of view, we can understand why Kant would suppose that, even if there could be no consciousness of a region of space apart from conceptualization of it, when concepts do in fact "determine" an intuition they always serve for the illumination of something whose nature is to some extent independent of themselves. If they did not, of course, Kant's theory of geometry would simply be unintelligible. This view, then, even if it allows the logical possibility of an internal state with the form of an intuition and yet lacking conceptualization, is perfectly compatible with denying that any such state would be a conscious one, at least in one very important sense of that term. So while in one sense we might concede the possibility of intuitions apart from concepts, they would not in that case any longer be intuitions. For they would no longer be conscious in the appropriate sense.

This point is connected with another one. The representational content of empirical concepts always involves, for Kant, rules for the synthesis of specific sorts of sense perceptions. They connect a concept with perceptions containing specific spatial and temporal forms as well as specific sensations. The significance of the concept *red*, for example, would presumably involve a system of rules relating to our expectations concerning specific sorts of sense perceptions different from those involved in the concept *green*. This does not mean that a red object can never reasonably be expected to appear to be green. But even though a green appearance might be, in the right circumstances, identifiable as an object that is really red, this would not imply that the system of rules constituting the representational significance of the concept involves its specific connection with such appearances. In general it seems obvious that if systems of rules constitute the significance of concepts, they do so by connecting concepts with specific sorts of perceptions, and awareness of the character of the latter will therefore always involve some sort of awareness not only of particular spatiotemporal forms but also of some content due to the particular sensations involved.

This seems to imply that, as such, we cannot be said to have a genuine "awareness" of the rules in question at all. For whatever process originally leads to the institution of specific empirical concepts, the rules that are involved are not of the sort that could ever be *formulated*. Of course once we have the concept *red* we can formulate a "rule" connecting red objects with specific sorts of sense perceptions, for example perceptions in which we are at least presented with objects that appear to be red. But this sort of rule would presuppose the concept in question, whereas the rules that Kant has in mind are supposedly ones whose institution is what first provides us with a concept. What we need to suppose, then, is that an organism can evolve a system in which certain sorts of potential concepts are connected in a rule-governed way with certain sorts of (intentional) objects *potentially* conceptualizable, but where the rules are not themselves conceptualizable with regard to whatever content is thereby involved. If concepts derive their significance from systems of rules, that is, the institution of the system in question must in some sense be a preconceptual one. As we have seen, Kant has a tendency to suppose that the preconceptual level is below that of genuine awareness. This may be why he speaks of productive imagination, essential to concept formation, as a "blind but indispensable function of the soul" (A78/B103). On the other hand it is not clear how an organism could develop a system of rules involving specific sorts of appearances *without* being aware of the latter. Presumably the most reasonable solution will acknowledge two notions of awareness. In one sense there can be no preconceptual awareness, in another sense there must be. The former is connected with the possibility of *self*-awareness, on Kant's view. That is the crux of the argument of his "transcendental deduction": the unity of synthesis provided by genuinely conceptualized awareness is a necessary condition for "unity of apperception," that is , for unity of self-consciousness (A107ff.; B131ff.). But Kant is also prepared to grant that the psyches of nonhuman animals, and even infants, are lacking in precisely that sort of unity.[17] Presumably he would not deny that they are altogether lacking in awareness. In any case Kant offers no account of just what is involved in the process whereby the rules determinative of conceptual content, and hence of genuine self-awareness, are instituted in the first place.

I shall conclude this section by returning to Kant's "phenomenalism." With respect to that doctrine it is important to be clear what his theory of concepts, taken by itself, does and does not assert. One might suppose that on Kant's theory what an empirical concept refers to is always a synthesis of possible perceptions. In this sense, one might conclude, material objects are syntheses or constructs out of nonmaterial entities. But it is not Kant's claim that concepts refer to syntheses of perceptions. A concept, considered as such, synthesizes a manifold of possible perceptions. That it "synthesizes" such a manifold means that the representational significance of the concept is a function of its rule-governed connection with the members of the manifold. This connection determines what the concept refers to. It does not follow that the concept refers to possible perceptions. What it refers to is the object (i.e., the specific kind of object) that is the object *of* those perceptions, given that those perceptions are in fact conceptualized in terms of it. Thus the manifold of perceptions of a possible tree of a certain sort is a manifold of perceptions of appearances of a tree. But qua object of the perceptions in question, as we have already seen, an appearance of a tree *is* a tree, or at least a possible one. Thus one of those appearances may be a (possible) tree of a certain description apprehended from a certain perspective; another will be a possible tree of a different but related description apprehended from a different but related perspective. Such "objects" are what a concept refers to. That a concept refers to such objects, i.e., that a perception "informed" by that concept is, phenomenologically, a perception *of* such an object, is determined by the fact that it synthesizes a certain manifold of perceptions. But it is not the perceptions that are referred to by the concept. What the concept refers to is a certain sort of *object* of possible perception.

Though the concept *tree* on Kant's account does not refer to a set of perceptions, it is still the case that in a certain sense the application of that concept in *judgment* refers to such a set. In the case of the "assertoric" judgment, for example, use of the concept asserts that something is a tree. That something really is a tree amounts to the fact that certain perceptions (beyond whatever given one is in question) are obtainable. So the judgment refers to a set of possible perceptions. But each of the latter, insofar as it is in fact conceptualized in terms of the concept, is a perception of a (possible) tree. It is the latter that the concept refers to, not some possible manifold of perceptions of a tree.

These claims may appear to be contradicted by some of Kant's own. When he introduces the notion of a concept as a rule, for example, Kant also asks what we mean by the "object" represented by a concept. This is where he introduces the notorious "transcendental object = x." What Kant appears to say is that a concept represents the unity of a manifold of perceptions: "This *unity of rule* determines all the manifold, and limits it to conditions which make unity of apperception possible. The *concept of this unity* is the representation of the object = x . . ." (A105); "[A concept] can be a rule for intuitions only in so far as it represents in any given appearances the necessary reproduction of their manifold, and thereby the synthetic unity in our consciousness of them" (A106). Two points should be made. First, it is perfectly possible that what Kant says a concept "represents" is really what he thinks is represented by the presence of a concept in a judgment. For judgments are the only use to which we put concepts. But a second point is more important. In the passages in question, Kant does not say that a concept represents a unity of possible perceptions. What it represents, he says, is a unity of the manifold of appearances that are possible perceptual *objects*. Thus the concept of a tree is the concept of a single (empirically real) object that is identifiable with a whole *manifold* of (possibly real) objects. Or to put it the other way around, to recognize any given appearance as a tree (i.e., as an object in space orientable and describable in some particular way) is ipso facto to judge it to be the same object as a whole manifold of differently oriented and describable objects. From the phenomenological point of view, each member of the manifold is a different "object" from the other. But from the point of view of empirical reality a number of these objects might all be identifiable as the same one. The ability to introduce an awareness of that sort of identity is precisely, on Kant's view, the contribution that concepts make to what are otherwise mere intuitions. The notion of the "transcendental object" merely gives expression to this point.

II. Concepts and Forms of Judgment

We have been considering "empirical" concepts so far, but there are also a priori concepts. Kant calls these the categories, or the pure concepts of the understanding. Empirical concepts must always be based on the categories for Kant. Hence they always contain an a priori conceptual element. But there are two differences between empirical concepts and the categories. Unlike empirical concepts, the categories do not involve rules relating to specific sorts of sense perceptions. Their significance is much more general. Secondly, a necessary condition for the application of any concepts to objects is that the concepts in question involve the categories. Indeed the latter are necessary for the very possibility of self-consciousness according to Kant. These are truths, he thinks, that can be established by reflection on the concept of judgment as such and on the concept of self-consciousness, without any empirical investigation.[18] But there is no specific empirical concept that necessarily is utilized by any being capable of self-awareness and by any being capable of conceptualizing in general, and no mere reflection on empirical concepts can justify our use of them. What matters is their utility as rules for synthesis of the specific sorts of sense perceptions available to us.

Though Kant does not introduce the categories as special sorts of rules, he does suggest that they are or contain rules of some sort: "Transcendental philosophy has the peculiarity that besides the rule (or rather the universal condition of rules), which is given in the pure concept of the understanding, it can also specify a priori the instance to which the rule is to be applied" (A135/B174–175; cf. B145). But this seems intended merely to express the fact that reflection upon the concept of an "object in general" (and the correlative concept of a unity of consciousness) provides us with the materials for the formulation of rules or principles that *contain* the categories. These of course would not be rules in the sense in which empirical concepts are consitituted by rules. For the principles in question are judgments that already contain concepts, namely the categories. These judgments, in Kant's view, express necessary truths about all objects or events to which we are able to apply specific concepts. It is only in this sense that the categories, which Kant often describes as constituting the concept of an object in general, can be regarded as rules or principles.

It is tempting to suppose that the categories are some sort of higher-order rules. It might be thought, for example, that empirical concepts function as rules relating to specific syntheses of sense perceptions, while categories function as rules governing the original institution of any such empirical rules. This would be a misleading suggestion. If there are specific sorts of syntheses involved in the constitution of empirical concepts, then we ought to be able to form some general conception of them. But we could not suppose that the categories *are* our conception of such syntheses. As Kant often reminds us, and as the specific examples of the categories show, the categories are concepts of certain features of perceivable objects (and events). Though some of them may also be applicable to perceptions as well as to objects of perception, they are not as such concepts that *refer* to perceptions. Now as we saw, this is so for empirical concepts as well and yet they also "serve as rules" for synthesis of perceptions. But it is difficult to see how this could be the case with the categories. If they do not serve as specific rules for synthesis of perceptions, the only way they could involve rules for such synthesis would be precisely if they were concepts of the general *forms* of such synthesis. But once again, they are concepts of features or aspects of possible objects of perception and of relations involving such objects, not concepts of relations among perceptions themselves.

Kant introduces the categories in connection with the "forms of judgment." This occurs in the section he calls the Metaphysical Deduction of the categories (A70/B95–A83/B109; the title occurs in a reference at B159). We have already had some acquaintance, in Chapter Two, with the distinction between the forms and the contents of judgments. The general point is this. Several different judgments might utilize the same empirical concept or concepts. Thus the concepts *tree* and *tall* might be combined into a number of judgments: "(All, some, this) *tree*(s) (is, are) (not) (possibly, actually, necessarily) (non-) *tall*." And even here, we are considering only the categorical, not the hypothetical (if/then) or disjunctive (either/or) forms. On Kant's view there is a sense in which the only concepts involved in all the judgments in question are the concepts *tree* and *tall*. The other factors relate to the form of the judgment. This point has an obvious parallel in modern symbolic logic. One of the most obvious differences, however, is that modern logicians regard the universal ("all") judgment as really hypothetical in form. Thus "All trees are tall" would be "(x) (Tree$x \supset$

Tall*x*)." But while Kant does not regard the universal judgment in this way, both approaches agree in supposing that the only concepts in question are *tree* and *tall*; the rest belongs to the "logical form" of the judgment.

There are also other differences between Kant's approach and that of the modern logician. For example, Kant regards the difference between "Trees are not tall" and "Trees are non-tall" as a difference in form. The modern logician is inclined to regard it as one of content: they involve two different concepts, *tall* and *non-tall*. Kant seems to suggest (A71–73/B97–98) that the latter case involves negation with respect to a certain range of *objects* in a way that the former does not. He seems to suggest a distinction between saying that whatever happens to fall under the concept *tree* is tall and saying *of* whatever *does* fall under that concept that *it* is (or they are) tall. As we saw in Chapter Two, however, it is not easy to see how Kant could permit such a distinction, insofar as it requires reference to things other than concrete individuals (and regions of space). At the very least, Kant would be required to extend the notion of "singular" judgments so as to include references to whole *classes* of objects, and hence to include what would seem to be "universal" judgments as well. In addition, presupposing such a distinction between merely descriptive and genuinely referential judgments, there would seem to be something very misleading about the whole Metaphysical Deduction. The well-established science of formal logic, Kant suggests, presents us with a list of judgmental forms. His own "*transcendental*" logic then faces the task of showing how these forms function in reference to concrete objects of intuition and as necessary conditions of unity of apperception, that is, how they function as "categories." The original grounding in formal logic is apparently supposed to guarantee completeness of the enterprise (A69/B94, A79/B105). One-one correlation of the categories with the forms of judgment will assure that nothing is left out:

> The same function which gives unity to the various representations *in a judgment* also gives unity to the mere synthesis of various representations *in an intuition*; and this unity, in its most general expression, we entitle the pure concept of the understanding. (A79–80/B104–105)

As it turns out, however, the original table of judgments already involves introduction of the distinction between purely descriptive and genuinely referential judgments. Since on Kant's view the latter always involves the attachment of concepts to intuitions, it follows that the original table was not in fact formulated purely with an eye on "formal" logic. Formal or what Kant calls "general" logic "abstracts from all content of knowledge, that is, from all relation of knowledge to the object, and considers only the logical form in the relation of any knowledge to other knowledge . . . " (A55/B79).

Thus formal logic considers concepts only in relation to other concepts, not in relation to objects.

Apart from this issue, Kant's connection of the categories with the forms of judgment may seem incoherent. On the one hand we are required to distinguish between the concrete concepts contained in a judgment and the judgmental forms it involves. In some sense the categories are identical with the latter. On the other hand the categories are obviously *concepts*. This brings us to one of the most notorious difficulties in Kant interpretation, the "schematism" of the categories (A137/B176ff). There the point seems to be that while the categories are indeed "identical" with certain judgmental forms, when these forms are applied to intuitions they in some sense *become* genuine concepts for the first time.

The Schematism chapter poses a problem concerning the applicability of categories to intuitions. If categories were simply rules, even higher-order rules, regarding the synthesis of intuitions, it would be difficult to see how such a problem could exist. In any case Kant asks, How can the categories be applied to appearances, since they are not "homogeneous" with them? The answer, he urges, lies in something that *is* homogeneous both with the category and also with appearances. This is the "schema" of the category (A137–138/B176–177). There are two difficulties. First, it is not obvious what concepts, if any, Kant has in mind when he says that the categories are not homogeneous with appearances. Second, it is not clear what he means when he says that they are not *homogeneous* with appearances.

With regard to the first issue two positions have been taken: (1) Kant distinguishes between *two sets* of categories. For example we need to distinguish between the abstract concept of a subject in relation to its predicates and the more concrete concept of a relatively permanent object in relation to its potentially alterable states; or between the abstract concept of a determining ground in relation to some consequence and the more concrete concept of an event of a kind that is necessarily followed by events of some other kind. It is the former with regard to which Kant poses the problem of schematism, whereas the latter are concepts that emerge in the course of his *solving* that problem. I shall call the latter "schematized" or "phenomenal" categories, and distinguish them from "unschematized" categories. The latter, it might seem, need not be restricted within the phenomenal realm.[19] (2) The problem concerns phenomenal categories only.[20]

A number of passages indicate that Kant's problem involves a distinction between two sets of categories. He tells us, for example, that it is by means of schemata that the pure concepts of the understanding "obtain relation to objects and so possess *significance (Bedeutung)*" (A146/B185). Apart from schemata and from any "sensible condition," though the categories do retain a meaning of sorts, it is a "purely logical meaning (*nur logische*

Bedeutung)" (A147/B186): they remain free of contradiction yet lack "all use and indeed all significance (*der ganze Gebrauch, ja selbst alle Bedeutung)*" (B308; cf. ff.). Thus schematization appears to involve providing reference for concepts that could not by themselves provide such reference. These would be unschematized categories.

Some passages appear to contradict the claim that there are concepts lacking the sensible condition provided by schemata. For example after maintaining that the categories do express, apart from schematization, the "thought of an object in general (*das Denken eines Objekts überhaupt)*" (A247/B304), Kant insists that apart from schemata we remain only with "pure forms of the understanding's employment through which alone no object can be thought (*ohne doch durch sie allein irgendein Objekt denken . . . zu können)*" (A248/B305). So apart from schemata there are no concepts at all and hence no categories, only mere *Gedankenformen* (B305–306). Kant puts the point explicitly: apart from conditions that determine a relation between concepts and their instances, concepts "would be without all content, and hence be mere logical forms *and not pure concepts of the understanding*" (A136/B175; emphasis added).

In addition to this problem, commentators have attacked Kant's claim that there is a special problem of "homogeneity" besetting categorial but not empirical concepts.[21] It is possible to see, I think, that Kant is indeed dealing with a problem peculiar to the categories which it is not unreasonable for him to have posed as a problem about homogeneity of representation. To see this we need to recognize that Kant himself was not perfectly clear about the relationship between forms of judgment and categories. It is of course Kant's view that the latter at least *contain* the former in some way. He tells us that elimination of schemata from phenomenal categories still leaves us with something, namely *Gedankenformen*.[22] Now supposing Kant was unclear about the distinction between the latter and categories, then we could understand why he denied that there are nonphenomenal categories yet also held that even after elimination of schemata a set of categorial concepts remains. We could also understand why he posed the problem as one concerning homogeneity. For if judgmental forms possess a genuine *representational significance* even though they are not concepts, then while they might represent "features" of possible appearances, they could not by themselves constitute any actual *concepts* of such features. To this extent they will fail to be "homogeneous" with appearances. The problem would then be that of producing, on the basis of mere *Gedankenformen*, concepts that do represent the features in question. This involves "schematizing" the forms of judgment.

Insofar as Kant was unclear about the distinction between forms of judgment and categorial concepts, he would be led to describe the problem as if it were concerned with the schematization of genuine but un-schematized categorial *concepts*.

Any attempt to pursue this suggestion must take more care than some commentators have in distinguishing between the forms of judgment and the concepts *of* judgmental forms. It is often observed that Kant attempted to derive the categories from a set of concepts of the various judgmental forms. This may suggest that he blurred the distinction between the two sets of concepts.[23] But it is unlikely that Kant confused, for example, the relation between a subject and a predicate concept in a *mental act* with a relation between possible subjects and their modifications in reality. Further, even if the categories were derived as suggested, this could not in itself explain the inconsistencies in the text. We would still need to ask whether the categories Kant took himself to be deriving were phenomenal or nonphenomenal categories. If the former, then we have simply opted for the second line of interpretation of the Schematism chapter; if the latter, we have failed to explain Kant's tendency both to assume that there are such concepts and yet to deny it.

There are two reasons why on Kant's view judgmental forms cannot be concepts. First, concepts are regarded as providing a specific representational content to mental states. Forms of judgment, on the other hand, are merely the various ways in which concepts, or the states that contain them, yield a judgment *with* some particular content. To talk about the ways in which contents are present in the mind would, it appears, not be to talk about some additional content present in the mind. Second, concepts are those elements whose presence in a mental state constitutes it as the awareness or conception of a certain kind of object. But it is difficult to see what sort of object the mere presence of judgmental form could bring before the mind. It does not for example make sense to suppose that some intuitive state is the (intentional) seeing of "all" or of "some," or that it is the seeing of "having a certain predicate." What we can see is all or some *animals*, or animals *being four-footed*. But this requires in addition to judgmental form an empirical concept. Judgmental form by itself does not yield the awareness of any kind of object.

In some crucial respects, accordingly, judgmental forms cannot be concepts even if they are necessarily involved *in* all concepts. There is also an important respect in which judgmental forms are like concepts. This, I suggest, is precisely what accounts for Kant's uncertainty whether judgmental forms are or are not concepts. The point is that judgmental forms, like concepts, are representationally significant. Their presence in or absence from a given judgment makes a difference in what the judgment *says about the world*. Indeed it seems possible to extend the notion of subsumption to judgmental forms, so that judgmental forms and not just concepts might be regarded as subsuming various sorts of objects under themselves. Thus what the form of the subject/predicate judgment subsumes under it, we might say, are all cases of something *having a certain characteristic*; the form of the universal judgment subsumes all cases of something's being *all* of a kind of entity. These of course are what we might call "states of affairs" rather than particulars, and it is reasonable, I think, to assume that states of affairs are just the sorts of entities that judgments do represent. Possible *particulars*, on the other hand, appear to be what Kant regards as the domain of representation of concepts. But as noted, it is Kant's view that all concepts contain the logical forms of judgment. So the presence of a concept in a mental state should yield not only the awareness or conception of a certain kind of particular but also the awareness or conception of a certain state of affairs. Thus the presence of the concept *animal* in an intuitive state of the visual sort should yield not only what may be properly described as the "seeing" of a (possibly nonexistent) animal but also what may be described as the (intentional) seeing of something's *being* an animal (though of course the seeing may be merely "problematic" and involve no actual belief that anything is an animal). Not only, therefore, may we regard the forms of judgment as possessing a representational significance of their own, but we may even regard them as in some sense "representing" something that any *concept* will necessarily represent. This is an additional reason why Kant may have been led to think of judgmental forms as a special kind of concept, despite the fact that he also had reasons for denying that judgmental forms are any kind of concept at all.

This point cannot be recognized if one goes too far in an attempt to purge Kant's theory of representation of all "mentalistic" elements. The point is that there must be some actual *aspect of a mental act* that is the embodiment in any given instance of whatever form of judgment is in question. In principle, therefore, it is an aspect distinguishable from whatever particular conceptual content might be instantiated in an act. Consequently all mental acts contain representationally significant features that may remain over even in abstraction from concrete conceptual representation. The point is the key to Kant's ambivalence concerning the possibility of representation apart from phenomenal conditions. But it can only be formulated in a "mentalistic" context. Suppose, for example, that we regarded the concept of judgmental forms as a purely linguistic concept. Then judgmental forms would be aspects or components of judgments viewed as linguistic entities. But judgments viewed as linguistic entities derive their sense only from the *interpretation* of those entities. (Presumably, a non-mentalistic approach would attempt to account for "interpretation" in behavioristic terms.) Judgmental forms could then only be regarded as features common to a certain range of interpretations of linguistic entities. Naturally, this approach would be especially congenial to those who regard the categories as "second-order" rules, merely expressing the general forms of possible concrete "synthesis." Equally obviously, judgmental forms on such a view could have no significance apart from their connection with concrete interpretation, that is apart from actual empirical synthesis. On the other hand it is perfectly possible to hold, if the concept of judgmental form is not a purely linguistic one, that such forms contain a representational sense even apart from their concrete employment in experience (though of course one that is always also contained *in* such concrete employment). That sort of view is clearly unpalatable to some. But it amounts to no more than the view, perfectly palatable to others, that at least some of the mind's representational capacity is a function of innate and unanalyzable "ideas" that it brings to experience rather than derives from it. Of course apart from schematization Kant himself hesitates to call them "ideas" (i.e., "concepts").

What remains to be done is to see how judgmental forms relate to the categories. Kant speaks, as we have seen, both of schematized (or phenomenal) and of unschematized (or pure) categories. The latter it seems are nothing but forms of judgment. The former, Kant tells us, are something more than bare forms of judgment, and he has no tendency at all to doubt whether they are genuine concepts.

A schematized category, I suggest, is a content potentially instantiable by mental states whose parts are to be related by judgmental form.[24] But it is not the only kind of content that satisfies this description. Consider the empirically derived thought of any particular subject/predicate relation, say that of animals being four-footed. Such a thought would contain the concept *animal* and the concept *four-footed*. It would, however, also involve the presence of an appropriate judgmental form relating these concepts—or, more precisely, the states containing them. We might employ the formula '*animal* R *four-footed*' to designate this whole content. It will be a content, then, whose presence in a nonintuitive mental state will yield a thought about four-footed animals. And its presence in an intuitive state (of the visual sort) will yield an intentional *seeing* of a four-footed animal, or the intentional seeing of something as *being* a four-footed animal. It will, in other words, be the empirical concept *four-footed animal*. The concept will be one that we have "constructed" with the aid of judgmental form.[25]

Let us return, then, to the (phenomenal) categories. I have employed the symbol '*animal* R *four-footed*' in order to designate the content that any state will contain just in case it involves the awareness or conception of something's being a four-footed animal. The *category* of substance and accident, we must assume, will be a content that involves the very same judgmental form. But it will lack empirical content. It may be designated by a symbol of the form '——— R ———'. The problem then is to see what could provide the content for mental states that would in this case be related by the judgmental form in question. The "form" of categorial thought is provided by a form of judgment. What provides its content? This is the problem of schematism for Kant.

The only apparent source for the contents in question is pure intuition:

> [S]ince concepts to which no corresponding object could be given, being objectless, would not even be concepts (thoughts through which I think nothing at all), just for that reason a manifold must be given *a priori* for those *a priori* concepts. And because it is given *a priori*, it must be given in an intuition without any thing as object, that is, given in the mere form of intuition . . . . [T]he rule of the schematism of concepts of the understanding is then applied to perceptions.[26]

For example, the content that the category of substance and accident involves is provided by our intuitive awareness of *permanence* and *succession*. The category may then be designated by the formula '*permanence* R *succession*'. In the Schematism chapter Kant took it for granted that this content could be derived from our pure awareness of the structure of time: "the schema of each category contains and makes capable of representation only a determination of time" (A145/B184). In passages added in the second edition Kant acknowledges the importance of our pure awareness of the structure of space as well (esp. B275–279, B288–294).

The construction of a representational complex by means of the provision of intuitive forms instantiable in mental states is the "schematization" of the judgmental forms. It was natural for Kant, I think, to have described this procedure as the production of a set of phenomenal categories on the basis of our possession of a set of nonphenomenal categories that are not "homogeneous" with appearances. Thoughts involving phenomenal categories do indeed contain a priori elements in addition to the intuitive forms provided by schematization. These are the forms of judgment. They may conceivably be present in a mental act even in the absence of the schemata in question. An analogous case in modern logic would be one in which a judgment contained only elements of logical form without any specific concepts. But it is important to see how the analogy fails in certain respects. The following might be offered as a purely formal judgment: (x) $(x = x)$. However, it is apparently not an example Kant could use, since Kant does not recognize identity as one of the forms of judgment. It could be argued that he ought to have done so. In fact Kant appears to acknowledge the shortcoming when he recognizes that some concept of "unity" is required beyond the one actually represented in the table of judgments, i.e., beyond the form of the "singular" judgment:

Combination is representation of the *synthetic* unity of the manifold. The representation of this unity cannot, therefore, arise out of combination. On the contrary, it is what, by adding itself to the representation of the manifold, first makes possible the concept of the combination. This unity, which precedes *a priori* all concepts of combination, is not the category of unity (§10); for all categories are grounded in logical functions of judgment, and in these functions combination, and therefore unity of given concepts, is already thought. (B130–131)

What Kant appears to be saying is that categories, functioning in concrete judgments, function in relation to our ability to identify single objects in the manifold of diverse appearances. This, as I have argued, amounts to the identification of one appearance with a "different" one. So insofar as the very notion of a concrete judgment presupposes that of such "unity," the notion is one of the a priori conditions of judgment. Why Kant did not then recognize it as one of the forms of judgment is unclear. Another judgment that a modern logician might regard as purely formal is: $(Ex)(Ef)(fx)$. This involves only the forms of existential judgment and predication. However it also involves quantification with respect to properties and not just possible particulars. Kant, as we have seen, tries to avoid regarding properties as objects of possible reference.

It is important to be clear in any case that the fact that the forms of judgment have a significance transcending concrete empirical employment does not *limit* their "transcendental" employment to judgments of a purely formal sort. One ought also to be able to consider judgments of a *mixed* kind. In such a case judgmental forms might occur both within a (phenomenal) category and also independently. Such would be the case, for example, when one judges that there exists something *phenomenally* whose existence is grounded in something that exists in itself. In that case the form of existential judgment occurs both in its schematized and in its unschematized mode.

To return then to the problem of schematism, it is perfectly understandable why Kant should have regarded the mere presence of judgmental form as the occurrence of a *thought* of some sort. It is also understandable why he should incline to see judgmental forms, just as such, as "concepts." Since they would then be concepts that are contained in all phenomenal categories and yet which remain even after removal of phenomenal conditions, they could be none other than "pure" categories. We have also seen why Kant would have been led to deny that mere forms of judgments are any sort of concept at all. This would lead him to maintain that the mere presence of judgmental form amounts only to the presence of the *form* of a possible thought, not to a genuine thought, and to deny that there are any such things as nonphenomenal concepts. The tension between these two ways of thinking may be what accounts for Kant's apparent claim in the Schematism chapter that there are unschematized categorial concepts that are not "homogeneous" with appearances but which can be *made* homogeneous with them. The tension between regarding judgmental forms as concepts on the one hand and merely as some sort of nonconceptual, yet "intellectual," representation on the other may be what led to the formulation of Kant's claim that mere judgmental forms are concepts that fail to be homogeneous with appearances. The process of schematization, in that case, would appear to be nothing other than a process of *making* those forms homogeneous with appearances. For it is a process of converting judgmental forms which already *represent* certain aspects of the world into genuine *concepts* of those aspects.

As I have suggested on a number of occasions, Kant's position requires that we be able to form intelligible even if highly "formal" and indeterminate thoughts about possible things transcending human intuition. This is because, on Kant's view, the empirical reality of the objects of human intuition "must" be conceived as grounded in a realm of non-phenomenal existence. We must thus at least be able to conceive that there is such a realm, even if we can form no more determinate idea about it nor regard ourselves as genuinely knowing anything about it. (It is also obvious that Kant's attempt to provide a "metaphysical foundation" for morality rests on the possibility of employing nonphenomenal "concepts" in judgments about reality.) On a number of occasions Kant himself insists upon this point. As we have also seen, he on other occasions appears inclined to insist upon the opposite point of view. The explanation, as I have argued, is that Kant found himself forced to recognize an element within the representational faculty of human cognition that is neither as such "intuitive" nor properly "conceptual."

Chapter 6

Self-Awareness
and the Flow of Time

I. The Problem of Inner Sense

I HAVE concentrated so far on the representational structure of outer intuitions and of judgments that conceptualize them. Outer intuitions, I have argued, are awarenesses of regions of space that might or might not be identifiable as (empirically) actual ones. When such awareness occurs in a purely imaginative manner, and when in addition the concepts that inform it are merely geometrical concepts, then we have an instance of what Kant calls "pure intuition." (Kant also uses the term to apply to a certain aspect of empirical intuitions.) This, as we have seen, fits with Kant's account of pure geometry. The key to that account lies in Kant's view that over and above the concepts informing any pure intuition, the latter also possesses a specifically *intuitional* aspect or "form." This is what guarantees that we are not in that case dealing with a purely conceptual event, but with a genuine kind of object-directed awareness (albeit imaginary). It therefore also guarantees that there will always be some intrinsic condition, internal to an intuition, with respect to what concepts are legitimately applicable to it. This is what grounds the "synthetic" character of geometrical judgments.

Apart from pure intuitions, there is of course also the case of empirical intuitions, or sense perceptions. This, on Kant's view, involves the presence of intuitional form in a state that is a sensory one, i.e., is founded on "sensations." The object of such a state may be variously described. This is because the way in which we describe the object of a cognitive state is always correlative with the internal character of the state itself. Or at least this is the case when we are regarding cognitive states in a purely phenomenological or intentional manner, and it is an essential part of Kant's view that all cognitive states are regardable in this manner. A perception, then, will always contain at least three elements: the intuitional form in virtue of which it is an awareness (in the case of outer intuition) of a possible region of space, the sensations in virtue of which the latter is also conceptualizable as an object *in* space, and, finally, whatever concepts (and forms of judgment) in fact determine the specific conceptualization. Consequently, the object of any perception, variously describable in accordance with the various concepts in question, will always be alternatively describable either as a possible material object or as a possible region of space. This is what legitimizes the application of geometry to the material world: with respect to its spatial structure, the object of sense perception is correlated with the very same "form of intuition" that constitutes the form of pure geometrical representations.

Now Kant also supposes that there is a form of temporal intuition. Can our general approach accommodate an extension in this direction? To be sure, critics sometimes suggest that Kant's own claims, especially those concerning the transcendental ideality of space and of time, are in fact more easily applicable to the former than to the latter of these two alleged forms of intuition.[1] It might make some sense, for example, to hold that spatial objects are real only in the sense that certain perceptions are possible, namely those in which intentional objects are conceptualizable in accordance with the appropriate sorts of "rules." Or at least this seems to make more sense than the corresponding supposition concerning temporal states of affairs. Consciousness at least, and hence the conscious subject, would seem to be temporal "in itself," even if everything else is spatial only in appearance. But in addition to this general difficulty besetting any interpretation of Kant, some special ones may seem to be posed by the claim that Kantian appearances are merely "intentional objects" whose general structures are dictated by forms of intuition internal to the apprehension of them and which are thus subject to whatever general rules govern the conceptualization of such structures—i.e., objects whose empirical reality is a correlate of conditions imposed by our own forms of intuition and understanding.

A unified interpretation along these lines requires the notion of a possible region (stretch) of time analogous to that of a possible region of space. In addition we need to distinguish between merely thinking or judging *that there is* (or was or will be, or might be or has been) a certain stretch of time and a genuinely object-directed *apprehension* of such an item. Finally, our distinction between the intuitive apprehension of a stretch of time and its conceptualization in beliefs and judgments must remain compatible with neutrality in regard to the *reality* of intuited stretches as such. That is, there must be a kind of immediate awareness of stretches of time that provides a reference of our concepts to possible realities that are judged to be (at least in the typical case) actual ones. This last condition may appear especially difficult to satisfy. We can consider a merely possible yet genuinely intuited region of space by considering the case of what we agree to be a merely imagined or hallucinated spatial expanse. (So long, that is, as we are sure to distinguish what is, phenomenologically, the imagining of a possible object from merely imagining *that there is* or might be such an object.) There still seems to be a point in saying, in such cases, that our concepts have been applied to an at least intended region of space, even if it proves to have been *merely* intended. But consider an intuitively apprehended expanse that also exhibits, at least in our apprehension of it, an instance of temporal succession. Then it seems we have a paradigm case of the intuitive awareness of a stretch of time. Unfortunately, it seems implausible to say that the stretch in question is one that might or might not be judged to be an actual one. Intuited regions of space might turn out to be unactualized possibilities. But the very fact that I am *aware* of them as (at least in my own apprehension) enduring through a stretch of time seems to imply that at least that stretch must itself be something actual. It is, after all, the time during which I had the experience in question. Kant himself in fact identifies our intuitive awareness of time with the intuitive awareness of our own conscious experiences:

> By means of outer sense, a property of our mind, we represent to ourselves objects as outside us, and all without exception in space. . . . Inner sense, by means of which the mind intuits itself or its inner state, yields no intuition of the soul itself as an object; but there is nevertheless a determinate form in which alone the intuition of inner states is possible, and everything which belongs to inner determinations is therefore represented in relations of time. Time cannot be outwardly intuited, any more than space can be intuited as something in us. (A22–23/B37)

There is, one soon discovers, considerable difficulty in identifying precisely what constitutes the domain, or the "manifold," of "inner sense" for Kant. In the passage just quoted Kant says that what we are aware of via inner sense is the mind (*Gemüt*), or at least its inner state (*innerer Zustand*) or its inner determinations (*innere Bestimmungen*; cf. A34/B50). Other times he speaks of modifications (*Modifikationen*: A99) of the mind or of alterations (*Veränderungen*) of it.[2] In the first edition *Critique* Kant is also more specific. In addition to the *denkendes Subjekt* he mentions thoughts, consciousness, and desires (A357); thoughts, feeling, inclination, and decision (A358); representations and will (A358); and, once again, representations and thinking (A359). The inclusion of thoughts (*Gedanken*) and thinking (*Denken*) is problematic in the light of further reflection. The second edition *Critique* limits the awareness of "spontaneous" activities to a purely *conceptual* sort of apprehension thereby excluding its presence from a manifold of intuition (B157). Kant is also explicit in the *Anthropology*:

> If we present [*vorstellen*] to ourselves the inner action (spontaneity) whereby a *concept* (a thought) is possible—*reflection*—and the receptivity whereby a *perception* (perceptio), i.e., empirical *intuition* is possible—*apprehension*—and in both acts do so with consciousness, than consciousness of oneself (apperceptio) can be divided into that of reflection and that of apprehension. The former is a consciousness of the understanding, the latter inner sense; the former can be called *pure*, the latter *empirical* apperception, so that the former would wrongly be called inner *sense*.[3]

Insofar as decision (*Entschliessung*) and will (*Wille*) are also characterized by "spontaneity" of action, the same point would appear to apply to them as well. I shall return to this issue. For now it is also worth noting that the status of feeling (*Gefühl*) also raises problems for Kant. Kant insists in the *Anthropology* (Pt. I, § 24) that there is only one inner sense (as contrasted with the five outer ones). But the Reflections indicate that he thought twice: "We have, however, several inner senses. Feeling."[4] In addition one might find it odd that even the most elaborate listings of the first edition *Critique* fail to include *Empfindung*. The omission might suggest a version of the subjectivist doctrine already encountered: as actual states of the perceiving subject, sensations are as subjective as *Gefühle*, and we are aware of them in whatever way we are aware of the latter, through inner sense; but unlike mere *Gefühle*, sensations are also projected "outward" as aspects of the objects immediately perceived through outer sense. In *that* context they are not objects of inner sense at all.[5] Of course I do not find this sort of reading agreeable.

Apart from such complications as these, it would presumably be safe to say that inner sense is a capacity for the immediate awareness of one's own "states of consciousness." Kant, that is, appears to be intending a distinction that is reminiscent of one that Locke had drawn earlier between "sensation," through the usual five senses, and that special sort of internal apprehension that Locke called "reflection." Locke appeared to regard the latter as sufficiently analogous to the former to warrant regarding it as a kind of "sense" as well:

> Secondly, the other fountain from which experience furnisheth the understanding with ideas is,—the perception of the operations of our own mind within us, as it is employed about the ideas it has got. . . . And such are *perception, thinking, doubting, believing, reasoning, knowing, willing*, and all the different actings of our own minds;—which we being conscious of, and observing in ourselves, do from these receive into our understandings as distinct ideas as we do from bodies affecting our senses. This source of ideas every man has wholly in himself, and though it be not sense, as having nothing to do with external objects, yet it is very like it, and might properly enough be called *internal sense*. But as I call the other Sensation, so I call this REFLECTION, the ideas it affords being such only as the mind gets by reflecting on its own operations within itself.[6]

Baumgarten, whose texts Kant annotated and employed in his courses, is less cautious:

> I possess a faculty of sensing, i.e. sense [Kant: *der Sinn*]. Sense represents either the state of my soul, inner sense, or the state of my body, outer sense. Hence sensation [Kant: *Empfindung*] is either inner through inner sense (consciousness more strictly speaking), or outer, produced through outer sense.[7]

One difference between Locke and Kant is that inner sense does not yield direct awareness of inner *activity* for Kant. A similarity lies, however, in their conception of the relation between inner sense and time. The former also provides, for both, a genuine experience of the latter (even if *concepts* of time might also be applied, in judgments, to outer items as well):

> That we have our notion of succession and duration from this original, viz. from reflection on the train of ideas, which we find to appear one after another in our own minds, seems plain to me, in that we have no perception of duration but by considering the train of ideas that take their turns in our understandings.[8]

It is noteworthy, too, that while Locke extends "reflection" to the apprehension of internal activities, the experience of internal time rests solely on an apprehension of the internal flow of "ideas," that is of those items toward which mental activity is presumably *directed*. In the light of this fact, and insofar as "inner sense" is supposed to be coextensive with the domain of immediate time-awareness, one might propose a correction with respect to our original suggestion. Instead of regarding it as the capacity for awareness of one's own "states of consciousness," one might regard it as awareness merely of one's own "ideas" or *Vorstellungen*, or at least of some of them. (Kant allows for unconscious *Vorstellungen*.)[9] At one point Kant in fact characterizes inner sense as the *Inbegriff aller Vorstellungen* (B220). That skirts the issue of activity or "spontaneity," though it leaves the problem of *Gefühle*, which are not strictly *Vorstellungen* (A801/B829).

Continuing to abstract from this problem, we should note an equally striking parallel between the two thinkers. As with what Locke called reflection, namely, Kant's faculty of inner sense is not explicable wholly in terms of some special formation process for accurate *beliefs* or *judgments*. It might be supposed, for example, that a person is immediately aware of his own conscious states simply in virtue of being in a position to form accurate judgments about their occurrence.[10] This at least would obviate the need for discovering an ingredient that plays a role in *generating* those judgments analogous to the role played by "sensations" in ordinary perceptual judgments. The latter, it seems, are not merely responses to some

underlying causal or dispositional mechanism. Rather, postulated mechanisms are themselves responses to an independent alteration within one's
state of consciousness, that is in one's "sensations." Of course, this point
would not be telling were the concept of sensation to be explicated wholly
by reference to the faculty of belief-formation in the first place. For Locke,
though, the formation of perceptual and reflective judgments presupposes
an original acquisition of the *concepts* they contain. This in turn must be
founded upon *experiences* of the ordinary perceptual and of the inner
reflective sort. So the notion of an "experience," whether inner or outer,
cannot itself be explicated in terms of specific alterations within one's
general capacity for the formation of judgments. That would presuppose
precisely what needs explaining. Now Kant does not put his own point,
primarily, in terms of an order of "explanation" of the genetic sort favored
by Locke. But a parallel conclusion, as we know, needs to be drawn, since
for Kant the *referential* element in any judgment must always hinge on
something other than the concepts it contains. This of course is because
concepts are general "representations." The formation of judgments referring to particular *instances* of concepts must therefore rest on a capacity
that is not itself purely conceptual, and inner sense accordingly involves
intuitions of one's own conscious interior (A22–23/B37) and not merely the
formation of thoughts and judgments about it. But then the problem
remains: what is there in inner consciousness *besides* certain, presumably
accurate, beliefs or judgments about oneself? And whatever there is, in
addition to the latter, is it something with regard to which the notion of
apprehending "intentional objects" is applicable? And is it something to
which a distinction can be drawn paralleling the distinction between
sensational "matter" and "form" in an outer intuition? These appear to be
problems to which Locke's formulations do not subject him. Baumgarten
appears to be in a stickier position, inasmuch as he uses the term *sensatio*
both as Kant does for a representation that "relates solely to the subject as
the modification of its state" (A320/B376), as well as with respect to the
distinction between inner and *outer* sensation. This appears to require that
a single internal condition function as the "material" for two distinct kinds
of perception.

   In a certain sense, the problem concerning matter and form in an inner
intuition might appear to be one we can dismiss. For in a certain sense we
cannot be expected to answer the corresponding question regarding outer
intuitions either. We say, to be sure, that the material of the latter is
provided by "sensations." We might be tempted to suppose that we know
what this means. As I have noted, after all, Kant himself sometimes uses
the term to refer to something with which we are all quite intimately
familiar, namely the material aspect of immediately apprehended "appearances." In this sense, for example, sensation is the very colors that we see

and the sounds that we hear, at least insofar as these are all in fact immediately experienced. As I have contended, however, the sense in which sensations are supposed to be the material aspect of immediately apprehended appearances is considerably different from that in which they are regarded as components of the cognitive states by which we *apprehend* appearances. The latter are not something with which we are acquainted, nor an aspect of such a thing—at least not in the sense in which we are "acquainted" with appearances. Sensations in this sense are introduced only as part of a theory aimed at *accounting* for the apprehension of appearances. [11]

However, even if we were relieved from specifying the material component of inner intuitions as cognitive states, we would not thereby escape a corresponding requirement regarding the *objects* of those states. The "formal" aspect of such objects is presumably provided by whatever stretch of intuited time is in question, qua stretch of time. What then serves as a "material" in relation to that form? What, that is, is presented as *filling* the stretch of time? Kant is the first to reject what might seem the most obvious answer, namely *ourselves*. For in whatever way self-awareness is conveyed by inner sense for Kant, it involves the conceptualization of a self as filling a time that it is precisely not *intuited* as filling—or at least, not in the sense in which matter is intuited as filling regions of space:

> Consciousness of self according to the determinations of our states in inner perceptions is merely empirical and always changing. No fixed and abiding self can present itself in this flux of inner appearances. (A107; cf. B133, B275)

> Although both are appearances, the appearance to outer sense has something fixed or abiding which supplies a substratum as the basis of its transitory determinations and therefore a synthetic concept, namely, that of space and of an appearance in space; whereas time, which is the sole form of our inner intuition, has nothing abiding, and therefore yields knowledge only of the change of determinations, *not of any object that can be thereby determined*. (A381; emphasis added)

These passages may appear to imply that whatever material might be involved in "inner" self-awareness, it is not something that is phenomenologically presented to us. In that case, however, we would seem to be deprived of a ground even for so much as postulating a matter/form distinction within an inner intuition corresponding to a parallel distinction in its object, for that, as we saw in the case of outer intuition, would have to rest on first taking the object in question as an *intentional* object. This is not to say that there would be no "inner intuitions," or that they would not have objects. But what might appear required is that we abandon a phenomenological approach to such objects. And once having abandoned that approach, according to which the objects of inner intuition would be in the first instance intentional objects, i.e., objects that, as phenomenological correlates of the apprehension of them, might or might not be judged to be realities, our only alternative might appear to lie in appeal to a *semantical* rather than a phenomenological notion of reference. Inner intuitions, that is, could be construed as the "singular terms," or perhaps (begrudgingly) the postulated "inner analogues" of singular terms, by means of which we refer to ourselves in at least the typical sorts of self-referential judgments. There is, of course, no reason to suppose that everything to which we "refer" is phenomenologically presented to us. Nor is there, it might seem, any reason to suppose that whatever inner items might underlie our references to some object must contain a structure that parallels a corresponding one in the object itself.

Kant himself provides what might appear the most natural suggestion, if we assume that inner sense provides no direct awareness of the "self" or the "subject" of experience. In that case, it would seem, inner sense must provide an awareness of at least some of those items that we might regard as "determinations" of the self. The list, we have seen, is not clear. It certainly includes *Vorstellungen*, which Kant often characterizes as "determinations" of the mind (cf. A197/B242). It also includes feelings and inclinations and perhaps even in some sense "acts" of thinking and willing. As to what Kant means by *Vorstellungen*, there will be differences of opinion. He pretty clearly has in mind, I think, what he also calls "appearances," which as we have seen he sometimes characterizes as something "in us" and as modifications of the mind. Taking the latter notions literally, one will espouse a subjectivism that I have endeavored to reject. On the other hand, following the suggestion that the appearances "in us" are merely intentional objects of awareness as such, the items in question will have little in common with the other items on Kant's lists. These others seem much more serious candidates for "determinations" of the self, namely feelings, inclinations, and acts of thinking and willing. In any case, introduction of these sorts of items would appear of little use in the formulation of a *phenomenological* approach to inner sense that is sufficiently comparable to that proposed for outer sense.

One way to attempt reinstatement of a phenomenological approach would be to distinguish between determinations of the self as it is *in itself* and determinations of the self as they *appear* to us. For Kant, after all, is insistent that inner intuition yields an awareness only of the latter (cf. A34/B5; A35–36/B52). The objects of inner intuition, then, might comprise that set of intentional objects that are appearances of our own mind in the way that certain others are appearances of things distinct from our mind. This suggestion might seem to be confirmed by the Kantian notion of "self-affection." What Kant maintains is that the mind, in becoming aware of itself, affects itself. And precisely because of this fact we can be sure that what one is thereby aware of is merely an "appearance":

> If the faculty of coming to consciousness of oneself is to seek out (to apprehend) that which lies in the mind, it must affect the mind, and only in this way can it give rise to an intuition of itself. But the form of this intuition, which exists antecedently in the mind, determines, in the representation of time, the mode in which the manifold is together in the mind, since it then intuits itself not as it would represent itself if immediately self-active, but as it is affected by itself, and therefore as it appears to itself, not as it is. (B68–69)

We know that it is Kant's claim that a necessary condition for awareness of an object distinguishable from my mind, and located somewhere in space, [12] is that this object produce an effect via stimulation of sense organs. The awareness of the object in question will then be an internal state with a twofold aspect. Its "formal" aspect will be one it might share with an awareness that is not sensory, that is with a "pure" intuition. This is the aspect in virtue of which it apprehends a possible region of space. The "material" aspect is that in virtue of which it apprehends that region in a sensory manner. Corresponding to this distinction, there will be a distinction with respect to the object in question, namely between the region of space as such and the material that we might conceptualize as *occupying* it. Are we now to suppose it Kant's view that a parallel account must be drawn for inner intuition? In that case, on the side of the intentional object in question we should find a stretch of time and also a certain "material" conceptualizable as occupying it. The latter would be what we conceptualize as determinations of our mind. The corresponding cognitive state, we would then assume, contains an aspect analogous to that produced by the stimulation of sense organs. (As we have seen, there is no reason to suppose that we are acquainted with this aspect as such.) But it would presumably be something generated not by the impingement of objects upon sense organs, but by the mind's impingement upon itself. [13]

Unfortunately this approach is not only implausible in itself, but contrary to what Kant says about self-affection. It is perhaps not unreasonable to say that we have a kind of inner awareness whereby a certain "material" is apprehended as filling a temporal "form." It may not even be unreasonable to claim that, in virtue of this particular form, the material is presented only as it appears and not as it really is in itself. What one might mean by this is simply that the temporal features of our internal states, as we are aware of them, merely reflect the mode of our awareness of those states and not any aspect that is proper to them as such. This is the sort of claim that philosophers sometimes make. Anyone will accept it, for example, who holds that with respect to reality in itself there is no "flow" of time and no past, future, or "now."[14] These features, it might be claimed, merely reflect the way in which reality presents itself to consciousness. If that is so, then there would be some point in saying that the material presented in inner awareness is presented in a form that applies only to its appearance. But the crucial problem concerns that material itself. We can characterize the material of outer intuitions as matter that might possibly occupy real space or might not. For this is precisely what is involved in regarding the objects of outer intuition as intentional objects that might in any instance fail to be something real. But it may seem impossible to characterize the material of inner awareness as anything other than our own internal states, at least as they appear to us. For that very reason, it may seem impossible to regard the objects of inner awareness as intentional objects that merely happen to be conceptualizable as real. They are as such realities, it would seem, that at most might fail to be apprehended precisely as they are in themselves.

In any case, no support can be found for the doctrine in question in Kant's claims about self-affection. The paragraph from which the above-quoted passage was extracted makes it clear that Kant is not talking about a process whereby some material is generated as the basis for conceptualization as this or that sort of object with this or that ontological status. Rather, Kant is speaking of some sort of "affection" that is in question precisely when our understanding introduces concepts into intuitions that it has *not* generated. The claim, with respect to inner intuition, is offered as a parallel to a point discussed earlier with respect to outer intuition:

> In confirmation of this theory of the ideality of both outer and inner sense, and therefore of all objects of the senses, as mere appearances, it is especially relevant to observe that everything in our knowledge which belongs to intuition . . . contains nothing but mere relations; namely, of locations in an intuition (extension), of change of location (motion), and of laws according to which this change is determined (moving forces). What it is that is present in this or that location, or what it is that is operative in the things themselves apart from change of location, is not given through intuition. (B66–67)

Kant concludes that, since "outer sense gives us nothing but mere relations," it presents us at most with appearances and not with things in themselves. What is the basis of this inference? As I suggested earlier, we need to take our clue from what Kant claims needs to be *added* to mere intuition, in order that it present us with something more than mere "relations." It is, as the passage makes clear, simply the *concept* of what sort of thing is present in some region of space, or is moving from one region of space to another. What Kant is saying, then, is that one is aware of an object that *occupies* a region of space only insofar as intuitions are conceptualized. Apart from that, intuitions at most relate to the presentation of a region of space that some object *might* be conceptualized as occupying. Since, I think Kant reasons, the representation of an object in space is only introduced by the conceptualization of intuitions, the "objects" in question must at most be intentional objects that are, as such, correlates of the very representation of them.

Kant's claims about self-affection must be read in this light. Here is the rest of the argument:

> . . . the time in which we set these representations, which is itself antecedent to the consciousness of them in experience, and which underlies them as the formal condition of the mode in which we posit [*setzen*] them in the mind, itself contains relations of succession, coexistence, and of that which is coexistent with succession, the enduring. Now that which, as representation, can be antecedent to any and every act of thinking anything, is intuition; and if it contains nothing but relations, it is the form of intuition. Since this form does not represent anything save in so far as something is posited in the mind, it can be nothing but the mode in which the mind is affected through its own activity (namely, through this positing of its representation), and so is affected by itself; in other words, it is nothing but an inner sense in respect of the form of that sense.

What Kant is saying, I think, is this. Awareness of oneself through inner sense requires that something, namely determination of our mind, be represented as occupying certain stretches of time. But the representation of anything as occupying a stretch of time requires the application of concepts to intuitions; apart from that, the latter at most relate to the presentation of stretches of time that certain items *might* be conceptualized as occupying. Whatever Kant means by self-affection, in other words, it has to do merely with the conceptualizations of intuitions and not with the generation of anything analogous to sensations. This should already be clear, I think, from the fact that the affection in question involves an activity (*setzen*) of a sort that Kant only attributes to judgment and from the fact that Kant expressly links it with the intentional activity of "seeking out" (*aufsuchen*) an object.[15] The same point is clear from Kant's later discussion:

> For we intuit ourselves only as we are inwardly *affected*, and this would seem to be contradictory. . . . It is to avoid this contradiction that in systems of psychology *inner sense*, which we have carefully distinguished from the faculty of *apperception*, is commonly regarded as being identical with it.
>
> What determines [*bestimmt*] inner sense is the understanding and its original power of combining the manifold of intuition, that is, of bringing it

under an apperception, upon which the possibility of understanding itself rests. Now the understanding in us men is not itself a faculty of intuitions, and cannot, even if intuition be given in sensibility, take them up *into itself* in such manner as to combine them as the manifold of its *own* intuition. Its synthesis, therefore, if the synthesis be viewed by itself alone, is nothing but the unity of the act, of which, as an act, it is conscious to itself, even without sensibility, but through which it is yet able to determine sensibility. (B153)

If this is the case then one might of course wonder why Kant does not also speak of "affection" in the case of outer intuitions, since these require conceptualization as much as inner intuitions do. Perhaps the reason is that Kant already had introduced a very different kind of affection in the case of outer intuitions, namely that involving the production of sensations. What he is now considering is a kind of "affection" that is not at all analogous to that. In any case, it is not inappropriate for Kant to speak of self-affection. For by conceptualizing any intuition, as I have argued, one is introducing a certain element *into* that intuition, thereby affecting it in its own internal quality and making something new of it. As we have also seen, Kant thinks of the conceptualization of intuitions as a process whereby intuitions are made fully *conscious*. In that sense we can even concede that the self-affection in question *produces* intuitions (i.e., qua conscious), though it does not produce their "material." Finally, we shall see in the next section how for Kant the "determining" of outer intuitions always *is* a determining of inner sense, though not in terms of a subjectivistic account.

II. Inner and Outer Sense

Kant's treatment of self-affection contains a claim that I have so far ignored. The claim, I think, is the key to his account of inner sense and the problem of its "material." The claim is simply this: that "the representations of the *outer senses* constitute the proper material with which we occupy our mind." This claim is so important that, given that the objects of outer intuition are themselves conceded to be mere appearances, Kant offers it as sufficient to establish the ideality of the objects of inner intuition (B67). What is equally striking, with respect to our earlier questions concerning feelings and acts of the will, Kant also maintains in the same passage that "feeling of pleasure and pain, and the will" must be excluded from his subsequent treatment of self-affection and awareness through inner sense (B66). I shall return to this point later.

The suggestion, then, is that the "material" of inner sense is the very same body of material as is involved in the case of outer sense. A number of passages make this claim. Some of them are passages that also tend to generate a supposition that I have already rejected, namely that the immediate objects of spatial perception are really internal states, somehow projected and spatialized by means of the process of perception itself. They are passages in which, for example, Kant says that all appearances exist only "in us" and as "determinations of my identical self" (A129), or in which he says that inner sense is the "sum of all representations" (B220) and that all conceptual activities directed toward the objects of outer sense must first "determine inner sense" (B150). It may be tempting to read these passages as entailing an extreme subjectivism, though I have argued to the contrary. I have argued, that is, that the point in calling outer appearances "determinations of inner sense" is, at least in part, simply to signal their status as intentional objects. However, there might also be a stronger claim to be made. The point already suggested is that on Kant's view the immediate object of outer awareness is an intentional correlate[16] of a perceptual state comprised of a sensory "material" plus an intentional element referring *through* that material to a possible region of space. The stronger claim is now this: this very same material also functions, in virtue of an additional intentional element, as the material of inner intuitions of regions of time. That is, a single manifold of material provides the basis for two distinct kinds of intuitions, inner and outer.

This is a claim to which Kant himself gives more explicit expression:

> Even time itself we cannot represent, save in so far as we attend, in the *drawing* of a straight line (which has to serve as the outer figurative representation of time), merely to the act of the synthesis of the manifold whereby we successively determine inner sense, and in so doing attend to the succession of this determination in inner sense. (B154; cf. B156, 163, 292)

This is quite the reverse of passages giving rise to a subjectivist reading. It does not suggest, in particular, that representations of outer awareness are really only constructions out of some properly inner material. Rather, the awareness of anything inner is itself said to presuppose the material of *outer* representation.[17] Naturally, the suggestion in question should also imply that it is properly *sensation* through which our own existence in time is made manifest. And so Kant says as well:

> Perception exhibits the reality of something in space; and in absence of perception no power of imagination can invent and produce that some-thing. It is sensation, therefore, that indicates a reality in space *and in time*, according as it is related to the one or to the other mode of sensible intuition. [emphasis added] (A373–374)

> The 'I think' expresses an indeterminate empirical intuition, i.e., percep-tion (and thus shows that sensation, which as such belongs to sensibility, lies at the basis of this existential proposition). (B423, note)

In order to proceed with these suggestions, we need to digress a bit, and to distinguish two very different kinds of "temporal awareness." More generally, we need first of all to note that in some instances "awareness" of a certain object or state of affairs is primarily determined by the content of whatever *concepts* are in question in those instances. That the (intentional) object of perception on some occasion is a tree, for example, depends on the presence of the concept tree in an intuition. Elements pertaining to the "form of intuition" determine merely that, phenomenologically, some region of space is presented as a region thus conceptualizable (given that we possess the relevant concepts). We are sometimes aware, then, of a certain sort of object only in the sense that an intuition, with a form of its own, is further informed by means of the concept of that sort of object. According to Kant, however, this cannot be the only sense in which we are aware of regions of space and of time. There is no doubt a sense in which, had we failed to conceptualize an intuition in terms of the concept *rectangular* (or *approximately rectangular*) then we could not be said to have perceived a rectangular region on some occasion. Nevertheless, we are also aware of the spatial form of any region to which we have applied a concept in something *more* than the sense that the concept refers precisely to a region of that form. Regions of space have a certain priority with respect to objects represented as occupying them. We are aware of the latter (phenomenologically) only in the sense that we are led to conceptualize presented regions of space in a certain way. We are not presented with those regions, in turn, only in the sense that something still more fundamental is conceptualized.

Now we need to apply this distinction to see that there are two very different ways in which a person might be said to apprehend a stretch of time or some instance of temporal succession. In one way, we apprehend such things simply in the sense that certain of our intuitions are conceptualized by the appropriate temporal concepts. This is a sense in which one often perceives instances of succession located in regions of space, hence (as we might put it) regions of space that are *also* regions of time, and vice versa. Obviously, therefore, Kant must have something else in mind when he also insists that time cannot be "intuited" outside us (A23/B37), something that he of course attributes to an appropriate form of intuition and not merely to certain concepts. What we need to consider is the possibility, then, that the very same sensory material might serve both as the vehicle for the conceptualization of regions of space as containing objects enduring, and altering, through stretches of time and also as the vehicle for a more immediate and *intuitive* awareness of time. The latter would be an awareness that, though carried by that same material, is more properly awareness of the flow of empirical consciousness itself than of the temporal features of the spatial reality that we are also aware of (i.e., conceptualize) as the object of that consciousness.

Now Kant is not the only philosopher to suppose that a single state of the perceiver might serve as the vehicle both for an intending of objects of consciousness and also for an awareness of the flow of consciousness itself. According to Brentano, for example, every psychological state has the property of referring to an intentional object and also that of referring to itself as an object of consciousness.[18] That is to say, we are not in the first instance aware of our own conscious states in virtue of additional states of which they are the objects. Rather, we apprehend the former in virtue of some respect in which they carry an awareness of *themselves*. A similar claim is made by Sartre.[19] But we need to see what Kant himself has in mind.

In trying to give some content to these claims, we need to notice that a certain metaphor is likely to influence our approach. Suppose that we use the picture of an arrow to represent our apprehension of objects distinct from ourselves. At one end of this arrow, then, will be the being whose states of apprehension are in question, i.e., ourselves. At the other end will be whatever, if anything, that being succeeds in apprehending by means of those states. Or if you will, at the other end will "be" all the intentional objects of its consciousness. In any case, it is tempting to introduce a second arrow to represent a special kind (an "internal" kind) of self-awareness. This arrow might be imagined as departing from either of two places. It might be supposed to depart from the same point of origin, the same "subject" of consciousness, as the original arrow. Or it might rather be supposed to depart, as Brentano's position would suggest, from some point on or within the original arrow itself. In addition, we might imagine different objects at which this second arrow ends up pointing. It might, for example, bend back and point at the original subject of consciousness. Or it might point instead at the first arrow. In either case, we are likely to be influenced, in thinking about this question, by the metaphor of some sort of "turning back" of the subject, or of its consciousness, upon itself.

The novelty of Kant's approach lies to a large extent in its independence of this (admittedly mixed) metaphor of boomeranging arrows. Kant's insistence that one and the same material provides a vehicle for the apprehension of spatial forms, and also for the apprehension of our consciousness *of* such forms, does lend itself to formulation in terms of the metaphor. But Kant, I think, adopts a different approach. For him the fact that the material of outer sense is also that of inner sense implies that whatever of our own "self" is presented in inner intuition is something that is at best reflected *in the very objects* that we also conceptualize as objects of outer sense, i.e., as bodies in space. The point might be put with the help of

another metaphor. Self-awareness is often regarded as a kind of "reflection." This in turn is often regarded, metaphorically at least, as a kind of
bending backward of the subject upon itself. But it might also be thought of
in a different way. It might be seen as more like the kind of reflection
involved when somebody looks in a mirror. We might think of a person's
consciousness as aware of itself in inner sense only to the extent that it is
"reflected" *in*, or mirrored *back*, from those very objects that it also
conceptualizes as objects distinct from itself.

Of course certain things need to be ignored to grasp the point of any
metaphor. Here in particular while inner intuition is supposed to provide a
kind of self-awareness, Kant, as we have seen, does not regard it as
presenting the "self" as an identifiable *object* of awareness. What I perceive in a mirror is of course a determinate object. It is my body. What
Kant by contrast is trying to capture is the kind of self-awareness involved
precisely when I feel the need to distinguish between all perceivable
bodies, including my own, and my consciousness *of* those bodies. It is the
kind of self-awareness, that is, where a person's consciousness is supposedly aware of *itself*. Now some philosophers maintain that this kind of
self-awareness must in turn involve the awareness of another object, an
object distinct from the body, namely that special object that we call the
"self" or the "ego." Kant denies this. There is, he grants, an inner self-
awareness. But insofar as it is purely "inner," the self is thereby not
presented as an identifiable object at all. Rather, it is merely presented as
the temporal flow of empirical consciousness itself. This requires some
qualification with respect to the mirror metaphor. Nevertheless, the
metaphor remains apt. For the flow of empirical consciousness is presented
as an "object" of consciousness, not by a kind of "bending back" of the self
(or of consciousness) upon itself, but rather by means of its own reflection in
the very objects that are also conceptualized as bodies in space:

> Motion, as an act of the subject (not as a determination of an object), and
> therefore the synthesis of the manifold in space [i.e.,—Kant's footnote—
> motion "as describing of a space"], first produces the concept of succes-
> sion—*if we abstract from this manifold* [emphasis added] and attend solely
> to the act through which we determine the *inner* sense according to its
> form. (B154–155) [W]e cannot obtain for ourselves a representation of time,
> which is not an object of outer intuition, except under the image of a line,
> which we draw. . . . (B156)

This proposition, as I noted earlier, provides one of the reasons leading
Kant to conclude that in inner sense the self is not apprehended as it is "in
itself" (A34/B51, A35–36/B52). For the material of inner sense is the very

same set of objects as are presented in outer sense, and these are mere appearances (B67).

Inner intuition, then, does not really change the direction of consciousness—away, for example, from an external realm into another special inner one. Rather, it simply involves being aware *in a special way* of the appearances presented in outer intuition. These may of course be conceptualized as material objects, or states of such, occupying stretches of time and exemplifying various temporal properties. But those same objects that, as originally presented intentional objects, might be thus conceptualized also serve as the vehicle for a properly intuitive awareness of temporal properties and of stretches of time. The temporal properties thereby in question, however, are not conceptualizable as perceptually presented features of material reality. Rather, they are conceptualizable only as pertaining to the flow of empirical consciousness itself. Of course, the "flow of empirical consciousness" will in that case constitute one among the intentional *objects* of consciousness. Thus it will have to be regarded as an object whose only claim to empirical reality must lie in whatever conformance is required by *criteria* of empirical reality, in precisely the way that the reality of apprehended regions of space must lie in their conformance with such criteria. This requires a distinction, accordingly, between consciousness as it presents itself as an intentional object of consciousness, i.e., consciousness as "reflected" in the manifold of intentional objects conceptualizable as bodies in space, and consciousness as it is "in itself," i.e., as the original capacity for *apprehending* such objects. But Kant's point precisely is that consciousness in the latter sense is not presented as an object at all, and certainly not presented through inner sense. We are "aware" of it, rather, merely as the capacity *for* the presentation of appearances that are conceptualizable as material bodies and of stretches of time that are conceptualizable as the flow of the very consciousness *of* those appearances. Consciousness "in itself" is not an object of inner sense for Kant. Inner sense acquaints us only with consciousness as it appears to us, i.e., as reflected in its own intentional object.

Kant's argumentation in The Second Analogy of Experience indicates, I think, this distinction between intuitive and merely conceptual aspects of temporal awareness.[20] First of all, Kant says, we do need to distinguish between two ways in which succession might be presented in the "synthesis" of appearances:

> The apprehension of the manifold of appearances is always successive. The representations of the parts follow upon one another. Whether they also follow one another in the object is a point which calls for further reflection . . . . The appearances, in so far as they are objects of consciousness simply in virtue of being representations, are not in any way distinct from their

apprehension, that is, from their reception in the synthesis of imagination
. . . . (A189–190/B234–235)

What, Kant then asks, "am I to understand by the question: how the
manifold may be connected in the appearance itself," precisely when the
latter is supposed to *be* distinguishable from the apprehension of it? The
answer is this:

> That which lies in the successive apprehension is here viewed as repre-
> sentation, while the appearance which is given to me, notwithstanding that
> it is nothing but the sum of these representations, is viewed as their object:
> and my *concept* [emphasis added], which I derive from the representations
> of apprehension, has to agree with it. (A191/B236)

Consider one of Kant's examples, a case in which what I visually apprehend would most naturally be conceptualized as a ship in a position on a
stream, followed by its absence from that and reappearance in a different
position downstream. The crux of Kant's argument is that, so far as immediate intuition goes, nothing that I have apprehended in fact constrains the
interpretation in question. That same experience might have been conceptualized in at least two different ways. One, as suggested, would take what I
apprehend as a successively composed event involving movement on an
actual stream. The other would be very different. It would suppose that the
only succession is in my *apprehension* of the stream. Perhaps I have simply
noticed, for example, a downstream object all along coexistent with an
upstream one remarkably similar to it, which I am now failing to notice.
Indeed, though rather less likely, the apparently continuous observation of
a ship's *movement* downstream might even turn out to have been a continuous and remarkably coordinated succession of noticings and failings to
notice of diverse but coexistent objects. The latter case would of course
require a very bizarre circumstance on the surface of the stream itself. But
that does not affect Kant's point, which is that so far as immediate intuition
goes, what appears to be the apprehension of a succession of observed
states of affairs might also be conceptualized as nothing more than an
instance of succession in the faculty of apprehension itself. This point could
as well be made by imagining a still more extreme case. After all, so far as
immediate intuition goes, there might not really have been a stream in
front of me in the first place.

Now these examples might appear to present us with something analogous to the situation regarding space. The immediate objects of spatial
intuition are regions of space that might or might not be regarded as real
expanses. So whenever one judges of an intuitively presented region that it
is a portion of real space, or even a material body, one is conceptualizing *as*

the apprehension of a portion of spatial reality an intuition that, in its intrinsic intuitional character, might not be the apprehension of any such reality at all. A similar point might now seem required with respect to intuited succession. As immediately apprehended, an instance of succession might or might not be an instance of succession in some object of perception. In the case in which one has veridically apprehended the movement of a ship downstream, on the other hand, a certain instance of possible succession has in fact turned out to *be* an instance of actual succession with respect to such an object.

However, this analogy cannot be wholly sustained. That Kant would not accept it, after all, should be evident from his claim, already emphasized, that outer sense does not yield an intuition of time (A23/B37). This claim seems to imply that while we may indeed apprehend an instance of outer succession in the sense that we have correctly "informed" our outer intuitions with the appropriate temporal concepts, we never really thereby obtain an *intuition* of that succession. What could Kant mean by this? Does he only mean, for example, that no sequence of intuitions ever *guarantees* that its object is an instance of objective outer succession? That can't be it. For no sequence of intuitions ever guarantees the reality of a spatial phenomenon either, and that does not lead Kant to say that we are never intuitively aware of regions of space.

What Kant must mean by this claim, I think, is that in the way in which we are at least entitled to *suppose* that particular intuited forms are regions of space occupied by material objects, we are not entitled to suppose that particular intuited successions are instances of succession *in* those regions. Though we may conceptualize our intuitions as perceptions of succession with respect to perceived objects, we may not identify any succession that we intuitively apprehend with whatever succession we might suppose to *characterize* those objects. We are indeed aware of succession intuitively, and not merely insofar as spatial intuitions are conceptualized in a certain way. But it would always be wrong to suppose that the very succession that we thereby apprehend *is* an instance of succession that occurs in some object of perception. The former is, rather, the succession of one's own internal experience. In other words, the sense in which I am aware of a set of regions of space that I can conceptualize as a set of states of a *ship moving* is different from the sense in which I am aware of the *motion* of that ship. The "motion" that I am aware of in that first sense, on the other hand—the motion that I am aware of in the same intuitive way that I am aware of the regions of space in question—is simply the "motion" of my own consciousness in apprehending the object in question. This, it is important to note, does not contradict Kant's insistence that we are immediately aware of objects in space, nor my claim that such "immediacy" is to be explained solely in terms of the conceptualizability of intentional objects of intuition.

For the point simply is that on Kant's view we are not *entitled* to conceptualize the intentional objects of our intuitions of motion as the motions of objects in space. We are at most entitled to conceptualize certain of the intentional objects that are apprehended in such motion as objects *that are* moving in space. The *motion* that is intuited is conceptualizable only as the motion of my own consciousness.

This, I think, is a position to which Kant is inevitably led, once he has rejected all accounts of inner awareness in terms of a metaphorical bending back of the (equally metaphorical) "arrows" of intentional direction. (Which in turn he must reject precisely because there is no special set of "material" for inner sense.) For if the very succession of which I am intuitively aware without that backward glance turns out to be an instance of succession in perceptual objects, then how indeed *could* I apprehend, in such cases, the succession of my own states of consciousness? I would have to bend over backwards precisely in order to become aware of the flow of my own inner life. In that case we would still need to face at least one of our original problems. Namely, how can we avoid supposing that the temporal flow of inner sense is the flow of consciousness as it is *in itself* and not merely as it is manifest phenomenally? For Kant is emphatic in maintaining that the succession apprehended in inner sense pertains only to objects that appear to a "subject" that is *not* thereby apprehended and not subject to the conditions of such succession:

> If we abstract from *our* mode of inwardly intuiting ourselves—*the mode of intuition in terms of which we likewise take up into our faculty of representations all outer intuitions* [emphasis added]—and so take objects as they may be in themselves, then time is nothing. It has objective validity only in respect of appearances, these being things which we take *as objects of our senses.* (A34/B51; cf. A35–36/B52)

This point is accommodated, on the account I have suggested, insofar as our awareness of the flow of empirical consciousness simply is our intuitive awareness of succession with respect to intuitively apprehended spatial forms (in abstraction, of course, from their identification as realities).

Now this might appear to imply precisely the subjectivism I claim to reject. That the succession intuitively apprehended in the objects of outer intuition is really only a succession within empirical consciousness might seem to imply that the *objects* of outer intuition are entities internal to that consciousness, hence merely subjective entities. What we need to remember, however, is that the level with respect to which Kant regards us as intuitively aware of succession in the objects of outer intuition is a level at which he is still abstracting from the identification of those objects as any kind of reality. It is a level, that is, on which we are dealing with pure intentional objects. So to say that an instance of succession is apprehended with respect to such objects is not at all to say that what is intuitively apprehended is a succession of *entities*, not to mention mental ones. There is no contradiction, accordingly, in taking any succession thereby apprehended precisely as defining an instance of succession within empirical consciousness itself. What we need to remember is simply that the reality of *empirical consciousness* is no less defined by structures governing the conceptualizability of pure intentional objects than is the world of material objects identified as the objects *of* that consciousness.

Unfortunately, it might be urged, this now threatens to undercut my original comparison between inner and outer sense as the apprehension of intentional objects. In the case of outer sense, this did not imply merely that any intuited region of space is as such ontologically neutral with respect to reality "in itself." It also implied that any such object is ontologically neutral with respect to empirical or *phenomenal* reality: it might or might not turn out to be a portion of empirically determinable space. The parallel with time may now appear lost, inasmuch as any instance of intuited succession is ipso facto a real instance of the flow of empirical consciousness. However, I have not quite committed Kant to supposing that instances of intuited succession are *as such* constitutive of real succession within empirical consciousness. The most I have committed him to is that any instance of intuited succession apprehended by me, or by any other empirically *real person*, must also be a real succession within empirical consciousness. This is compatible with maintaining that, with respect to nothing more than its intrinsic intuitional character, it is precisely not yet made out whether or not a representational state is a portion of anybody's empirical consciousness. It is also compatible with an additional claim that Kant makes in the Transcendental Deduction, namely that the *conceptualizability* of any representational state is at the same time its containability within some person's consciousness: "The abiding and unchanging 'I' (pure apperception) forms the correlate of all our representations in so far as it is to be at all possible that we should become conscious of them" (A123). It is Kant's view that consciousness, in the full sense, requires the conceptualization of intuitions, and this presupposes the possibility of connecting the latter with other intuitions into a single person's consciousness. Both of these claims are compatible with insisting, as Kant does, that such connections are not given in the bare intuitional character of an intuition as such. Perhaps that leaves it as a logical possibility that there be intuitions that are not thus connected. Kant, as we have seen, appears ambivalent with respect to this point. Or perhaps we only need to say that, apart from such connection, we would be left with representational states that *would* be intuitions were they thus connected. In any event, we would seem to be left with something like Leibniz's unconscious "perceptions." Kant, as noted earlier, displays in fact a certain tolerance with respect to that motion.

I want to proceed, in the next section, to relate these remarks to Kant's distinction between the self as it is "in itself" and the self as an object of possible intuition, and particularly to his claims concerning the nontemporality of the former. Before doing so, let me conclude the present section by summarizing our general situation so far. The crux of Kant's doctrine, I have argued, is that self-awareness through inner sense is simply awareness of the flow of our own conscious life as manifested in the flow of the objects of outer sensibility, qua pure intentional objects. Conceptualization of such objects in terms of our concepts of material reality may thus be said to involve the "determination" of inner sense by reference to outer perception. As we shall see in the next section, the second-edition Refutation of Idealism is concerned with asserting precisely the necessity of such determination, though this necessity is also perfectly compatible, for any *given* object, with abstracting from questions concerning the reality of that object. (We cannot of course abstract from questions concerning the reality of the *stretch of time* that we are thereby apprehending.) Thus when dealing with the objects of inner sense one is not dealing with a domain of objects distinct from the realities outside of ourselves. In most cases the objects of inner sense are in fact realities existing in space; it is simply that we abstract from that reality when we are concerned with inner sense. That is part of what it means to say that we are then concerned only with "inner" sense.

Strictly speaking, one of the "objects" of inner sense is not the sort of thing that could be a reality existing in the space outside our own consciousness. This arises in the case in which we focus on the very *flow* of intentional objects in inner sense. Those objects might or might not, in any instance, be realities outside of us, but their intuited flow is never anything outside of us. The temporal properties of objects perceived in space are never themselves perceived. That is something about which we can only judge on the *basis* of what we perceive. This may appear to conflict with Kant's aim of overcoming doctrines that place a "curtain of ideas" between consciousness and realities in space. And to a certain extent this is so. But Kant, I have argued, is forced to the position precisely because it is the only one allowing both for a properly intuitive apprehension of the flow of one's own consciousness and also for an avoidance of doctrines based only on metaphor. It is in any case important to remember that the position in question is perfectly compatible with granting that we perceive bodies in space, and many of their properties, even if it forces us to deny that we perceive the *temporal* properties of those bodies.

Now I have said that part of what we mean in speaking of "inner" sense is that we are considering the intentional objects of outer awareness purely *as* intentional objects. But there is more to it than that. This, as I suggested earlier, has to do with our ability to regard such objects as "reflections" of our own internal qualities—qualities of which, in themselves, we never can be intuitively aware, but only insofar as they are thus reflected. In some areas we have already seen how this is so. The matter and form of outer objects, qua immediately apprehended, is a reflection of certain, otherwise inapprehensible factors within our own cognitive state, namely sensations and the forms of intuition. In addition we have noted that, from the phenomenological point of view, one's *conceptual enrichment* of intuition is also reflected in the objects of that intuition. We are never intuitively aware of a concept as such, but we are intuitively aware of concepts at least insofar as they are "reflected" in the very objects of our own intentional activity, qua intentional.

It may seem that there must be more than this to the inner awareness of our own conceptual activities, and as we shall see later Kant does not deny this. In any case, it might appear that Kant is in an even less tenable position with respect to certain other items of obvious inner awareness. These are the items that we left in abeyance earlier, namely feelings and acts of the will. The latters' character as acts of "spontaneity" would of course place them alongside other instances of conceptual activity. So the situation in their regard would perhaps be as follows. As we shall see, Kant admits that there is an awareness of conceptual activity that is not exhausted by our intuitions of its "reflection" in outer objects. This, however, is a purely intellectual awareness, and not a matter of intuition at all. It is presumably in the same way, then, that we must be aware of our own acts of will. Whether Kant's account of that awareness is acceptable of course remains undecided. But it is at least reasonable to suppose that the issues in question do not differ from those involved in the awareness of any ordinary judgment, and Kant, as I have indicated, is prepared to concede that a complete account of the latter cannot be provided wholly by appeal to inner sense. The status of "feelings" is rather different. This is because the only indication that Kant provides of a self-awareness that transcends inner intuition relates to the possibility of an awareness of our own spontaneous acts, and feelings are not spontaneous acts.

In a certain way the problem of feeling is insoluble within the terms that Kant lays down. But in another respect I think Kant himself has indicated its solution. The problem remains if we refuse to acknowledge a correspondence between an intentional object and our feelings in regard to it that is analogous to the way in which an object's perceived "material" corresponds to our sensations in perceiving it. To be sure, Kant is consistent in denying that no *material* in the composition of an object corresponds to our feelings in regard to it.[21] Accordingly, nothing that might correspond to our feelings in regard to some object could constitute an element bearing on our judgments concerning its reality. However, this is consistent with conceding that something in an object always corresponds to our feelings in regard to it. The claims are compatible, at least, so long as we are abstracting from the reality of apprehended objects and considering them purely as intentional objects.

Now except for one sort of case, Kant would definitely refuse to grant the sort of correspondence I have suggested. For excluding that one exception, Kant clearly regards the connection between the representation of an object and our feelings in regard to it as a purely causal connection. The feelings in question do not enter into the representation of the object, but are at most produced by it, or by certain of our thoughts about it. Such cases, for Kant, are those in which one has feelings involving *desire* for an object, which of course are always cases in which the reality of the object is a relevant consideration. Kant sharply distinguishes them from cases in which one experiences feelings that are connected with purely aesthetic appreciation. Here one's feelings relate to an object purely as apprehended and in abstraction from questions concerning its material reality. It can be argued that even in these cases one's feelings are merely causally connected with the representation of an object. What is special about such feelings, one might claim, is simply the operative causality. It is Kant's view that the feelings in question involve an apprehension of an especially fitting "harmony" of perceived sensory form in relation to the possibility of its conceptualization. One might argue, then, that what characterizes a purely aesthetic pleasure is simply that such a harmony is its cause. There would then be no ground for supposing that the term 'harmony', in these cases, expresses a feature that is actually apprehended in an object, over and above its intuitional form and sensory material. There would be no ground for supposing, that is, that there are special aesthetic qualities connected with our perception of the (natural) beauty of objects.[22]

I think it can be argued that the contrary view is more in keeping with the direction of Kant's thought in his analysis of aesthetic judgment. Since I have argued the point at some length elsewhere,[23] I shall not do so here. I would, however, note that if Kant's view is in fact such as suggested, we ought nonetheless not be surprised that he does not present it in as clear a fashion as possible. As I have argued, it was already an accomplishment on Kant's part to recognize the immediate objects of perceptual apprehension as intentional objects containing an aspect corresponding to a person's sensations. This is because the perspective required for this recognition, namely the intentional or phenomenological perspective, makes it extremely difficult to find a terminology appropriate for designating the aspect in question. Kant of course describes it as the "material" of an object. But that term is likely to suggest the presence of some material *reality*, and so it cannot be wholly adequate. The term that we need should be one that is neutral with the regard to the existence of a perceived reality corresponding to someone's sensations. Precisely this fact, as I have suggested, accounts for Kant's tendency to employ an equally misleading term, namely 'sensation' itself. But now we are called upon to go even beyond those aspects of objects that we are naturally tempted to identify with material reality (and not merely with the *possibility* of judgments concerning such reality). This requires adherence to a perspective that might be difficult to maintain, namely one that totally abstracts from concern with the reality of an apprehended object and concentrates only on objects as they are intended by the consciousness of them. It requires, that is, suspension of what Husserl has called the "natural" standpoint.[24] In any case, once we distinguish internal states from aspects of intentional objects that nevertheless "reflect" them, then there can be no a priori reason why "mere" feelings, in addition to sensations proper, should not be thus reflected, at least in those cases where they are more than merely externally connected with the representation of an object. But to "see" the reflection one of course needs to abstract from features relevant to our judgments concerning the mind-independent reality of an object.

Granting this point of view with respect to purely aesthetic feeling still leaves the problem of all other sorts of feelings. For it is only with respect to the former that Kant at least comes close to recognizing the phenomenon of intentional "correspondence" or "reflection." However, as feelings they all seem equally accessible to inner awareness. With respect to this difficulty, I can only conclude with the observation that what I have suggested is the Kantian insight has in fact been extended by certain other thinkers. This has been done by Edmund Husserl, for example, whose phenomenological approach dictates that corresponding to *all* dimensions of judgment and attitude in an intentional state will be phenomenologically descriminable aspects of its object qua intentional.[25]

III. Transcendental and Empirical Consciousness

Through inner sense, Kant maintains, we are not aware of the self as it is "in itself," but only as it appears. Furthermore, the temporal forms that apply in the latter context do not apply to the self as it is in itself. Now it would no doubt be absurd to suppose that the succession of intentional objects apprehended by ourselves is not at least the phenomenological correlate of a sequence of cognitive states of a subject that is as real in itself as anything could possibly be, and hence really endures through time. So Kant probably did not mean to deny this. But he might nevertheless have supposed that the cognitive states of the subject in question do not endure through the stretches of time that are apprehended by them in the same *sense* that empirically identifiable individuals do. I want to examine how this might be so. Naturally, we are also required to examine precisely how we are able to be aware, if at all, of a nonempirical subject in the first place.

So far, all we can say about a nonempirical subject—if there be such—is that it comes to be, or perhaps even determines itself to be, in various states whose intentional objects are those stretches of intuited time the apprehension of which I ascribe to myself as stretches of my own empirical consciousness. This is compatible with supposing that, considered by itself, the "identity" of the subject in question is an unsteady one:

> . . . we can conceive a whole series of substances of which the first transmits its state together with its consciousness to the second, the second its own state with that of the preceding substance to the third. . . . The last substance would then be conscious of all the states of the previously changed substances, as being its own states, because they would have been transferred to it together with the consciousness of them. (A363)

To be sure, Kant then concludes that this last substance "would not have been one and the same person" as those earlier in question. But the context makes it clear that the sense in which it would not be the same is perfectly compatible with whatever *unity of empirical consciousness* grounds our ordinary judgments of self-identity. Along the lines so far pursued, what this would appear to mean is that the succession of intentional *objects* apprehended within the stretches of time in question continue to be interrelated within, i.e. to "reflect," a single empirical consciousness.

The integrability of a succession of intentional objects into a single life-history is of course only a necessary condition for an empirical unity of consciousness. The additional requirement is what Kant indicates in the passage just quoted. *Consciousness* of any later member of that life history must also include a *consciousness* of the earlier members, and of their relation to the later. (Presumably, details can be introduced allowing for gaps of various sorts.) It is obvious, I think, that along the lines of the sort of interpretation that I have been offering, once we are talking not simply about intentional objects but about the consciousness *of* them, we are talking about items that must be, in as proper a sense as one could find, "states" of a nonempirical subject of consciousness, and I think that Kant is committed to this. But the point remains that there is still no intuitive *apprehension* of any of those states for Kant. That is to say, none of them are representations that "turn back on themselves." Instead, intuitive awareness of one's own states of consciousness is nothing more than intuitive awareness of successions of intentional objects and of their integrability into a whole with others that are themselves no longer intuited (or if never in fact intuited, are represented as intuitable). Insofar as the objects in question "reflect" the consciousness of them, and only to that extent, is one intuitively aware of that consciousness itself.

Now by supposition any intuitional consciousness will possess both the internal form of an intuition and whatever conceptual elements are involved in the recognition of the region of space or stretch of time that is apprehended by it. It is not necessary, as we have seen, that every region of space that is intuitively apprehended be conceptualized as a region of real space, to say nothing of a region that is really occupied by some portion of matter. But insofar as we are now considering instances of *consciousness*, in the fullest sense, it must at least be the case that the stretches of time in question are conceptualized as empirically real, namely as real portions of some person's empirical consciousness. At the very least, then, Kant demands that, as he puts it, the "I think" must be able to accompany all those intuitions that are in fact mine (B131–140). These concepts must of course suffice precisely for the conceptualization of the various intuitions in question as interrelated within a single empirically determinable system of times. Without such concepts, those items would not comprise a sequence of stretches of any one's consciousness. And then of course it becomes problematic to what extent they could be regarded as consciously apprehended at all. Like Leibniz's unconscious perceptions, they would at least be inaccessible to any form of *self*-consciousness, i.e., to what both Kant and Leibniz refer to as "apperception."

What Kant calls the "transcendental unity of apperception" appears to be the general form of order involved in the possibility of conceptualizing any intuition as relating to others within a single empirical consciousness:

> This transcendental unity of apperception forms out of all possible appearances, which can stand alongside one another in one experience, a connection of all these representations according to laws. For this unity of consciousness would be impossible if the mind in knowledge of the manifold could not become conscious of the identity of function whereby it synthetically combines it in one knowledge. The original and necessary consciousness of the identity of the self is thus at the same time a consciousness of an equally necessary unity of the synthesis of all appearances according to concepts . . . . For the mind could never think its identity in the manifoldness of its representations, and indeed think this identity a priori, if it did not have before its eyes the identity of its act, whereby it subordinates all synthesis of apprehension (which is empirical) to a transcendental unity, thereby rendering possible their interconnection according to *a priori* rules. (A108; cf. B133–134)

The key to Kant's Transcendental Deduction is the claim, in turn, that this unity, necessary for the self-ascribability of experiences, at the same time requires conceptualization of one's experiences in terms of the concept of a (possible) *object* of experience:

> The original and necessary consciousness of the identity of the self is thus at the same time a consciousness of an equally necessary unity of the synthesis of all appearances according to concepts, that is, according to rules, which not only make them necessarily reproducible but also in so doing determine an object for their intuition, that is, the concept of something wherein they are necessarily interconnected. (A108)

Thus the transcendental unity of apperception is correlative, in the first edition Deduction, with the concept of the "transcendental object" of one's intuitions. The second edition Deduction makes the same point, but without the use of the latter terminology: "The transcendental unity of apperception is that unity through which all the manifold given in an intuition is united in a concept of the object" (B139). As we have seen, conceptualizing a given intuition as one of my own at least requires conceptualizing it as an intuition of an empirically real stretch of time, namely one occupied by myself. The Transcendental Deduction demands more than this, insofar as it also demands conceptual acts involving the concept of an objective reality *apart* from oneself. This point is also presented in the Refutation of Idealism added in the second edition. I shall not undertake an analysis of these claims.[26] I would simply note that, whatever Kant has in mind by them, it is compatible with conceding that the intentional object of any *given* intuition might not itself be a reality apart from oneself:

> From the fact that the existence of outer things is required for the possibility of a determinate consciousness of the self, it does not follow that every intuitive representation of outer things involves the existence of these things, for their representation can very well be the product merely of the imagination (as in dreams and delusions). . . . All that we have here sought to prove is that inner experience in general is possible only through outer experience in general. (B278)

In addition to speaking of a transcendental unity of apperception, Kant also speaks of a transcendental apperception *simpliciter*, distinguishing it from the "empirical" apperception that he equates with inner sense (cf. A107). Kant also contrasts the latter with "pure" or "original" apperception (B132; cf. B153) and in the *Anthropology* (Pt. I, § 4), as we have seen, with an apperception "of the understanding." This is an important point. It might be tempting to suppose that Kant's doctrine of transcendental apperception simply refers to the fact that there are necessary conditions of empirical self-consciousness. In that case, we do not need to distinguish between two *kinds* of self-consciousness, not to mention between two kinds of *self* of which we are conscious. All we would need to deal with are the general forms or structures required for ordinary, everyday empirical consciousness. Thus the term 'transcendental' would not point to the possibility of apprehending anything other than ordinary empirical objects, including ourselves qua empirical object. It would only point to the general *form* of our apprehension of such objects. But the truth is that Kant himself supposes that there is more to it than that, and this, I think, is just as we should expect. What Kant calls "empirical apperception," or "inner sense," is the awareness of oneself insofar as one is aware of particular stretches of intuited time "synthesizable" together with others into the right sort of whole. One can of course speak of the general "forms" of the synthesis or syntheses in question, and Kant attempts to do this in terms of his doctrine of the "categories." But precisely what we need to remember is that all such syntheses relate to possible objects of consciousness. What about the consciousness *of* them? As we have seen, we are aware of it empirically only insofar as it is reflected in those very objects. But precisely because this cannot be the only way in which we are aware of it, Kant is forced to speak not simply of a transcendental (i.e., necessary) unity of self-consciousness, but of a transcendental self-*consciousness*, that is of a "pure" kind of self-consciousness that is totally "original" and hence not explicable, but necessarily presupposed, by all appeals to empirical consciousness itself.

The reason that Kant needs to appeal to a nonempirical self-consciousness is very simple. It lies in the fact that empirical intuition, even in inner sense, never yields an awareness of mental *activity*, but only of certain *objects* of such activity. Any being that is capable of ascribing experiences to itself must obviously be in some way aware not simply of the objects that are presented to its own conscious activity, but of various instances of that activity itself. In that case, however, the kind of awareness in question could not be by means of inner intuition. Kant himself draws the only possible conclusion from this. The kind of awareness in question must not be intuitive at all, but purely conceptual:

> On the other hand, in the transcendental synthesis of the manifold of representations in general, and therefore in the synthetic orginal unity of apperception, I am conscious of myself, not as I appear to myself, nor as I am in myself, but only that I am. This *representation* is a *thought*, not an *intuition*. (B157)

In this passage Kant speaks not of a transcendental apperception, but of a unity *of* apperception. This may suggest that he does not mean to speak of an awareness that refers to something other than an empirically definable self. In that case, one might argue, when Kant speaks of a transcendental "representation" of the self, all he really means to do is speak about the general *form* of, or the necessary *conditions* for, the representation of an empirically definable person. This might appear to be confirmed by Kant's further contention that the intellectual factors operative in "transcendental" self-consciousness will indeed yield determinate knowledge of the empirically identifiable self just as soon as they are combined with empirical intuition:

> Certainly, the representation 'I am', which expresses the consciousness that can accompany all thought, immediately includes in itself the existence of a subject; but it does not so include any *knowledge* of that subject, and therefore also no empirical knowledge, that is, no experience of it. For this we require, in addition to the thought of something existing, also intuition, and in this case inner intuition, in respect of which, that is, of time, the subject must be determined. (B277; cf. B157)

A similar point might seem to be conveyed by the following claim concerning the transcendental representation "I think":

> All the manifold of intuition has, therefore, a necessary relation to the 'I think' in the same subject in which this manifold is found. But this representation is an act of *spontaneity*, that is, it cannot be regarded as belonging to sensibility. I call it *pure apperception*, to distinguish it from empirical apperception, or, again, *original apperception*, because it is that self-consciousness which, while generating the representation '*I think*' (a representation which must be capable of accompanying all other representations, and which in all consciousness is one and the same), cannot itself be accompanied by any further representation. (B132)

All these passages may seem to imply that transcendental self-consciousness is at most an indeterminate sort of awareness of the existence of the empirical subject, if it is a genuine sort of awareness at all, and an awareness that is simply to be made more concrete in combination with actual intuition. Or more likely, transcendental self-consciousness is really not any sort of awareness at all; the term in question simply refers to the general form of, or conditions for, any possible empirical self-consciousness.

However, other things that Kant says seem to imply something much stronger. They imply that transcendental self-consciousness is not merely a kind of intellectual function which, when applied to intuition, yields concrete awareness of an empirically identifiable individual. For even in abstraction from such further determinations, transcendental self-consciousness involves an awareness of a spontaneous power of cognitive *activity* that is never presented in intuition of either the outer or the inner sort. When the functions of transcendental apperception are applied, as they must be, to the concrete content of intuitions, they serve to unify those intuitions by means of the concept of a single person's experience. This of course requires application of the "synthetizing" activities of the understanding. According to Kant, there is some sense in which we are actually *aware* of those activities:

> This transcendental unity of apperception forms out of all possible appearances, which can stand alongside one another in one experience, a connection of all these representations according to laws. For this unity of consciousness would be impossible if the mind in knowledge of the manifold could not become *conscious of the identity of function* whereby it synthetically combines it in one knowledge. The original and necessary consciousness of the identity of the self is thus at the same time a consciousness of an equally necessary unity of the synthesis of all appearances according to concepts . . . For the mind could never think its identity in the manifoldness of its representations, and indeed think this identity *a priori*, if it did not have before its eyes the *identity of its act*. . . . (A108; emphasis added)

> [The understanding's] synthesis, therefore, if the synthesis be viewed by itself alone, is nothing but the unity of the act, *of which, as an act, it is conscious to itself* [emphasis added], even without sensibility, but through which it is yet able to determine the sensibility. . . . Thus the understanding, under the title of a *transcendental synthesis of imagination*, performs this act upon the *passive* subject, whose *faculty* it is, and we are therefore justified in saying that inner sense is affected thereby. Apperception and its synthetic unity is, indeed, very far from being identical with inner sense. (B153–154)

The same point is made in the earlier quoted passage from the *Anthropology* (Pt. I, § 4).

The passages imply that we are aware of our own mental activity in some way that transcends its mere "reflection" in the intentional objects of that activity. As we have seen, this implies for Kant that the awareness in question could not be intuitive, though it needs, as he also insists, to be brought into relation with intuition in order to constitute awareness of an individual person, qua individual. In abstraction from that relation the awareness in question is of a purely general sort. As Kant puts it in a passage quoted earlier, it is an awareness *that there is* a subject whose nature transcends its determination by empirical intuition. It does not, apart from the determination introduced by the latter, actually *refer* to any such subject.[27] This distinction is precisely like that between the awareness "of" an ordinary material reality, in the sense that there is awareness *that there is* a certain sort of instance of it, and awareness that is directly of some particular instance *of* that sort. The difference lies in Kant's concession that there can also be such awareness, of the general sort, of the existence of something that is not an empirical reality at all, i.e., of something that is "intuitable" neither in inner nor in outer perception. As for the nature of the awareness in question, Kant does not provide an account, except insofar as he says that it is a purely intellectual matter. That by itself is compatible with maintaining that there is no more to it than the subject's pre-"programmed" ability to form certain accurate sorts of *judgments* about its own mental acts when they occur. If Kant thinks there is more to it than this, he offers no account of what might be involved. Certainly, no appeal to some prior "intuition" of the acts in question could be offered as part of that account.[28]

It follows that, while Kant acknowledges a nonempirical "awareness" of acts of consciousness, he cannot consistently acknowledge such an awareness of particular *instances* of any such activity, except insofar as the particularization in question can be defined, or "determined," empirically:

> The 'I think' expresses the act of determining my existence. Existence is already given thereby, but the mode in which I am to determine this existence, that is, the manifold belonging to it, is not thereby given. . . . Now since I do not have another [nonempirical] self-intuition which gives the *determining* in me (I am conscious only of the spontaneity of it) prior to the act of *determination*, as time does in the case of the determinable, I cannot determine my existence as that of a self-active being; all that I can do is to represent to myself the spontaneity of my thought, that is, of the determination; and my existence is still only determinable sensibly, that is, as the existence of an appearance. But it is owing to this spontaneity that I entitle myself an *intelligence*. (B157, note)

This would appear to imply that, in abstraction from inner intuition, we are at most aware *that there are* instances of spontaneously creative activity responsible for the conceptualization, or the "determination," of whatever stretches of intuited time present themselves as portions of our own empirical consciousness. It is only by reference to such intuitions, on the other hand, that the awareness in question could be supposed to be the awareness of the activity *of* some particular person and ascribable *to* that person. It is only by reference to that activity's "reflection" in the intuitions in question that it is representable not simply as the activity of a subject, but as *my* activity.

I have given some reason, then, to suppose that there must be a subject of consciousness, for Kant, of which we can have no empirical awareness as such. We do have a kind of *non*empirical awareness of it, but it is of a purely general sort, and when we attempt to proceed from generalities to specifics, we merely succeed in capturing its "reflection" in the intentional objects of its own consciousness. In that sense the self is necessarily "transcendental" for Kant. I want to conclude this chapter, then, with a final reflection regarding this self. This concerns Kant's claim that the empirical "forms" of temporal reality do not apply to the entity in question.

As I suggested earlier, Kant's claims about the nontemporality of the self "in itself" would seem to make little sense if taken to deny that its conscious states form a temporal sequence. But Kant might not have meant to deny this. Instead he might simply have meant to insist that, in whatever *sense* the states in question might form a temporal sequence, it could not be in virtue of occupying any of the stretches of time that are presentable in inner intuition. This of course is much stronger than the claim that those states, as opposed to their mere "reflection," are not themselves present-able in inner intuition. It is the claim that those states, when they are considered as anything more than such reflection, cannot even be sup-posed to *occupy the stretches of time* that are presented in inner intuition. Making this distinction requires us to be clear, of course, that stretches of time, and not simply possible occupants of them, are indeed presented as intentional objects in inner intuition.

It is not difficult to surmise, it seems to me, how Kant might have been led to such a conclusion. We have seen that the stretches of time apprehended in inner sense are intentional objects that, just as such, might or might not be accorded empirical reality but, insofar as the awareness of them is representable as ascribable to any particular *subject* of conscious-ness, must in fact be accorded such reality. They must, that is, be concep-tualized as stretches of time actually occupied by the subject in question, at least qua empirically real. But what could it possibly mean to accord an intuited stretch of time an empirical reality? Kant's position on this ques-tion is bound to run parallel to the position that he was forced to adopt with respect to the ontological status of intuited regions of space. Intuited regions of space, being intentional objects of consciousness, are simply not the sorts of things whose qualification as empirical reality could be a function of their construability as realities "in themselves." As intentional objects, they can at most be such that the apprehension *of* them is pro-duced, at least partly, in virtue of some affection by things that exist in themselves. They themselves cannot literally be such things. If they were, we would have to regard the distinction between merely intentional and genuine empirical reality as a distinction between two statuses ascribable to one and the same item, an intuited region of space. But that would require regarding an intuited region of space, purely qua intuited, as indeed an item in its own right, over and above the apprehension of it. That would contradict our supposition that, purely qua intuited, a region of space is a merely *intentional* "item." Accordingly, as I argued earlier, the reality of regions of space, and of any material that occupies them (insofar as the latter is itself empirically identifiable), can lie in nothing other than the satisfaction of appropriate conditions by the *apprehension* of such items—conditions which, in that case, must concern more than the internal constitution of any given apprehension and hence its connectability with other *possible* apprehensions, in accordance with the general "categorial" criteria for such connectability.

Kant, I suggest, reasoned in a parallel fashion with respect to intuited stretches of time. How could we ever suppose that such items are real in themselves? Their reality can be at most of the sort that lies in their conceptualizability as related to *other* intuitions. Of course, in another sense, their reality might be regarded as lying simply in the fact that they are intentional correlates of acts of consciousness that, in *their* turn, are real "in themselves." But that must be a secondary sense, with respect to our ordinary empirical judgments. For on Kant's view it is impossible to refer to the occurrence of acts of consciousness, unless in a purely general way, except insofar as we have *already* conceptualized certain intuited stretches of time as empirically real. So the conclusion is unavoidable: no intuited stretch of time, qua empirical reality, is real in itself. From this it would appear to follow that no intuited stretch of time could literally be *occupied* by an act of consciousness ascribable to the "transcendental" subject. Or if you will, such acts can occupy those stretches of time only in the sense that they are reflected in those stretches as intentional objects. That of course is quite different from the sense in which empirically identifiable objects might be regarded as occupying those same stretches of time. As for the latter sort of occupancy, we might then inquire what it could possibly involve. It is difficult to see what this could amount to for Kant without going outside the realm of inner sense entirely, since in that realm no enduring being is discovered. Having thus also excluded the self "in itself," we seem to have no option but to conclude that the self that occupies any stretch of time that is also occupable by its own states of consciousness must (whatever we say about those states themselves) also occupy space:

> Thus the permanence of the soul, regarded merely as object of inner sense, remains undemonstrated, and indeed indemonstrable. Its permanence during life is, of course, evident *per se*, since the thinking being (as man) is itself likewise an object of the outer senses. (B415)

It follows that, in a certain sense, there are two "subjects" of consciousness. There is the empirically identifiable person that occupies regions of space. We ascribe certain states of consciousness to this subject, namely all those that are "reflected" in the intuited stretches of time that it is also judged to occupy. (Of course, it may also be judged to occupy stretches of time that are not in fact intuited.) Kant does not make it clear in precisely what sense such "ascription" is to be taken. But in any case it must be in a different sense from that in which those same states of consciousness are ascribable to the "transcendental" subject of which we have no intuitive awareness. Does that mean that there are two *me*'s? Yes and no. At least we need to remember that the transcendental "me" is me precisely only *because* its consciousness is reflected in those stretches of intuited time that are conceptualizable as occupied by myself as an empirically identifiable subject. Apart from the latter possibility, in whatever sense such consciousness might be thought to belong to the subject in question, they would not be ascribable to me. Perhaps the most fitting conclusion, then, amounts to a conversion of my earlier point concerning noumenal and phenomenal "persons" with regard to Kant's ethical theory. A phenomenal person, I maintained, is really a kind of logical composite of an empirically identifiable object (a body that manifests certain behaviors) and a noumenal subject. Now it appears we need to conclude that any such noumenal "subject" must also be a kind of logical composite. For it *is* such a subject only to the extent that its consciousness is in turn reflected in empirically determinable phenomena. Where that leaves angels and disembodied souls remains a mystery.

Notes

1. The Background of Kant's Representationalism

1. References to the *Critique of Pure Reason* will appear in standard form, in the Norman Kemp Smith translation, occasionally revised.

2. Cf. Gerold Prauss's claim that "only within the framework of such a theory [as Kant's] does it become explicable . . . that experience can not only be, as interpretation [*Erdeutung*], a success, but rather also as misinterpretation a failure": *Kant und das Problem der Dinge an sich* (Bonn: Bouvier Verlag Herbert Grundmann, 1974), p. 66. With respect to the historical analyses of this chapter, note also Prauss's claim that prior to Kant, and since Plato and Aristotle, adherence to a conception of knowledge as a "receptive copying" (*rezeptives Abbilden*) of objects has prevented recognition precisely of the fundamental question, namely that concerning the possibility of *false* representation (p. 105). In general, though (see passim and, e.g., pp. 105ff.), Prauss formulates the problem in terms of true and false *judgments*, placing the entire burden of representational content on the latter. I attempt to accord a more central role to the representational forms of the *sensibility* that underlies judgment.

3. St. Thomas Aquinas, *Summa Theologica*, I, Q78, A3, ans., trans. Anton C. Pegis, *Basic Writings of St. Thomas Aquinas* (New York: Random House, 1945). For relevant passages in Aristotle, see *De Anima* 424a15ff.; 425b20ff.; 429a10–432a10.

4. Ibid. Q84, A2, ans. It can be argued that, at least with respect to the reception of sensible form, St. Thomas's talk about "immateriality" is not meant to exclude a purely physicalistic interpretation. See Sheldon M. Cohen, "St. Thomas Aquinas on the Immaterial Reception of Sensible Forms," *Philosophical Review*, XCI (1982): 193–209.

5. Ibid., Q84, Aa. 6–7; Q85, A1.

6. Ibid., Q84, A3, ans.

7. Descartes, "Replies to Objections V," *Philosophical Works*, trans. Elizabeth S. Haldane and G.R.T. Ross (London: Cambridge University Press, 1934), II, p. 231.

8. Ibid.

9. Descartes, "Dioptric," *Philosophical Writings*, trans. Norman Kemp Smith (New York: Random House, 1958), p. 146. See also pp. 146–147 and "Rules for the Direction of the Mind," *Works*, I, pp. 37ff.

10. First passage: "Dioptric," *Writings*, p. 145. Second passage: "Replies VI," *Works*, II, p. 251.

11. Kant, *On the Form and Principles of the Sensible and Intelligible World*, trans. G. B. Kerferd, *Selected Pre-Critical Writings* (New York: Barnes & Noble, 1968), II, 4–6 (*Ak.* II, pp. 392–394). References in the latter form will, throughout

this book, be to volumes of the Prussian, later German, Academy edition of Kant's works.

12. Ibid., II, 3 (*Ak.* II, p. 392).

13. Ibid., II, 4 (*Ak.* II, p. 392).

14. Ibid., II, 4 (*Ak.* II, pp. 392–393), restoring Latin *species* for the translation.

15. Kant, *Prolegomena to Any Future Metaphysics*, trans. Lewis White Beck (Indianapolis: Bobbs-Merrill, 1950), I, 9 (*Ak.* IV, p. 282).

16. St. Thomas Aquinas, *De Veritate*, 2, 3, 9, trans. Ausonio Marras in "Scholastic Roots of Brentano's Conception of Intentionality," in Linda L. McAlister, ed., *The Philosophy of Brentano* (Atlantic Highlands, N.J.: Humanities Press, 1976), p. 134.

17. St. Thomas, *Summa*, Q85, A2, ans.

18. Ibid., Q17, A3, Reply 1; cf. Q85, A1, Reply 1, Q85, A3, ans., Q85, A6, ans.

19. Ibid., Q85, A1, ans.

20. Cf. Ibid., Q85, A2, Reply 2.

21. Ibid., Q86, A1, ans.

22. The difference between the phantasm and the forms abstracted by intellect, of course, is that the former also contains features irrelevant to the *essence* of the thing in question. Cf. ibid., Q85, A1.

23. Cf. Anthony Kenny, *Descartes* (New York: Random House, 1968), pp. 113–116.

24. Descartes, *Works*, II, p. 254 ("Replies VI").

25. Ibid., pp. 367–368 ("Replies III").

26. Ibid., pp. 105–107 ("Replies IV").

27. Ibid., I, p. 248 ("Principles," I, 69).

28. It is important not to conflate the distinction between sensations and other ideas with that between ideas that are less or more "adequate." For the ideas that we have *of* sensations, when contemplating them—when, for example, I think about red, but don't actually see it—might also be, and usually are, "confused." Cf. *Principles*, I, 46 and 66. Descartes himself seems not always to keep the distinction between sensations and ideas *of* them clear: cf. *Works*, II, pp. 106–107 ("Replies IV").

29. Ibid., II, p. 252 ("Replies VI").

30. If this is so, then "sensation"—in the sense of immediate awareness of (and not just thought about) colored *shapes*—is indeed, as for Leibniz, a kind of "confused" *intellection* (cf. *Works*, I, p. 192: "Meditation VI"). But it isn't clear, I think, that this is Descartes's considered view, since most of his talk about the confusion involved in sensation concerns only the inadequate intellectual ideas we have *of* sensations. Descartes's failure to distinguish the sense of 'idea of extension' that applies to merely *seeing* some shape from the sense in question when one merely thinks about and *understands* what one sees contributes of course to the unclarity.

31. Ibid., p. 52 ("Definitions" following "Replies II").

32. Ibid., p. 105 ("Replies IV").

33. Ibid., p. 52 ("Definitions").

34. Ibid., I, p. 138 (Preface to "Meditations").

35. Ibid., II, p. 10 ("Replies I").

36. Ibid., p. 53 ("Definitions").

37. Ibid., p. 107 ("Replies IV").

38. Unlike the Scholastics, too, Descartes had a special problem concerning the "connection" between images produced in the brain and the "ideas" that the mind "derives" from them. At best the relation is *causal* for Descartes, but it is difficult to

see how a state of the brain could causally *determine* the mind to act in a certain way. So he concludes that the causal stimulation at most provides an "occasion" for the mind to act. This, as he grants, seems to threaten the whole notion of an idea "derived from" experience. Ibid., I, p. 443 ("Notes Against a Programme"). For the Scholastic, the action in question was never of the material organ (containing the phantasm) *on* the intellect in the first place, but rather one of the latter "turning to" the former. Descartes presumably could make no sense of this notion, except insofar as it *was* taken causally.

39. Some of the points in this section are also argued by John W. Yolton, "Ideas and Knowledge in Seventeenth-Century Philosophy," *Journal of the History of Philosophy*, XIII (April 1975): 145–165. Cf. also Brian E. O'Neil, *Epistemological Direct Realism in Descartes's Philosophy* (Albuquerque: University of New Mexico Press, 1974), Ch. 3; Thomas A. Lennon, "The Inherence Pattern and Descartes's Ideas," *Journal of the History of Philosophy*, XII (Jan. 1974): 43–52; and my *Intentionality: A Study of Mental Acts* (University Park: Pennsylvania State University Press, 1977), Ch. 1.

40. Leibniz, "Correspondence with Arnauld," July 14, 1686; trans. Leroy E. Loemker, *Philosophical Papers and Letters* (New York: Humanities Press, 1970), p. 337.

41. Ibid., pp. 207–208 ("What Is an Idea?").

42. Ibid., p. 339 ("Correspondence with Arnauld," October 9, 1687).

43. Ibid., p. 644 ("Monadology," sec. 17).

44. Ibid., p. 648 ("Monadology," sec. 56–57).

45. Ibid., pp. 493–494 ("Clarification of the Difficulties which Mr. Bayle has Found").

46. Leibniz, p. 457 ("A New System of the Nature and the Communication of Substances," sec. 14).

47. Ibid., p. 609 ("Correspondence with Des Bosses," April 21, 1714).

48. Hide Ishiguro, *Leibniz's Philosophy of Logic and Language* (Ithaca: Cornell University Press, 1972), pp. 98–101. For the contrary view see Nicholas Rescher, *The Philosophy of Leibniz* (Englewood Cliffs, N.J.: Prentice-Hall, 1967), pp. 71ff.

49. Leibniz, p. 268 ("First Truths").

50. Ibid., p. 207 ("What Is an Idea?"); cf. p. 649 ("Monadology," sec. 63).

51. Michelangelo Ghio, "Leibniz e l'espressione," *Filosofia, Nuova serie*, XXXX (July 1979), p. 336.

52. Franz Brentano, *Psychologie vom empirischen Standpunkt*, ed. Oskar Kraus (Hamburg: Felix Meiner, 1924), vol. I, Bk. 2, Ch. 1, sec. 5; translation by D. B. Terrell in Roderick Chisholm, ed., *Realism and the Background of Phenomenology* (Glencoe, Ill.: Free Press, 1960), p. 50. For a discussion of Brentano's relation to the Scholastics, see Herbert Spiegelberg, " 'Intention' and 'Intentionality' in the Scholastics, Brentano and Husserl" and Ausonio Marras, "Scholastic Roots of Brentano's Conception of Intentionality," in McAlister, op. cit.

53. Cf. *Wahrheit und Evidenz*, ed. Oskar Kraus (Leipzig: Felix Meiner, 1930), trans. Roderick Chisholm, *The True and the Evident* (New York: Humanities Press, 1966), p. 78: "I allowed myself the term 'immanent object', in order to say not that the object exists, but that it *is* an object whether or not there is anything that corresponds to it. Its *being* an object, however, is merely the linguistic correlate of the person experiencing *having* it as object, i.e., his thinking of it in his experience."

54. Brentano, *Psychologie*, vol. II, suppl. essay #1.

55. Leibniz, p. 644 ("Monadology," sec. 14).

56. Ibid., p. 557 ("Reflections on the Doctrine of a Single Universal Spirit").

57. Regarding the general comparison with Brentano, one might note the comments of J. N. Findlay, *Kant and the Transcendental Object* (Oxford: Clarendon Press, 1981), pp. 362–363. Findlay suggests that Brentano's *Vorstellungen* are comparable to Kant's intuitions and concepts, as opposed to any "judgments" that might involve them. It would be more fitting, on my own approach, to compare them simply with Kant's intuitions (both pure and empirical), assimilating concepts more closely to those additional factors involved, as we might say, in "judgmentalizing" our intuitions. A comparison between Kant and Brentano is also made by Rolf George, "Kant's Sensationism," *Synthese*, 47 (1981): 229–230. Like George, I connect Kant's need to introduce an element of intentionality with the fact that "sensation" as such does not constitute mental "reference." If mere sensation is in any sense representational, it is not as such the representation of *objects*. However, George follows an interpretation according to which the introduction of the needed intentional element rests on our ability, in perception, to turn our own *sensations* into objects. On the other hand, he agrees that judgmental or conceptual forms are intended by Kant as constituting a (quasi-)semantical reference quite *beyond* the realm of sensations (pp. 241ff.). This leads him to be less charitable than I am regarding Kant's identification of the basic forms of perceptual and "semantical" reference (pp. 245–246).

58. Brentano, *Psychologie*, vol. II, suppl. essay #2.

59. Ibid., vol. I, Bk. 2, ch. 2, sec. 8; vol. II, suppl. essay #2.

60. Leibniz, p. 549 ("On What Is Independent of Sense and Matter").

61. Ibid. p. 647 ("Monadology," sec. 49).

62. Leibniz, p. 644 ("Monadology," secs. 12 and 13).

63. Ibid., p. 516 ("Correspondence with De Volder," March 24/April 3, 1699); p. 607 ("Correspondence with Des Bosses," Sept. 20, 1712): "Why actually an infinity of monads? . . . otherwise phenomena would not correspond to all assignable percipients. Indeed we know some confusedness in our perceptions, however distinct they may be, and so there are monads corresponding to these confused ones as there are monads corresponding to the greater and more distinct ones."

64. Ibid., p. 517.

65. *Prolegomena*, "Introduction" (*Ak.* IV, p. 260).

66. John Yolton, *Locke and the Compass of Human Understanding* (Cambridge: Cambridge University Press, 1970), Ch. 5.

67. Cf. Edwin B. Allaire, "Berkeley's Idealism," *Theoria*, 63; repr. in Allaire, et al., eds., *Essays in Ontology* (Iowa City· University of Iowa, 1963). Also P. Cummins, "Perceptual Relativity and Ideas in the Mind," *Philosophy and Phenomenological Research*, XXIV (1963):202–214.

68. Berkeley, *Principles of Human Knowledge*, sec. 49. Cf. Third "Dialogue Between Hylas and Philonous," *The Works of George Berkeley*, 9 vols. (Edinburgh: Nelson & Sons, 1948–1957), p. 237.

69. "Third Dialogue," *Works*, p. 250.

70. Ibid., p. 234.

71. Cf. L. Nathan Oaklander, "The Inherence Interpretation of Berkeley: A Critique," *Modern Schoolman*, LIV (March 1977):268–269. Oaklander, however, does not say that "ideas" are "intentional objects" in the sense in question. He argues that the mind's "relation" to them is like that of a thought's relation to what the thought is *about*. This, as it stands, is compatible with the fourth interpretation that I suggest below. For additional criticism of the "inherence" account, see George Pappas, "Ideas, Minds, and Berkeley," *American Philosophical Quarterly* 17 (1980):181–194.

72. Berkeley, *Principles*, sec. 142.

73. George Pitcher, "Minds and Ideas in Berkeley," *American Philosophical Quarterly*, 6 (July 1969). Pitcher contends, with some qualification (p. 203, n. 8), that this is also Descartes's view of sensation.

74. Berkeley, *Principles*, sec. 5.

75. It has been objected against "entitative" interpretations of Berkeley that they make Berkeley's insistence that ideas cannot exist apart from the perceiving of them seem arbitrary. Certainly, there would be no *contradiction* in the notion of an unperceived idea, whereas Berkeley himself seems to imply that there is. Cf. Pitcher, pp. 205–206, and, for an attempt to respond to the difficulty, Pappas, pp. 193–194.

76. Berkeley, *Principles*, sec. 41.

77. David Hume, *A Treatise of Human Nature*, ed. L. A. Selby-Bigge (Oxford: Clarendon Press, 1888; repr., 1964), p. 1: "Those perceptions, which enter with most force and violence, we may name *impressions*; and under this name I comprehend all our sensations, passions and emotions, as they make their first appearance in the soul. By *ideas* I mean the faint images of these in thinking and reasoning. . . ." The difference from Berkeley is only terminological.

78. Ibid., p. 96: "An opinion, therefore, or belief may be most accurately defin'd, *a lively idea related to or associated with a present impression.*" For a fuller discussion of Hume's view of impressions and ideas, and of mental "states" as relational *states of affairs* containing them as objects, see my *Intentionality*, pp. 3ff.

79. Berkeley, *Principles*, sec. 142.

2. Concepts and Intuitions

1. There is also a third possibility, namely that intuitions are, as such, neither. Passages to the contrary would either spring from confusion, or else be provisional expressions of the fact that our representational faculty involves the *conceptualization of* intuitions. Apart from this, intuitions would merely be the material *for* representation. Thus there would be no special preconceptual "form" of sensibility. This in effect equates intuition with *sensation*, at least insofar as the former is supposed to be distinguishable from the factors that conceptualize it. Cf. Gerold Prauss, *Kant und das Problem der Dinge an sich* (Bonn: Bouvier Verlag Herbert Grundmann, 1974), pp. 63, 8off., 119, 210. This is of course a position with which I take issue in this study.

2. Cf. Rolf George, " 'Vorstellung' and 'Erkenntnis' in Kant," presented in a special section on translation problems in Kant at the American Philosophical Association, December 1980, and to be published along with other papers from that section by University of Iowa Press as *Interpreting Kant*, ed. M. S. Gram: "Kant here allows for representations that do not represent" (p. 4). Cf. also George's "Kant's Sensationism," *Synthese*, 47 (1981):229ff.

3. In a number of places in his logical writings and lectures Kant does say that intuitions are "individual" or "singular" concepts. Here he must either be using 'concept' very broadly to mean representation generally, or else to stand for a kind of *judgment*. As we shall see shortly, Kant does regard at least certain "concepts" as certain sorts of judgments. Acceptance of the suggestion that intuitions are certain sorts of judgments will of course require acknowledging a point that is often denied, namely that intuitions can themselves *contain* concepts. Though without consideration of this possibility, for a detailed criticism of the claim that intuitions are, or even could be, kinds of concepts, see M. S. Gram, "The Sense of a Kantian

Intuition," presented on the occasion mentioned in the preceding footnote and forthcoming as indicated.

4. A number of passages suggest this. A320/B377: concepts refer to an object "by means of a feature which several things may have in common"; *Immanuel Kants Logik*, ed. Gottlob Benjamin Jäsche (Königsberg: Friedrich Nicolovius, 1800), I, 1: a concept is "a representation of what is common to several objects" (though Kant proceeds to equate this claim with the claim that concepts are representations in virtue of themselves being *contained* in several representations). Cf. also *Reflexion* 2276, where a *Merkmal* is something of which I am conscious *an einem Dinge*, and 2278: "Every concept always represents a Merkmal of certain things" (*Ak*. XVI, p. 297). For more on *Merkmale*, and especially their status as "partial" representations, at most contained in other representations, see Rainer Stuhlmann-Laeisz, *Kants Logik* (Berlin: Walter de Gruyter, 1976), pp. 89ff.; on "singular concepts," pp. 77ff.

5. *Logik*, "Introduction," V.

6. Ibid., "Introduction," VIII.

7. *Refl*. 2286 (*Ak*. XVI, p. 299); cf. *Logik*, I, 1.

8. *Anthropologie*, Pt. I, sec. 28 (*Ak*, VII, p. 167).

9. E.g., A320/B377; *Logik*, I, 1. Immediacy, however, is almost always included, though it is omitted in the passage from the *Logik*.

10. Emphasis on singularity of reference has been fairly typical of recent discussions. See M. S. Gram, *Kant, Ontology, and the A Priori* (Evanston: Northwestern University Press, 1968), esp. Ch. 2, and the paper referred to in note 3 above; Jaakko Hintikka, *Knowledge and the Known* (Dordrecht: D. Reidel, 1974), Chs. 6, 8; Richard A. Smyth, *Forms of Intuition* (The Hague: Martinus Nijhoff, 1978), pp. 139ff; Manley Thompson, "Singular Terms and Intuitions in Kant's Epistemology," *Review of Metaphysics*, XXVI (1972):314–343. Some of these studies, e.g., those of Hintikka and Smyth, are willing to blur the distinction between intuition and concept. Insofar as the emphasis is on (quasi-semantical) singular *reference*, there is undeniably a need for the conceptualization of intuitions, though this hardly implies that intuitions can ever themselves be concepts.

11. *Anthropologie*, I, 7 (*Ak*. VII, p. 140).

12. Letter to Beck, Jan. 20, 1792; trans. Arnulf Zweig, *Kant: Philosophical Correspondence* (Chicago: University of Chicago Press, 1967), p. 184.

13. Cf. *Logik*, "Introduction," VII.

14. Cf. George, "Kant's Sensationism," p. 243: "One may wish to insist that the mental event that occurs when one sees a house is *not* the term of a judgment, and that even though one can say that, both in judging that Caesar is mortal, and in looking at a house, an object is before the mind, the two cases are *toto coelo* different. . . ." For the conflation in question of perceptual and semantical reference, no argument appears to be found in Kant (p. 244). Cf. also Smyth, pp. 139ff., who, unlike George, appears to favor a *reduction* of all reference to the semantical. On the other hand, on George's view (p. 240) perceptual "reference" for Kant involves a process whereby one's own *sensations* becomes objects of their own reference.

15. Cf. Stuhlmann-Laeisz, p. 76, who cites the example I discuss in the text. Cf. also T. K. Swing, *Kant's Transcendental Logic* (New Haven: Yale University Press, 1969), p. 8, who claims that "the whale is a mammal" is a paradigmatic singular judgment for Kant.

16. In the published text, '*Erscheinungen*' appears in place of '*Anschauungen*,' Kant made the correction in his *Handexemplar*. See *Ak*. XXIII, p. 45.

17. See Alvin Plantinga, *"De Re et De Dicto,"* Nous, III (1969):235–258, for a general discussion of the distinction. For an argument on behalf of a de re (more specifically, an "indexical") interpretation of reference to generalities, see Hilary Putnam, "The Meaning of 'Meaning'," repr. in *Mind, Language and Reality* (Cambridge: Cambridge University Press, 1975). On Kant and the distinction in general, cf. Robert Howell, "Kant's First-Critique theory of the Transcendental Object," *Dialectica*, 35 (1981); esp. pp. 96ff. According to Howell, de re judgments require two kinds of factors bearing on the *individuation* of their objects, perceptual (demonstrative, indexical) and descriptive. These correspond to Kant's distinction between intuition and understanding. Cf. "Intuitions, Synthesis, and Individuation in the *Critique of Pure Reason,*" Nous, VII (1973):207–232. The primary difference between Howell's and my own approach concerns his attempt to substitute the Kantian notion of an irreducible "form of intuition," and what I argue is its attendant notion of "appearances" as intentional objects that might or might not comprise an actual world, with certain notions drawn from the "semantics of possible worlds." The strategy is to construe Kant's "manifold of appearances" as a set of "perceptual alternatives" to the actual world, or as a set of possible worlds compatible with what one is perceiving in the actual world. The notion that the "descriptive" aspect of identifying reference functions by way of syntheses of "possible worlds" (or at least possible objects) is similar to my own position concerning concepts and judgment. However, what seems to me a reductive approach to forms of intuition aligns Howell's interpretation with those construing "appearances" in terms of a more fundamental conception of (actual) things *that* appear in perception. See "Kant's First-Critique Theory," pp. 114ff., and Hintikka, Ch. 10. (I criticize this approach in later chapters.) In addition, the notion of perceptual alternatives presupposes that of perception in general, whereas Kant's introduction of "forms of intuition," and the attendant notion of an appearance," seem to me part of a deeper attempt to see how perception itself is possible, that is, how it is *possible* for there to be "perceptual alternatives."

18. Cf. *Logik*, I, 21: "Caius is mortal." For examples of intuitions (or "singular concepts": see note 3 above): Rome, Bucephalus (*Ak.* XXIV, 1, p. 257), Socrates, Julius Caesar (*Ak.* XXIV, 2, pp. 754–755), the Sun, the Earth (*Ak.* XXIV, 2, p. 905). I take these last references, from various versions of Kant's lectures on logic, from George, "Kant's Sensationism," p. 244.

19. Letter to Beck, July 3, 1792; Zweig, pp. 192–193.

20. Bertrand Russell, "On Denoting," *Mind*, XIV (1905), repr. in Robert C. Marsh, ed., *Logic and Knowledge* (London: Macmillan, 1956).

21. As Jonathan Bennett points out, Kant confuses entertaining the idea *that* something is possible with merely entertaining a certain possibility, as one does, say, in connection with the unasserted (hence merely problematically represented) antecedent of a conditional judgment: *Kant's Analytic* (Cambridge: Cambridge University Press, 1966), pp. 78–79.

22. Zweig, p. 193.

23. *Logik*, I, 1.

24. Ibid., I, 18.

25. The emphasis on the *reference* of singular reference, as opposed to the mere singularity, is especially prominent in accounts that explicate Kantian intuition in terms of some notion of *demonstrative* reference, or even of "ostension." Cf. Ralf Meerbote, "Kant on Intuitivity," *Synthese*, 47 (1981):204–228. Cf. also Howell, "Intuitions, Synthesis, and Individuation in the *Critique of Pure Reason.*" My qualification, with respect to acceptance of this approach, should become clearer in

. section III. It involves, first of all, a notion of intuitions as sensory or imaginative awarenesses of possible objects to which various sorts of references are *possible* (depending upon the manner in which those intuitions are conceptualized). An account that appeals to a notion of ostension, further, seems to take, as the basic notion, that of ostensions involving objects in real spatiotemporal locations (cf. Meerbote, p. 206). This distinguishes it from the Brentanian approach that I maintain is Kant's.

26. Thus we must reject, e.g., Thompson's argument (pp. 328–329) that intuitions cannot function as subject terms precisely *because* concepts must function in the subject of a judgment.

27. This suggestion derives from Wilfrid Sellars, "Naming and Saying," *Science, Perception and Reality* (New York: Humanities Press, 1963), pp. 233ff. Sellars does not apply the point to Kant.

28. Cf. Richard Rorty, "Strawson's Objectivity Argument," *Review of Metaphysics*, XXIV (1970):218.

29. Cf. Robert Paul Wolff, *Kant's Theory of Mental Activity* (Cambridge, Mass.: Harvard University Press, 1963), pp. 151–152.

30. Kant himself speaks not simply of predicating a concept of an object but of using it *for* an object: *Ak.* XXIV, 2, pp. 908–909; cf. Stuhlmann-Laeisz, p. 77. Indeed, given that intuitions may be, perhaps must be, conceptual as well as intuitive, it is no surprise that we sometimes find Kant speaking of intuitions *as* concepts.

31. *Logik*, I, 15.

32. A problem that Kant never faces squarely enough is just what makes (empirical) imagination empirical, if it does not involve present "sensation." One response might make a Humean appeal to some residual or relatively "faint" *counterpart* of sensation in imagination. If so, Kant would of course have to insist on regarding this counterpart as providing at most the "material" aspect of an imaginative awareness, not as constituting it completely. In Ch. 4, sec. IV, I suggest a different approach.

33. Smyth, p. 143, refers to a passage in Kant's *Opus Postumum* in which Kant classifies as an intuition a representation to which no imaginative content can apparently be given, namely our idea of "the absolute totality of all things." The reason Kant offers is that the representation has only a single object. However, if we accept the general implication that Smyth draws from this, then it would seem to follow that *any* definite description which is satisfied by some particular object— even if we have no idea which object it is—will express an intuition. This seems un-Kantian. One way to deal with the difficulty might be to regard the idea in question as a special case in which only one thing *could* possibly satisfy the corresponding description. Another response might dismiss the example altogether on the ground that Kant himself, in the "Antinomies" chapter, seems to argue that "the totality of things" should not be regarded as a particular object at all. Regarding Kant's own view of Space and Time as infinite "wholes," see next chapter. The irrelevance of phenomenological content is also argued by Hintikka, who takes the role of free variables in algebra as paradigmatic of the role of intuitions in Kant (p. 166). Hintikka's approach is also extended and developed by Gordon Brittan in *Kant's Theory of Science* (Princeton: Princeton University Press, 1978), Ch. 2. However, it seems impossible to suppose that Kant regarded numbers as individuals. Apparent names for numbers seem rather to indicate the possibility of certain *operations*. This, presumably, is why Kant associates mathematical intuition with our intuition of *time*: *Prol.*,§ 10 (*Ak.* IV, p. 283).

34. The attempt to find some way of regarding "sensuous content" as intrinsic to

a sensuous judgment is also made by Romane Clark in "Sensuous Judgments," *Nous*, VII (1973):45–56. I extend the point to an analysis of the role of thought in emotions in "Causes and Constituents of Occurrent Emotion," *Philosophical Quarterly*, 25 (1975):346–349. In that discussion, however, I made no attempt to distinguish a referential dimension attributable to a unique form of intuition as *opposed* to thought. Clark directed his own discussion against some views of Wilfrid Sellars, e.g., *Science, Perception, and Reality*, pp. 90–91. These views have an obvious influence on Sellars's conception of intuitions, which he regards as "minimal conceptual episodes" (thoughts, though not what we would ordinarily call judgments), for an explanation of the occurrence of which, "sense impressions" are postulated as in a merely causal relation with such episodes. Cf. *Science and Metaphysics: Variations on Kantian Themes* (New York: Humanities Press, 1968), esp. pp. 17ff., "Kant's Transcendental Idealism," *Proceedings of the Ottawa Congress on Kant* (Ottawa: University of Ottawa Press, 1976), pp. 168–169.

35. The notion of concepts "informing" intuitions seems to me basically what Husserl had in mind, when he supposed that one and the same Meaning might be instantiated in a multiplicity of mental acts in the same way that a single color might be instantiated by a number of objects. See Edmund Husserl, *Logical Investigations*, trans. J. N. Findlay (New York: Humanities Press, 1970), Investigation I, sec. 31.

3. Matter and Form in Intuition

1. John Locke, *An Essay Concerning Human Understanding*, ed. A. C. Fraser (New York: Dover Publications, 1959), Bk. II, Ch. I, sec. 2.

2. *Refl.* 268 (*Ak* XV, p. 102).

3. *Anthropologie*, I, sec. 19 (*Ak.* VII, p. 156).

4. *Refl.* 268, 279, 293 (*Ak.* XV, pp. 102, 105, 110).

5. *Refl.* 293 (*Ak.* XV, p. 110).

6. *Anthropologie*, I, sec. 16 (*Ak.* VII, p. 154).

7. Ibid., I, sec. 19 (*Ak.* VII, p. 156). For a discussion of inner intuition, see Ch. 6.

8. *On the Form and Principles of the Sensible and Intelligible World* ("Inaugural Dissertation"), trans. G. B. Kerferd, in G. B. Kerferd and D. E. Walford, eds., *Kant: Selected Pre-Critical Writings* (New York: Barnes & Noble, 1968), II, 4. (*Ak.* II, pp. 392–393; Kerferd, p. 55).

9. *Anthropologie*, I, sec. 7 (*Ak.* VII, p. 141).

10. Cf. Hans Vaihinger, *Commentar zu Kants Kritik der reinen Vernunft*, Vol II (Stuttgart: Union Deutsche Verlagsgesellschaft, 1892), pp. 69ff., 165; Norman Kemp Smith, *A Commentary to Kant's "Critique of Pure Reason"* (New York: Humanties Press, 1962; repr. of 1923 ed.) pp. 85ff., p. 101; T. E. Wilkerson, *Kant's Critique of Pure Reason: A Commentary for Students* (Oxford: Clarendon Press, 1976), p. 26. A related position is defended by Rolf George in "Kant's Sensationism," *Synthese*, 47 (1981):229–255, though on George's position the "appearances" in question then function as part of our reference to objects ("appearances" in another sense) that are not made up of sensations.

11. Cf. H. J. Paton, *Kant's Metaphysic of Experience* (London: George Allen & Unwin; New York, Macmillan, 1936), vol. I, pp. 111–112; A. C. Ewing, *A Short Commentary on Kant's Critique of Pure Reason* (Chicago: University of Chicago Press, 1965; repr. of 1950 ed.), p. 34; Jonathan Bennett, *Kant's Analytic* (Cambridge: Cambridge University Press, 1966), pp. 15ff. P. F. Strawson, *The Bounds of Sense* (London: Methuen & Co., Ltd., 1966), distinguishes between an "austere"

and a "transcendental idealist" interpretation of Kant's views on a priori form (pp. 47ff.). On the austere interpretation, Kant simply maintains that space is an a priori form in that objects of perception necessarily exhibit it; on the transcendental idealist interpretation, the claim is added that this necessity springs from the nature of the perceptual faculties themselves. In either case the only "form" in question is the spatial form exhibited by objects of perception. A further approach entirely, one might note, will deemphasize necessary conditions of sensory *appearance* as such and focus rather on necessary conditions for *knowing an object*. I offer some comments on this sort of approach in the next chapter (section I).

12. Cf. A278, 376; *Anthropologie*, I, sec. 24, 28 (*Ak*. VII, pp. 161, 167).

13. Emphasis on the distinction between causal and *referential* relations has been made by others. Cf. Rolf George, "Transcendental Object and Thing in Itself," *Akten des 4. Internationalen Kant-Kongresses, Kant-Studien*, 65 (1974), Supplementary Volume, pp. 186–195; Robert Howell, "Kant's First-Critique Theory of the Transcendental Object," *Dialectica*, 35 (1981):86. The main source of my disagreement with these authors rests on my conception of intuitional "form" as an irreducibly basic intentionality that is an intrinsic property of a perceptual state and which brings with it an equally basic notion of an intentional object as *what gets conceptualized* by the judgments directed to such a state.

14. *Anthropologie*, I, sec. 5 (*Ak*. VII, pp. 135–136).

15. Locke, Bk. II, Ch. I, sec. 3.

16. Kant himself appears to regard the possibility of "comparative" reduction as incompatible with the claim that a genuine form of intuition is in question. Thus he argues at one point that sensations of taste and smell lack the form of (outer) intuition on the ground that they provide an awareness of spatial locations and relations only in the sense that comparative judgments may link them with the distances in question: *Refl*. 265 (*Ak*. XV, p. 100). The passage at A20–21/B35, regarding the imaginative "taking away" of qualities from a sensory representation, may also be taken as part of Kant's rejection of the approach in question.

17. ". . . substance is not without accidents, but these are modifications of space and of time . . ." (*Refl*. 265; *Ak*. XV, p. 100). Similarly, the point at B66–67 appears to be that, apart from conceptualizing factors, outer intuitions would merely refer to regions of space; conceptualization (of the appropriate sort) *of those regions* is in turn the perceptual recognition of objects that are regarded as "occupying" them. See Ch. 4, note 26.

18. Ewing, p. 30.

19. Paton, p. 166.

20. As Philip Kitcher has recently shown, any useful notion of knowledge a priori will in fact need to say something about the type of process by which the knowledge is acquired: "A Priori Knowledge," *Philosophical Review*, LXXXIX (Jan. 1980): 3–23.

21. It can be argued that the primary notion that Kant connects with that of knowledge a priori is not so much the negative one of independence from sense perception (in whatever sense this is in turn to be defined), but the more positive one of a method of justification that yields a *certainty of the highest possible kind* (hence higher than anything derivable from sense perception). This, one might note, introduces an ambiguity with respect to the use of such terms as 'necessarily.' Sometimes saying that something must necessarily be so merely indicates (belief in one's) possession of a certainty of the highest possible kind. That is an epistemological notion, and it is sometimes contrasted with a different notion of "necessity," namely one according to which I might *judge* that something is necessarily so while

conceding that the certainty in question falls short of the highest certainty that is in general obtainable. This has been called a "metaphysical" as opposed to an epistemological notion. That some sort of distinction is required by Kant himself is evident from the fact that he regards acceptance of a proposition as expressing a causal law as acceptance of it as expressing some kind of "necessary truth" (cf. Bxiii, A113–114, A534/B562, A766/B794), even though we obviously can have no knowledge a priori of such truths. The point seems to be that whatever degree of certainty we might have, concerning the obtaining of such necessities, being merely "derived from experience," it falls short of certainty of the highest possible kind.

22. A couple of by now "classic" discussions of Kant's distinction between analytic and synthetic judgments are Lewis White Beck's "Kant's Theory of Definition" and "Can Kant's Synthetic Judgments Be Made Analytic?" both reprinted in Beck's *Studies in the Philosophy of Kant* (Indianapolis: Bobbs-Merrill, 1965) and also in Robert Paul Wolff, ed., *Kant: A Collection of Critical Essays* (Garden City, N.Y.: Doubleday, 1967). Also see Moltke S. Gram, "The Crisis of Syntheticity," *Kant-Studien*, 71 (1980): 155–180. Gram argues that there are insurmountable difficulties involved in regarding synthetic judgments as those in which two concepts relate in some way different from their relation in an analytic judgment. Rather, Kantian synthetic judgments are best regarded as judgments that relate concepts to *intuitions*, and hence to some individual or individuals, rather than to other concepts.

23. Cf. Hilary Putnam, "Is Semantics Possible," reprinted in *Mind, Language and Reality* (Cambridge: Cambridge University Press, 1975), esp. p. 143. (For further discussion of the notion of "meaning" and what is "contained in" the meaning of a term, see also "The Analytic and the Synthetic" and "The Meaning of 'Meaning'," reprinted in the same volume.)

24. At A152–155/B191–195 Kant himself makes the distinction clearer. He says that while it is an analytic judgment that no one who is young is also old, when we apply the concepts in question to *objects* we cannot assert that proposition without qualification. Instead we must say that no one who is young is old *at the same time*. The temporal condition is not required for the analytic judgment as such. This presumably is because Kant thinks of that judgment as merely expressing a relation between the concepts in question, which of course exclude one another by their nature or content. But it is not the case that the *individual* to whom those concepts might be referred excludes either one by its nature.

25. In the *Critique* Kant connects time with the "general doctrine of motion" (B48–49). In the *Prolegomena*, §10 (*Ak*. IV, p. 283), he connects it both with arithmetic and with "pure mechanics." In fact it appears that Kant regarded both time and space as essential to arithmetic: "Inaugural Dissertation," II, 12 (*Ak*. II, p. 397). Cf. Philip Kitcher, "Kant and the Foundations of Mathematics," *Philosophical Review*, LXXXIV (1975):33ff.

26. In an earlier paper, I discussed Kant's treatment of spatial representations as intuitive, with respect to the need to relate that claim to the representation of regions of space rather than of space "as a whole." Cf. my "The Relationship Between Pure and Empirical Intuition in Kant," *Kant-Studien*, 68 (1977): 275–289. In that paper, though, I did not do the justice to Kant's recognition of the *irreducibility* of intuitional form that I have attempted to do in other papers and, of course, in this book. For a recent discussion of the tension between apparently absolutist and nonabsolutist pronouncements concerning the representation of space, see Günter Wohlfahrt, "Ist der Raum eine Idee? Bemerkungen zur transzendentalen Ästhetik Kants," *Kant-Studien*, 71 (1980), pp. 137–154.

27. See "Concerning the Ultimate Foundation of the Differentiation of Regions in Space," trans. D. E. Walford, in Kerferd and Walford, eds., *Kant: Selected Pre-Critical Writings*; "Inaugural Dissertation," III, 15 (*Ak.* II, p. 403); *Prolegomena*, §13 (*Ak.* IV. pp. 285–286).

28. That the appearance in question is that "of" a scalene triangle is presumably a function of its connection with the concept *scalene*. This of course does not imply that the concept is actually being applied to it.

4. Pure Intuition and Transcendental Idealism

1. A standard objection is that even if geometrical intuitions involve insight into our own cognitive faculties, we lack reason for supposing that those faculties are not subject to radical change. One response is that the difference between, say, Euclidean and non-Euclidean worlds would be so vast as to preclude the possibility of a being retaining its own cognitive *identity* through the change: A. C. Ewing, *A Short Commentary on Kant's Critique of Pure Reason* (Chicago: University of Chicago Press, 1938), p. 43. For further discussion, in connection with some Strawsonian aspects, see Ralph C.S. Walker, *Kant* (London: Routledge & Kegan Paul, 1978), pp. 55ff.

2. Kant himself distinguishes between an empirical and a "transcendental" distinction between things in themselves and appearances (A45/B62ff). According to the latter distinction, all things knowable in space and time are mere appearances, at least qua knowable in space and time. According to the former distinction, however, we still need to distinguish between those objects, qua knowable, and appearances of them, hence between appearances and appearances *of* appearances. The transcendental distinction is our primary concern in this chapter. For some recent surveys and discussions, see Gisela Shaw, "Das Problem des Dinges an sich in der englischen Kant-Interpretation," *Kant-Studien (Ergänzungsheft)*, 97 (1969); John Hoaglund, "The Thing in Itself in English Interpretations of Kant," *American Philosophical Quarterly*, 10 (1973):1–14; Karl Ameriks, "Recent Work on Kant's Theoretical Philosophy," *American Philosophical Quarterly*, 19 (1982):1–11.

3. Cf. Ralf Meerbote, "The Unknowability of Things in Themselves," in *Kant's Theory of Knowledge: Selected Papers from the Third International Kant Congress*, ed. Lewis White Beck (Dordrecht: D. Reidel, 1974), p. 170; Henry Allison, "The Non-Spatiality of Things in Themselves for Kant," *Journal of the History of Philosophy*, XIV (1976):313–321. Meerbote limits himself to Kant's claims about the *unknowability* of things in themselves; Allison extends the approach to Kant's claims about their nonspatiotemporality.

4. Cf. Arthur Melnick, *Kant's Analogies of Experience* (Chicago: University of Chicago Press, 1973), pp. 151ff. This approach, as we shall see later, may also take a phenomenalistic form, though it does not in Melnick's case.

5. Cf. D. P. Dryer, *Kant's Solution for Verification in Metaphysics* (Toronto: University of Toronto Press, 1966), p. 514: "By a thing in itself is meant any thing whatever considered apart from relations in which it stands." This is of course compatible with various approaches, depending upon which relations are in question. In addition, the claim in question is compatible with denying that all empirical concepts are concepts *of* things *as* standing in those relations.

6. Cf. Ameriks, pp. 2, 7.

7. The approach in terms of negative concepts is adopted by Kant himself in his concept of the "noumenon" (B307ff.), but there seems to me to be a distinction between that concept and the concept of the "thing in itself." The former may be

connected (positively, if possible) with that of a faculty of purely "intellectual intuition" of which it might be the object, or at least (negatively) with that of a faculty of "nonsensible" intuition. By "things in themselves," on the other hand, I argue that Kant simply means things that exist in a nonphenomenalistic way. However, even if differing in meaning, the terms should necessarily apply to the same *entities*, if they have any applicability at all.

8. Cf. Bxxvii, A42/B59, B69, A538/B566.

9. Cf. *Refl.* 6312, 6323, (*Ak*. XVIII, pp. 612, 643). My attention was called to these passages by Paul Guyer.

10. Gerold Prauss, *Kant und das Problem der Dinge an sich* (Bonn: Bouvier Verlag Herbert Grundmann, 1974), Ch. 2.

11. Cf. passages at A42/B59, A282/B346, A521/549, A740/B768, and a number of passages at A505–506/B533–534 and A491–494/B519–522. Cf. also the use of *'für sich,'* which modifies *'bestehend,' 'wirklich,'* and *'existieren'* at several points: Bxx, A35/B42, B412, 413, 417, A506/B534, A797/B825; *Prolegomena*, §57 (*Ak*. IV, p. 354).

12. For an argument that Kant's "possible perceptions" are really necessary ones, in a sense to be explicated by reference to counterfactual conditionals, see Bella K. Milmed, " 'Possible Experience' and Recent Interpretations of Kant," *The Monist*, 51 (1967), repr. in Lewis White Beck, ed., *Kant Studies Today* (LaSalle, Ill.: Open Court Publishing Co., 1969).

13. The first occurrence ("in themselves") does not involve the transcendental use of *'an sich.'* If it did, this would contradict the double aspect interpretation. Here Kant simply means to call attention to appearances as such, precisely as appearances. As the second occurrence ("in itself") indicates, appearances considered in themselves in *this* sense are precisely *not* something in themselves in the transcendental sense. This is because they do not exist apart from possible perceptions of them.

14. One might of course defend the intelligibility of judgments to the effect *that there are* things in themselves in causal relations with us, without admitting judgments de re, with respect to particular *ones*, that *they* stand in such relations. Cf. Robert Howell, "Kant's First-Critique Theory of the Transcendental Object," *Dialectica*, 35 (1981):85–125.

15. This point of view seems to be that of H. J. Paton: *Kant's Metaphysic of Experience* (London: George Allen & Unwin, 1936), I, pp. 95–96, 422; II, p. 451. However, it is not always clear when Paton's statements are meant to relate to the general analysis of empirical concepts. That appearances "are" also things in themselves, as they appear to us, need not be taken with such a bearing.

16. A phenomenalistic version of the double aspect approach *need* not take the form of a "predicate" phenomenalism. It does not, for example, in the case of Gerold Prauss, who defends the double aspect approach in combination with a view of appearances as intentionally "projected" (*entworfene*) objects (pp. 107ff.). As suggested earlier, one part of my disagreement with Prauss concerns his equation of the "projection" in question with conceptual and judgmental factors (cf. pp. 63ff., 100ff.). Apart from that, Prauss holds that appearances, while no more than intentional projections of the understanding, must also be regarded as something "in themselves." The point of so regarding them, apparently, is to allow for a distinction between successful and unsuccessful projections. Cf. pp. 124ff., 133ff., 145; also "Intentionalität bei Kant," in 5. *Internationaler Kant-Kongress* (Proceedings), ed. Gerhard Funke, et al. (Bonn: Bouvier Verlag Herbert Grundmann, 1981), I.2, pp. 763–771. This approach seems to me to equate the notions of

phenomenal "actuality" (existence) and "reality in itself," whereas Kant himself consistently emphasizes that considerations of things in themselves must appeal to *non*-phenomenal categories. In addition, Kant allows that some things might exist in themselves but not "appear" at all (B306). A view apparently similar to Prauss's is also presented by Nicholas Rescher, in "On the Status of 'Things-in-Themselves' in Kant," in Funke, et al., eds., I.1, pp. 437–447, and *The Primacy of Practice* (Oxford: Basil Blackwell, 1973), pp. 75–76, 77, note 12. It is not always clear, however, to what extent Rescher is intending to adopt a phenomenalistic approach.

   17. How the empirical distinction is drawn of course varies from theory to theory. On my own view, which seems to me to have affinities with Sellars's (see previous references), empirical appearances are intentional objects of perception, and in a sense so are empirical *realities*. The difference is that empirical reality is defined in terms of what perceptions *would* be obtained under the appropriately specified circumstances. In Kant's own example (A45/B62ff.), he somewhat arbitrarily restricts the circumstances of possible perception in such a way as to imply that a rainbow is not to be viewed as an empirical thing in itself, but merely as the appearance of raindrops, which are so to be viewed. On Prauss's view, appearances in the empirical sense seem to be equated with the "sensations" that get animated by intentional projection: *Kant un das Problem der Dinge an sich*, pp. 63ff., 124ff., 210.

   18. That Kant himself wavered between an "appearing" and "appearance" approach is maintained by Stephen F. Barker, "Appearing and Appearances in Kant," *The Monist*, 51 (1967):426–441 (repr. in Beck, *Kant Studies Today*), and Robert Howell, "A Problem for Kant," in *Essays in Honour of Jaakko Hintikka*, ed. E. Saarinen, et al. (Dordrecht: D. Reidel, 1979). I find, however, that those who see the distinction in Kant tend not to recognize that a "theory of appearance" (i.e., a sense datum approach) is perfectly compatible with a "theory of appearing" (i.e., a form of double aspect view), according to which empirical predicates designate merely the "ways in which" things in themselves appear (through sense data) to us. Nor does it seem clearly enough recognized that the *language* of appearing, suggestive of the double aspect approach, might not strictly speaking involve a double aspect approach at all (*nor* one that involves sense data). Cf. my "Intentional Objects and Kantian Appearances," *Philosophical Topics*, 12/2 (1981):9–37; also section V of this chapter. One might of course also distinguish a form of sense datum phenomenalism that rejects things in themselves as entities in their own right.

   19. "Is Sensation the Matter of Appearance?" presented at the American Philosophical Association, December, 1980; forthcoming in M. S. Gram, ed., *Interpreting Kant* (Iowa City: University of Iowa Press).

   20. Kant also describes the "material" aspect of an object, corresponding to possible sensations, in dynamical terms with respect to the presence in regions of space of powers to affect our sense organs (B208, A168–169/B210–211). This may seem to contradict the notion of matter defined with respect to that of an intentional object. All that is required, however, is that we regard the sensation present in perception as that aspect of the perceptual act in virtue of which its object is conceptualizable not simply as a region of space, but as a region of space occupied by causal powers that we happen to be perceiving. As intentional objects of perception, then, perceived objects are (possible) regions of space that *might or might not* contain such powers, and the sensible "qualities" phenomenologically apprehended in those regions are therefore themselves qualities that might or might not really *be* the powers in question. This is compatible with the intentional object approach, and, so long as the "reality" of the powers in question is constru-

able phenomenalistically, it is also compatible with denying that the objects of perception involve as their material causal powers that belong to things in themselves.

21. This of course requires distinguishing between the cube (as an empirical thing) "in itself" and that same cube as it appears. As I argue, this is not incompatible with construing both notions in terms of that of (actual or possible) apprehensions of intentional objects.

22. For an interesting discussion of this kind of identification, see Panayot Butchvarov, *Being Qua Being* (Bloomington: Indiana University Press, 1979), esp. Chs. 1 and 2. The same notion is present in Brentano, *Psychologie vom empirischen Standpunkt*, ed. Oskar Kraus (Hamburg: Felix Meiner, 1924), II, Supplementary Essay 4. Brentano gives the example of "attributive" identity, which involves identifying "the most diverse objects with one another," e.g., a round object (qua intentional object) with a red one (qua intentional object), when we judge that some round thing that we see also is a red one. We might also appeal to the notion of "possible worlds," regarding Kantian appearances (of empirical realities) in terms of the identification of particular objects through the various possible worlds in which they (might) appear. Cf. Howell, "Kant's First-Critique Theory." On Howell's view, however, it is necessary to regard those same objects as existing in themselves (pp. 115ff.). Hence the approach is basically a double aspect approach, combined with a particular sort of logical apparatus. The same goes for Jaakko Hintikka, *Knowledge and the Known* (Dordrecht: D. Reidel, 1974), Ch. 10.

23. Throughout I follow English usage in not distinguishing, in such cases, between empirical "reality" and "actuality." In fact *Realität* is not quite the same as, though closely related to, *Wirklichkeit*. For the former, cf. A166/B207; the latter, A218/B266ff. It is the latter about which I am speaking. For a discussion of the distinction, see Hans Seigfried, "Kant's 'Spanish Bank Account': On *Realität* and *Wirklichkeit*," forthcoming in Gram, *Interpreting Kant*.

24. This leads to a sort of "double affection" theory, according to which phenomenalistically interpretable causal relations are "appearances" of a network of causal relations among things existing in themselves, including the perceiver. For the classic statement see Erich Adickes, *Kants Lehre von der doppelten Affektion unseres Ich* (Tübingen: Mohr, 1929). For a criticism of the approach, and of various approaches resting on a notion of causal "affection," see M. S. Gram, *"How to Dispense with Things in Themselves: I,"* Ratio, XVIII (1976):1–16, and "The Myth of Double Affection" in W. H. Werkmeister, ed., *Immanuel Kant: Reflections on His Philosophy* (Tallahassee: Florida State University Press, 1974). For a defense, see Wilfrid Sellars, *Science and Metaphysics: Variations on Kantian Themes* (New York: Humanities Press, 1968), p. 52.

25. That the reality of appearances is causally grounded in that of things existing in themselves is also evident, e.g., at A494/B522ff., and *Prolegomena*, I, Anm. II (*Ak.* IV, pp. 288–289). Presumably, this does not involve an actual causal relation between things in themselves and appearances. Rather, a set of causal relations between things in themselves and the perceiver, as a thing in itself, is regarded as the "ground" of those *perceptual necessities* that define material reality. So things in themselves "affect" appearances only in the sense that they affect the *reality* of appearances.

26. Another passage suggestive of the double aspect approach is B66–67. Here Kant says that our representation of regions of space "contains nothing but mere relations; namely, of locations in an intuition (extension), of change of location (motion), and of laws according to which this change is determined (moving

forces)." This fact, Kant infers, leads to "transcendental idealism." The fact is often taken to be that in intuition we apprehend things only in certain relations to ourselves, i.e., as they appear to us. These things then presumably have a reality apart from that relation. Context makes it clear, however, that Kant's point is different. The point is that, apart from *conceptualization*, there would be no sense in which intuition presents us with any particular sort of object. At most it would present us with a region of space. Representation of an object as *occupying* that region hinges on the specific concepts attached to the intuition. How does this constitute an argument for "idealism"? I suggest the following. If *what* a person apprehends is something that can be constituted by the presence or absence of certain concepts within a perceptual state, then the "objects" of the consciousness in question must be, so far considered, merely intentional objects. I comment in Ch. 6 on the bearing of this passage on the temporality of objects.

27. The relation between O_1, considered independently of its identification as a real piece of paper, and O (the paper itself) is of course the "empirical" relation between appearances and things in themselves, as opposed to the transcendental one.

28. Cf. *Foundation of the Metaphysics of Morals*, trans. Lewis White Beck (Indianapolis: Bobbs-Merrill, 1959), pp. 71, 73 (*Ak*. IV, pp. 451, 454); *Critique of Practical Reason*, tr. Lewis White Beck (Indianapolis: Bobbs-Merrill, 1956), pp. 98, 101 (*Ak*. V, pp. 95, 97).

29. This same point might be put by saying that while a phenomenal and a noumenal "subject" are not literally one entity regarded in two ways, the phenomenal character (or personality) *of* that subject, and its noumenal character, are merely two aspects of a single reality. But notice, a "personality" or a "character" is not itself a thing, but a set of facts. This set of facts, we may suppose, will necessarily involve two "aspects" so long as an empirical person is in question. It will involve certain facts about an underlying noumenal ground, and also certain facts about the ways in which this ground appears in sense perception. Cf. John Atwell, "The Intelligible Character in Kant's First Critique," in Funke, et al., eds., I.1, pp. 493–500.

30. For a discussion of some other difficulties, more specifically related to Kant's views on morality, see my "Things in Themselves and Appearances: Intentionality and Reality in Kant," *Archiv für Geschichte der Philosophie*, 61 (1979):293–308.

31. Cf. Kemp Smith's notes to the passages; also *Ak*. XXIII, pp. 46, 48. The de re/de dicto distinction is of course relevant here. See note 14. It is also worth bearing in mind that the points I make by reference to questions concerning the "notion" or "concept" of existence can all be taken in a way that does not prejudge Kant's own concern whether there *is* a concept of existence at all, phenomenal or otherwise (A597/B625ff.).

5. Concepts and Judgments

1. Jonathan Bennett, for example, suggests that this is how Kant regarded concepts in his less considered moments: *Kant's Analytic* (Cambridge: Cambridge University Press, 1966), p. 54. Bennett mistakenly assumes, one might note, that if concepts are anything more than certain sorts of abilities or dispositions for Kant, then they *must* indeed be "introspectible particulars," which is how, he grants, Kant does have a "mild tendency" to think of them.

2. Thus some commentators find any sharp distinction between concepts and intuitions plainly inconsistent with Kant's claim that intuitions without concepts are

blind, at least when the claim is taken in accordance with Kant's "final critical teaching." Cf. Norman Kemp Smith, *A Commentary to Kant's "Critique of Pure Reason"* (New York: Humanities Press, 1962; repr. of 1923 edition), p. 168. Also Robert Paul Wolff, *Kant's Theory of Mental Activity* (Cambridge, Mass.: Harvard University Press, 1963), pp. 151–152.

3. Cf. Richard Rorty, "Strawson's Objectivity Argument," *Review of Metaphysics*, XXIV (December 1970):241–244.

4. Cf. Richard Rorty, *Philosophy and the Mirror of Nature* (Princeton: Princeton University Press, 1979), pp. 137–139; "Strawson's Objectivity Argument," p. 237.

5. Cf. Rorty, "Strawson's Objectivity Argument," pp. 236–244.

6. *Immanuel Kants Logik*, ed. Gottlob Benjamin Jäsche (Königsberg: Friedrich Nicolovius, 1800), "Introduction," VII.

7. Kemp Smith sees two competing lines in Kant's thought regarding synthesis. On the "subjectivistic" approach, objects of empirical cognition are the product of empirical operations upon sense data or sensations. On the "phenomenalistic" approach, objects are the product of activities taking place on a pre-empirical level of noumenal conditioning. Cf. Kemp Smith, pp. 270ff.

8. One line of interpretation sees this section, and others, as patched together out of conflicting doctrines stemming from different periods in Kant's development. The most prominent exponents of a "patchwork" approach are Vaihinger, Kemp Smith, and Robert Paul Wolff. For a good presentation of the general issue see Moltke S. Gram's essay in M. S. Gram, ed., *Disputed Questions* (Chicago: Quadrangle Books, 1967), pp. 13–22, as well as the essays by Vaihinger and Paton therein reprinted.

9. This is why, for example, Strawson speaks of some peculiar relation whereby for Kant merely imagined perceptions must be "alive" in every actually occurrent one, and not merely connected by "an external, causal connection": "Imagination and Perception," in Lawrence Foster and J. W. Swanson, eds., *Experience and Theory* (Amherst: University of Massachusetts Press, 1970), p. 40.

10. Robert Paul Wolff has argued that Hume's approach proves to be surprisingly close to the apparently conflicting Kantian view: "Hume's Theory of Mental Activity," *Philosophical Review*, LXIX (1960), repr. in V. C. Chappell, ed. *Hume: A Collection of Critical Essays*, pp. 99–128.

11. This in effect is the upshot of the Sellarsian approach, with which I find myself otherwise in almost total agreement. For Sellars the "form" of an intuition is as such conceptual, even if not explicitly "judgmental." Cf. "Kant's Transcendental Idealism," in *Proceedings of the Ottawa Congress on Kant* (Ottawa: University of Ottawa Press, 1976), esp. pp. 168–171; also *Science and Metaphysics: Variations on Kantian Themes* (New York: Humanities Press, 1968), 31–50. Most recently, though apart from the connection with Kant, cf. "Mental Events," *Philosophical Studies*, 39 (1981):325–345. See Ch. 2, notes 41 and 42, above.

12. The crux of the interpretation to follow develops ideas first presented by Wilfrid Sellars. See, for example, *Science and Metaphysics*, Ch. 3. Also for more general discussion of the theory of intentionality there presented, and other references, see my *Intentionality: Study of Mental Acts* (University Park: Pennsylvania State University Press, 1977), Ch. 5.

13. Cf. Wilfrid Sellars, "Notes on Intentionality," repr. in *Philosophical Perspectives* (Springfield, Ill.: Charles C. Thomas, 1967), p. 317.

14. Cf. Sellars, *Science and Metaphysics*, pp. 75–77.

15. It is worth recalling how central a role the notion of "spontaneity" in fact

plays in Kant's treatment of *ought*'s in the explicitly moral sphere (A547–548/B575–576).

16. Cf. A89/B122, A90/B123, A111, A124, B129. Cf. also *Refl.* 244 (*Ak.* XV, p. 93): "Also giebt es einen Begrif, der vor Erscheinung, und eine Erscheinung, die vor einen Begrif gehalten wird."

17. *Anthropologie*, Pt. I, sec. 1 (*Ak.* VII, p. 127).

18. This may make it less than clear why Kant refuses to regard the propositions in question as "analytic" truths. It is clear, in any case, that their validation is based wholly upon an examination of concepts: cf. A9/B13, A724/B752, A736/B764.

19. Cf. D. P. Dryer, *Kant's Solution for Verification in Metaphysics* (Toronto: University of Toronto Press, 1966), pp. 254ff.; S. Körner, *Kant* (Baltimore: Penguin Books, 1955), pp. 70ff.; H. J. Paton, *Kant's Metaphysic of Experience* (London: New York: Macmillan, 1936), vol. II, pp. 42ff.

20. Cf. George Schrader, "Kant's Theory of Concepts," *Kant-Studien*, 49 (1958), repr. in Robert Paul Wolff, ed., *Kant: A Collection of Critical Essays* (Garden City: Doubleday & Co., 1967), p. 145. A third main approach may also be mentioned. This finds Kant's argument to embody a confusion of two distinct problems, one essentially involving pure categories and one not. Cf. M. S. Gram, *Kant, Ontology and the A Priori* (Evanston: Northwestern University Press, 1968), p. 114 n. and pp. 127–129; H.W.B. Joseph, "The Schematism of the Categories in Kant's *Critique of Pure Reason*," in *Essays in Ancient and Modern Philosophy* (Oxford: Clarendon Press, 1935), pp. 266–302; Josef Spindler, "Das Problem des Schematismuskapitels der Kritik der reinen Vernunft," *Kant-Studien*, 26 (1935), pp. 266–282.

21. I have discussed this issue in "Categories, Schematism and Forms of Judgment," *Ratio*, 18 (1976), pp. 31–49.

22. "We demand in every concept, first, the logical form of a concept (of thought) in general, and secondly, the possibility of giving it an object to which it may be applied. In the absence of such object, it has no meaning and is completely lacking in content, though it may still contain the logical function which is required for making a concept out of any data that may be presented" (A239/B298). Part of the point appears to be the idea that the representational significance of a concept is essentially connected with the possibility of employing it in judgment. Thus it is part of the concept *tree* that a tree is the sort of thing that one can judge there to be one or some or all of, in a given case, or to undergo alteration while remaining "substantially" the same, etc. A more specific point seems also to relate to the category of cause and effect, insofar as the notion of "necessity" connected with the application of any concept (A104, 106) seems to involve the idea of causality. The point seems to be that part of the recognition of something as of a certain sort is our judgment concerning what sorts of perceptions necessarily will occur, given the appropriate conditions.

23. The claim that Kant illegitimately transformed a set of "formal" into a set of "material" concepts is argued by T. K. Swing, *Kant's Transcendental Logic* (New Haven: Yale University Press, 1969), pp. 43ff., 93ff.

24. This characterization is perhaps best suited for cases in which judgmental form is of the sort that relates concepts to one another. Kant's formulations in fact suggest that all judgments involve combinations of concepts, and that judgmental forms concern the ways in which such combination occurs. But Kant himself is constrained to recognize formally distinct judgments involving only a single concept. Such for example is the case in distinguishing the judgment that there *is* a God from the judgment that there *may* be a God (A599/B627). Consider also the distinction between the judgment that there is a God and the judgment that there

are *non*-Gods. Obviously, judgmental form does not always relate distinct conceptual contents. Where it does not however, Kant would presumably at least insist that it involves a particular way in some conceptual content may be related to the mind *itself*. We need to include this possibility when considering the claim that judgmental forms function within representational states by relating distinct "parts" of those states.

25. We have already noticed, in Ch. 2, a sense in which all concepts are really a kind of "judgment."

26. Letter to Beck, January 20, 1792, trans. Arnulf Zweig, *Kant: Philosophical Correspondence* (Chicago: University of Chicago Press, 1966), p. 184. Cf. A138–139/B177–178. Gram (*Kant, Ontology and the A Priori*, pp. 128–129) argues that the point of the Schematism chapter is precisely to determine how pure intuition *could* provide the referent for categorial concepts. He appears to take the formulation of this problem in terms of "homogeneity" to be based upon a confusion.

6. Self-Awareness and the Flow of Time

1. Kant responds to the objection at A36–37/B53–54. The objection, as offered by Lambert, Mendelssohn, and Schultz, and Kant's response to it are discussed by Hans Vaihinger, *Commentar zu Kants Kritik der reinen Vernunft*, Vol. II (Stuttgart: Union Deutsche Verlagsgesellschaft, 1892), pp. 309–404. By contrast, Jonathan Bennett argues for an interpretation according to which the claim in question is true, but trivial: *Kant's Analytic* (Cambridge: Cambridge University Press, 1966), pp. 45–52.

2. Cf. *Anthropologie*, Pt, I, 4, note (*Ak.* VII, p. 134).

3. Ibid.

4. *Refl.* 224 (*Ak.* XV, p. 85).

5. Cf. Norman Kemp Smith, *A Commentary to Kant's "Critique of Pure Reason"* (New York: Humanities Press, 1962; repr. of 1923 ed.), pp. 293–294. On Kemp Smith's view, the temporal form of inner sense arises *in the course* of that activity in virtue of which the subject projects certain of its own internal contents into space. Cf. H. A. Prichard, *Kant's Theory of Knowledge* (Oxford: Clarendon Press, 1909), p. 108; also H. J. Paton, *Kant's Metaphysic of Experience* (London: George Allen & Unwin; New York: Macmillan, 1936), vol. II, p. 389.

6. John Locke, *An Essay Concerning Human Understanding* (New York: Dover Publications, 1959), Bk. II, Ch. I, sec. 4.

7. A. G. Baumgarten, *Metaphysica*, sec. 535; reprinted in *Ak.* XV, p. 13.

8. Locke, Bk. II, Ch. XIV, sec. 4.

9. Cf. *Anthropologie*, I, 5 (*Ak.* VII, pp. 135–136). Here Kant emphasizes unconscious representations that are contained as parts of conscious states. But his own more general admission of a "feeling" state of the sort possessed by children before they develop a sense of "self" (and of animals that never do, presumably) would, assuming that the latter is on Kant's view essential for consciousness in the *fullest* sense, imply the possibility of total representational states that are not conscious in the sense in question: *Anthropologie*, Pt. I, sec. 1 (p. 127).

10. Cf. D. M. Armstrong, *A Materialist Theory of the Mind* (New York: Humanities Press, 1968), Chs. 10, 15. Though Armstrong calls the direct awareness of our own mental states "inner sense," his account is very different from what Kant has in mind. On the other hand, I argue in section III of this chapter that there is another kind of self-awareness that Kant is constrained to introduce, and which may be closer to what Armstrong has in mind.

11. Cf. Wilfrid Sellars's claim that sensations are not "apperceived": *Science and Metaphysics: Variations on Kantian Themes* (New York: Humanities Press, 1968), pp. 9ff. Cf. also "Empiricism and the Philosophy of Mind," reprinted in *Science, Perception, and Reality* (New York: Humanities Press, 1963), pp. 190ff. If of course sensations are like theoretical postulates, they appear to be postulated as aspects of reality "in itself," in particular of the self in itself. This raises problems, not squarely faced by Kant, concerning claims to scientific knowledge about the production of sensations by material objects, Cf. Gerold Prauss, *Kant und das Problem der Dinge an sich* (Bonn: Bouvier Verlag Herbert Grundmann, 1974), pp. 192ff.

12. The qualification is meant to allow for the logical possibility of extrasensory awareness of other minds.

13. As indicated in note 5 above, a somewhat different view would regard the "impingement" in question as resulting from a further act performed upon the sensations produced by external affection. My criticism of the present view applies equally to that alternative. On both approaches, the self-affection of which Kant speaks is supposed to be what accounts for the presence of temporal form in an intuition. As I argue, Kant is rather talking about a self-affection that is involved in the conceptualization of a temporal form that is *presupposed* by such activity.

14. Cf. Adolf Grünbaum, "The Meaning of Time," in *Basic Issues in the Philosophy of Time*, ed. Eugene Freeman and Wilfrid Sellars (La Salle, Ill.: Open Court Publishing Co., 1971), pp. 195–228.

15. So inner sense is by definition a function of the understanding as well as of sensibility. It can be argued that the same should be so for outer sense. However, as we saw in the preceding chapter, Kant is ambivalent with respect to the question whether unconceptualized outer intuitions are possible, though if possible they would at least not be conscious in the fullest sense. Why is Kant not equally ambivalent in the case of inner sense? One might of course reply that inner sense is by definition a faculty for the *consciousness* of one's own inner states. But the reply would be trivial once we have specified what we mean by the *kind* of consciousness that is supposed to be in question. Perhaps a deeper answer emerges from the account offered in section II. There the point is that self-awareness in inner sense rests precisely on a distinction between the immediate objects of consciousness qua objects that *might* be judged to be external realities and those same objects as they are ordinarily conceptualized. If the subject does not actually *draw* that distinction, then there would simply be no contrast in question. On "projectionist" approaches to inner sense, the answer would have to be different. There the point is that self-awareness through inner sense arises precisely in the course of the mind's spatializing projection of the material of outer sense (which apart from that is presumably neither inner nor outer). On that account, accordingly, the projecting mechanism must be by its very nature conceptual. That not only contradicts Kant's insistence upon an irreducible form of intuition, but leaves unintelligible his very *ambivalence* with respect to the possibility of unconceptualized, hence unconscious, outer intuitions.

16. The meaning of this claim will vary depending on whether or not we are considering awareness solely "de dicto," and its objects without regard to their identifiability as phenomenally real. This, as I argue, is the point of view characteristic of inner sense. The alternative point of view is of course closely connected with it since it does not involve any kind of *object* not already in question. It simply involves a judgment that identifies a whole manifold of such *possible* objects as one and all the same phenomenal reality. Strictly speaking, this would then limit the notion of "outer sense" to the apprehension of outer *reality*, thus making it a more

restricted notion than that of outer *intuition*. Cf. B276–277, note, and B278–279. It would also make the former, unlike the latter, an essentially conceptual affair.

17. This would also seem the point, despite a somewhat misleading presentation, of Pt. I, sec. 24, of the *Anthropology* (pp. 161–162). Strictly, Kant there appears to hold that a manifold of inner sense is a manifold of objects that might be *taken* as the presentation of some external reality, but ought *not* to be since its causal conditions are internal to the subject. I assume, though, that Kant does not quite mean this and emphasizes the case of internal causation for reasons connected with more particular concerns of the section in question. The more general idea that emerges is simply that of a manifold of objects that might be taken *either* as hallucinations or figments produced by purely internal conditions *or* as themselves (phenomenally) actual external realities.

18. Franz Brentano, *Psychologie vom empirischen Standpunkt*, ed. Oskar Kraus (Hamburg: Felix Meiner, 1924), vol. I, Bk. II, Ch. II, sec. 8 (pp. 179ff.).

19. Jean-Paul Sartre, *Being and Nothingness*, trans. Hazel Barnes (New York: Washington Square Press, 1966), pp. 10–15. Unlike Brentano, Sartre draws the conclusion that the self is aware of itself (apart from an objectifying "bad faith") only as reflected in its own *objects*. Cf. *Being and Nothingness*, p. 438: "This *lateral* escape, this wrenching away from self which characterizes pain-consciousness does not for all that constitute pain as a psychic object. It is a non-thetic project of the For-itself; we apprehend it only through the world. For example, it is given in the way in which the book appears as "about to be read in a hurried, jerky rhythm" where the words press against each other in an infernal, fixed round, where the whole universe is pierced with *anxiety*." Cf. *The Transcendence of the Ego*, trans. Forrest Williams and Robert Kirkpatrick (New York: Noonday Press, 1957), pp. 48–49: "When I run after a streetcar, when I look at the time, when I am absorbed in contemplating a portrait, there is no *I*. There is consciousness *of the streetcar-having-to-be-overtaken*, etc., and non-positional consciousness of consciousness. In fact, I am then plunged into the world of objects; it is they which constitute the unity of my consciousness; it is they which present themselves with values, with attractive and repellant qualities. . . ."

20. On the relation between the Second Analogy and inner sense, my own approach appears to have affinities with that of Klaus Düsing, "*Objektive und subjektive Zeit*," *Kant-Studien*, 71 (1980), pp. 11, 19ff., 27. Paton takes Kant's position in the Analogies to imply not only a distinction between "immediate" and "mediate" objects of intuition (vol. I, pp. 148–149), which to a certain extent I am also prepared to grant, but also that the former are "states" of one's own mind (p. 150).

21. Cf. *Kritik der Urteilskraft*, Introduction, VII (*Ak*. V, p. 189); sec. 3 (p. 206).

22. Probably the most thorough analysis of Kant's doctrine along these lines is presented by Paul Guyer, *Kant and the Claims of Taste* (Cambridge, Mass.: Harvard University Press, 1979).

23. See my "A New Look at Kant's Aesthetic Judgments," in *Essays in Kant's Aesthetics*, ed. Ted Cohen and Paul Guyer (Chicago: University of Chicago Press, 1982). This is an expanded version of a paper appearing earlier in *Kant-Studien*, 70 (1979).

24. Edmund Husserl, *Ideas: General Introduction to Pure Phenomenology*, tr. W. R. Boyce Gibson (New York: Collier Books, 1962), ch. 3, pp. 91ff.

25. Ibid., ch. 9, secs. 88–91 (pp. 237ff.). See also note 19, above.

26. I have said something about the relation between the Transcendental Deduction and the Refutation of Idealism in "Personal Identity and Kant's 'Refutation

of Idealism'," *Kant-Studien* 70 (1979), pp. 259ff. Cf. also Paul Guyer, "Placing Myself in Time: Kant's Third Paralogism," *Akten des 5. Internationalen Kant-Kongresses*, ed. Gerhard Funke, Manfred Kleinschnieder, Rudolf Malter, Gisela Müller (Bonn: Bouvier Verlag Herbert Grundmann, 1981), pp. 524ff. My approach in this book is no doubt compatible with a number of different approaches to Kant's arguments both in the Deduction and in the Refutation. That further concern with those arguments is "beyond the scope of the present work" should not be taken to indicate that I in fact have much to say on the subject, beyond what is to be found here.

27. Roderick Chisholm suggests (*The First Person* [Minneapolis: University of Minnesota Press, 1981], p. 85) that Kant is prepared to distinguish between a kind of self-reference that is not mediated by "representations" of a self and one that is. The former involves "direct attribution" of a property to the subject "transcendentally," as opposed to when one ascribes properties to the empirical subject as such: "I suggest that, when Kant speaks of 'attaching the "I think" ' to a representation, he is speaking of what happens when one directly attributes to himself a self-presenting property. . . . He says: 'It is obvious that in attaching "I" to our thoughts we designate the subject of inherence only transcendentally, without noting in it any quality whatsoever—in fact without knowing anything of it either by direct acquaintance or otherwise' [Chisholm's reference to A355]." As argued, it seems to me that the evidence rather suggests that the purely transcendental representation of the subject does not by itself serve for any genuine reference. At most it serves for "attribution" of a property to *a* subject that, in conjunction with the representation of an empirical subject, *then* constitutes reference. Kant, that is, refuses to divorce "reference" (as opposed to mere "description") from the possibility of an intuitive presentation *of* the thing referred to.

28. It might be argued, and certainly Fichte thought it was so, that the awareness of our own moral actions conveys a genuine intuition of transcendental consciousness as such. At present, I see no reason to suppose either that this is so or that Kant thought it was.

Index